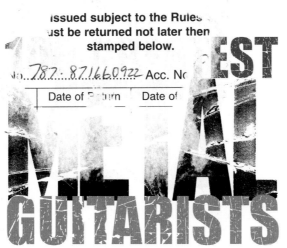

THE
100 GREATEST
METAL
GUITARISTS

JOEL McIVER

The 100 Greatest Metal Guitarists
Joel McIver

This book is dedicated to Chuck Schuldiner, Jesse Pintado, 'Dimebag' Darrell Abbott, Thomas 'Quorthon' Forsberg, Denis 'Piggy' D'Amour, and Øystein 'Euronymous' Aarseth. Not only is it dedicated to their memories, it is specifically intended to keep their awe-inspiring legacies alive. Please buy their albums.

A Jawbone Book

First Edition 2008

Published in the UK and the USA by Jawbone Press

2A Union Court, 20–22 Union Road,

London SW4 6JP, England

www.jawbonepress.com

ISBN: 978-1-906002-20-6

EDITOR: Tharg Axebringer

DESIGN: Paul Cooper Design, Johnathan Elliot at Mental Block Ltd

JACKET: Balley Design Limited

Origination and print by Colorprint (Hong Kong)

1 2 3 4 5 12 11 10 09 08

CONTENTS

FOREWORD
by Glen Benton of Deicide

When Joel asked me to write the foreword to this book, I asked myself where I should begin – so I figured I'd start with the first concert I went to by a guitar hero, which was Eric Clapton back when I was 14. I was in total amazement and awe as I watched the legendary Clapton, performing just a few feet from where I was seated, never knowing his personal struggles and substance abuse issues.

Now – at 40, and having recorded and performed with some of the greatest guitarists in my genre of music – I often find myself thinking that these guys are as eccentric as any other artist in any other form of the arts, from Vincent Van Gogh hacking off his ear to the suicidal endings of so many of the greats. Many were great at what they do, and yet they were overwhelmed by insanity.

When you think about it, it's hard to think of any great guitarist who wasn't addicted to something or who didn't suffer from some kind of mental instability – 'guitaritis', as I call it. From my perspective, I'm sure it has a lot to do with the never-ending flow of air being blown up their asses by their fans and fellow guitarists, which can lead to an incredibly egomaniacal path of self-destruction. I can only think of one guitarist who was as much of a saint as he was one of the greats: Randy Rhoads, whose tragic demise came while he was still in his prime.

Performing with a great metal guitarist has (and has always had) its challenges: there are truly great guitarists, and then there are the ones who merely get on the bandwagon and enjoy the free ride. This book will reflect on the ones who have made names for themselves among the true greats.

People in this business say that guitarists are a dime a dozen. This has the ring of truth to me: it is only the great ones who go from spare change in the pocket to become legends.

Glen Benton

INTRODUCTION

I remember it as if it were yesterday. It was the spring of 1988. I was 17 years old, an idiot teenager with zits, a line in unfunny sarcasm, and a training mullet. My friend Jon, who lived across the road in a small and frankly unremarkable village called Backwell in Somerset, was a confirmed headbanger ages before me. I thought Duran Duran and Soft Cell were as cool as music could get.

What a twit I was, for when Jon fired up his crappy Alba stereo and put on an LP by Metallica called *Master Of Puppets*, all the preconceptions of my short and naïve life thus far were blown away. The album starts with the song 'Battery', which begins with that pleasant acoustic introduction before the wall of riffs descends with sudden, terrifying volume. This moment marked my conversion to become a disciple of the heavy metal guitar, a path I have consistently trodden since then.

Two decades later, I have a job writing books about rock and metal bands, and I contribute to magazines such as *Total Guitar*, the bible in the field of the axe. It's a whole new era, in guitar terms, compared to the halcyon days of the 80s, when any fool with a Gibson Flying V could hoodwink people into thinking that he was a guitar god.

Back then, the lines between rock, metal, and even pop weren't as clearly defined as they are today. It's hard to believe now, but at one point the Michael Jackson song 'Beat It' was featured in the heavy metal charts of a prominent music magazine that shall remain nameless (OK, it was the UK weekly *Sounds*), just because it featured a shred guitar solo by Eddie Van Halen. If you wore spandex, indulged in the dark pleasures of the home perm, and placed your guitar at lower than chest level, you could be called a heavy metal musician, whatever you really played.

All this has changed, and this book of the most accomplished heavy metal guitarists of all time reflects this. There's rock, and there's metal – and in this book the twain do not meet. I admire the skills of Randy Rhoads, Angus Young, Yngwie Malmsteen, Buckethead, and Nuno Bettencourt as much as the next guy, but they're not known for metal: they play hard rock.

Similarly, if you were expecting to see Slash, or Steve Vai, or Joe Satriani, or even the aforementioned Eddie Van Halen (EVH as we in the shred fraternity nerdily call him), you'll be disappointed.

All of them are virtuoso guitarists, but they're primarily rock musicians, not metal musicians, and so they're not here. If this offends you, please feel feel to email me saying things like: "U R stupid & a Wanker, Steev Vye plays Gitar much beter than him out of Meggadeth!"

But seriously. These days, heavy metal is an international phenomenon generating hundreds of millions of dollars. It is fuelled by the masters of the almighty riff, whom I've seen fit to rank from 1 to 100 in this book – listing them in reverse order just to add to the suspense. (Try not to skip to the end – although I know you will – because the Number One choice makes most sense when you've read the 99 that come before it.)

I have not taken to this task lightly. The 100 musicians have been selected from a vast field of guitarists after exhaustive analysis of their technique, how innovative and groundbreaking I consider them to be, and how far (if at all) they have extended the boundaries of the heavy metal guitar.

It's not just about how dexterous they are on the axe, although that's a large part of it. The vocabulary of the modern guitarist has to include tricks such as sweep picking, tapping, string skipping, and hybrid playing, as well as breathtaking picking-hand precision in the rhythm parts.

That's not to say that only shredders are included. For example, Max Cavalera of Soulfly and Sepultura is a songwriter and sound experimentalist extraordinaire, but he cheerfully admits that he couldn't solo if his life depended on it. So he's somewhere down in the nether regions of the list.

This is a metal book with everything that term implies, so I've extracted players from all the relevant subgenres. The death metal scene has supplied a stack of players, mostly from the more melodic, technical end of the genre, which has flourished in the USA, Sweden, and Poland – although there are a few guitarists from the old-school brutal death metal scene too.

Black metal, by its nature, is more raw and atmospheric than death metal, and so only the most prominent BM players are here. This also applies to the doom metal scene. Power metal and progressive metal, of course, both rely on speed and melodic dexterity on the guitar, so there are loads of those guys in this book. Add to these the classic heavy metal players who pioneered the genre, and the view here is both wide and balanced. Where possible, I've included a quote from each musician taken from my own interviews, in most cases done specifically for this book.

You may have come across a Top 100 of metal guitarists that a certain American guitar magazine ran a couple of years ago. While it contained many of the names in this book, the editors also saw fit to include those well-known heavy metal artistes Neil Young, Brian May, Jeff Beck, Robert Fripp, and of course Pete Townshend. Yes, really. It makes you wonder why they didn't include Keith Richards and John Lennon while they were at it. Don't worry, though – you won't find anything as halfwitted as that here.

You may still find some of my choices controversial. My top two will surprise a few people, for example – although not anyone who really knows how demanding metal guitar can be. Elsewhere, there are a few young guitarists whom I've placed a long way ahead of their elders and betters, and this might raise the hackles of the traditionalists among you. I've only done this after much considered thought about what each player can actually do with those six (or seven, or even eight) strings, rather what the date on his birth certificate is.

We're at the beginning of a golden age in the guitar world, as a whole new crop of musicians emerge from the underground with awe-inspiring skills. Those skills would have made them freaks 20 years ago, but now they are regarded as the norm. This book celebrates and quantifies this new development. Whatever you think of my Top 100, the heavy metal guitar's time is now. Enjoy the ride.

Joel McIver – Buckinghamshire, England, August 2008

EURONYMOUS (Øystein Aarseth)
Mayhem

> "
> **Aarseth's death attracted international attention to Norwegian black metal, and the style became more and more successful.**
> "

Øystein 'Euronymous' Aarseth is often labelled as The Godfather Of Black Metal. He redefined the landscape of black metal not once but twice. When he formed his band, Mayhem – they were named for the Venom song 'Mayhem With Mercy' – it triggered the rise in Norway of a new black metal scene, fuelled by Aarseth's distaste for the then-hip death metal sound, which he regarded as a mere trend.

Aarseth and his band reverted to the values of the first wave of black metal bands – Venom, Mercyful Fate, and Bathory – and adopted a Satanic stance, soon gathering an Inner Circle of like-minded bands around them, which centred on Aarseth's Oslo record store, Helvete (it means Hell). These included Burzum, Immortal, Emperor, and other soon-to-be-legendary bands from the scene.

Their members were soon making tabloid headlines by burning down churches and vandalising graveyards, in a naïve attempt to return Norway to its pre-Christian roots. Matters took a serious turn after two murders were traced to members of the Inner Circle and reached their nadir when Aarseth himself was murdered in August 1993 by Burzum's Varg Vikernes (stage-name Count Grishnackh), a former friend of the Mayhem guitarist.

Aarseth's death attracted international attention to Norwegian black metal, and the style became more and more successful. Today it is the country's most profitable export. Aarketh's murderer, Vikernes, was imprisoned for 21 years, and he continues to issue racist, quasi-Nazi writings from his prison cell. He is due for release as you read this.

As a guitarist, Aarseth pioneered the raw necro sound that was such an important element of the second wave of black metal. Delivered on a Gibson Les Paul, his riffs were tinny, cold, and relentless, perfectly complementing the icy vocals and lyrics of his bandmates in Mayhem. To this day, the sole full-length album recorded by the Aarseth line-up – 1994's *De Mysteriis Dom Sathanas* – provides the template that many black metal bands seek to match.

▶▶❙ **Genius moment**
'Funeral Fog', the opening track on *De Mysteriis*, is a perfect example of Aarseth's cold, machine-like delivery of riffs.

PETER LINDGREN
Opeth

Peter Lindgren was a member of the remarkable Swedish progressive metal band Opeth for 16 years, and he developed a poised, experimental guitar style over several key albums. He was a creative counterfoil to the accomplished Mikael Åkerfeldt and

has a style ranging from the harshest of death metal to the most delicate, atmospheric playing – a range that made Opeth an unclassifiable musical force and gave them their fame.

Like Åkerfeldt, Lindgren initially joined Opeth as a bass player before switching to guitar. On the band's early albums, when death metal was still their priority, he used a relatively smooth tone that served the overall sound perfectly. Lindgren alternated solos with Åkerfeldt – famously, each man handed a lead part over to the other if it proved difficult to execute – but he is equally fêted for his remarkable grasp of textures and atmospherics.

Opeth are known for their love of 70s progressive rock, with all the multiple layers of sound and complex song structures that this implies. Lindgren's clean guitar parts, as well as his riffs, were a crucial part of the band's sound, but he left them in 2007, to the surprise of many observers, saying he had a less-than-complete commitment to the forthcoming 18-month world tour. The parting was amicable and he remains a much-respected member of the Swedish metal scene.

▶▶▏ **Genius moment**

The opening riff of 'The Grand Conjuration', one of the outstanding tracks on Opeth's 2007 album *Ghost Reveries*, is a masterpiece of timing and economy, with an interplay between the guitarists that is razor-sharp.

MATT WILCOCK
Akercocke, The Berzerker

Matt Wilcock is in the progressive death metal band Akercocke, but the Australian guitarist honed a deeply impressive rhythm and lead style with his home country's most extreme acts, Abramelin and The Berzerker, before relocating to the UK in the early 2000s.

Although Abramelin was a generic death metal band, The Berzerker – effectively the studio musician and vocalist Luke Kenny plus touring musicians – are a fearsomely powerful act who cross into gabba and techno territory, anchored by distorted twin kick-drums and powerful, bass-heavy riffs. The result is a fearsome wall of sound.

On albums such as *Dissimulate*, The Berzerker took this approach to its limits, with Wilcock's riffs benefiting from an ultra-tight picking style. The frequency-spanning assault of The Berzerker's music, as well as the phenomenal speed of its execution, demanded such accuracy in order to be tolerable.

Wilcock demonstrated this on a DVD, *The Principles And Practices Of The Berzerker*, and continues to apply such discipline in Akercocke. In that group, however, he also manages to exercise a talent for melodic solos that were almost entirely absent in the work of his previous band. Keep an ear open for the picked and swept licks that he and fellow Akercocke guitarist Jason Mendonça trade throughout the band's albums.

> **"** a fearsomely powerful act who cross into gabba and techno territory, anchored by distorted twin kick-drums and powerful, bass-heavy riffs. **"**

98/100

98/100

> ▶▶❙ **Genius moment**
> In 'Axiom', on Akercocke's fifth album, 2007's *Antichrist*, Wilcock and Mendonça embark on a staccato riff with a pinch harmonic that requires remarkable palm-muting and picking accuracy. This occurs after the final section of the acoustic introduction at 1:35. The song is stuffed with other notable riffs, such as the Chuck Schuldiner-style groove riff that follows a few seconds later.

Wilcock on technique

"Paul Gilbert tops my list as the most accomplished metal guitarist, primarily for his work with Racer X. As well as possessing unbelievable technique, he has so much attitude in his playing: whether he plays one note or 32, he makes his guitar scream. Technique-wise, I think his playing is unsurpassed: the solo in 'Superheroes' is a blur of notes, both picked and legato. 'Poison Eyes' has cross-string 16th-note lines that skip over six strings flawlessly, and 'Technical Difficulties' has ascending pentatonic lines at a million miles an hour. All this blistering speed, combined with the attitude and personality that comes through in his playing, makes Gilbert my top vote for the greatest metal guitarist."

> " he makes his guitar scream. Technique wise, I think his playing is unsurpassed. "

JIM MARTIN
Faith No More

'Big' Jim Martin is not a shredder in the conventional sense, but more a guitarist with an effortless grasp of textural riffage. He knows how to interact with a band that can play almost any kind of music and is an alternative-rock icon and metal guru. His band, Faith No More, may be missed more than any other: their split in 1998, after more than a decade of leftfield music-making, deprived the scene of a unique, hard-to-define force.

The band began life as Faith No Man, auditioning a variety of singers (including the young Courtney Love) before settling on Chuck Mosely. At first they played a raw form of hardcore with slap bass and Martin's heavy riffage, but by the late 80s the San Francisco band had replaced Mosely with Mike Patton and found their niche, boosted by the sparing, economical use that Martin made of his vast guitar sound.

Faith No More was a truly uncategorisable band, indulging in easy listening, pop-rock, funk-metal, and other, often technically challenging styles. Martin – who normally revelled in a hugely-boosted guitar tone mixed high in the sound – developed an economy of style that gave his relatively infrequent riffs a notable presence.

> ▶▶❙ **Genius moment**
> The guitar parts in 'From Out Of Nowhere', which range from simple punk downstrokes to uplifting harmonies, provide an object lesson in how to combine a keyboard wash with rock riffs.

97/100

LEFT Matt Wilcock, once of the Australian grindcore act The Berzeker, who now supplies expert riffs and leads to the British progressive death metal band Akercocke.

Occasionally, as with the song 'Surprise! You're Dead!', Martin was given full rein, delivering a full-on metal storm with a relentless barrage of changes of key and tempo. But most of the time, Faith No More's approach was more subtle than that. Eccentric, wilful and always ahead of their time, the band peaked critically and commercially with 1992's *Angel Dust* album, and then made a slow decline before that final split in '98. Martin now runs a pumpkin farm, a typically unpredictable career move.

MICHAEL ROMEO
Symphony X

The complex music of American power metal band Symphony X centres on the neoclassical influences of guitarist Michael Romeo, who trained as a pianist in his youth. He developed a guitar style similar in complexity and flamboyance to that of Yngwie Malmsteen and Randy Rhoads, and then assembled Symphony X. The band recorded a series of albums that quickly gained the approval of progressive-metal fans.

Listen out for Romeo's excellent command of sweep picking as well as the artificial harmonics that he scatters throughout his rhythm parts. ('Sweep picking' is where the player sweeps his pick, or plectrum, smoothly across the strings in one fluid motion while his fretting hand performs an arpeggio. 'Artificial harmonics' are notes plucked at certain harmonic points on a string relative to where it is fretted, resulting in a distinctive 'pinging' harmonic sound.) These trademark elements of his playing help make Romeo one of the more recognisable players in a field populated by guitarists who often sound similar.

Symphony X, effectively a vehicle for Romeo's playing, have released nine albums since 1994 and toured extensively – a remarkable achievement given the turn of musical fashions since then.

Neoclassical heavy-metal guitar has its roots in the 80s, but it had almost died out by the middle of the following decade – and in the mid 90s, grunge made extrovert guitar solos look obsolete, while the nu-metal movement was on its way. All the more surprising, then, that a band like Symphony X could survive, and even flourish, before the classic metal sound became acceptable once more in the early 2000s. The credit for this must go to Symphony X's songwriting and to Romeo's awe-inspiring guitar skills.

> "
> in the mid 90s, grunge made extrovert guitar solos look obsolete, while the nu-metal movement was on its way.
> "

▶▶| Genius moment

Symphony X's 2001 concert album *Live On The Edge Of Forever* is a run-through of the band's best-known songs to that point. Try 'Egypt', a seven-minute progressive opus, for a selection of rhythm parts and leads that depict Romeo at his fearsome best – and all with no studio refinements.

96/100

RIGHT Dan Swanö, the legendary Swedish songwriter and producer, once played in death metal monsters Bloodbath (Swanö pictured centre).

DAN SWANÖ

94/100

95

JOE DUPLANTIER
Gojira, Cavalera Conspiracy

French death metal has never been the most vibrant musical scene – at least not until the arrival of Gojira, whose excellent, complex music combines the technical elements and raw aggression of the original 90s death sound.

Founded in 1996 by guitarist Joe Duplantier and his drumming brother Mario, Gojira originally called themselves Godzilla before refining that name to its original Japanese form, for legal reasons. Duplantier's superb riffing precision and inventiveness have sustained the band through four albums so far, although their rise to prominence can more accurately be attributed to a series of high-profile tours. A US jaunt in 2007 at the bottom end of a heavyweight bill led by Lamb Of God, and including Trivium and Machine Head, was crucial to their growing prominence.

Duplantier also plays bass to a high standard, which explained his temporary recruitment to Cavalera Conspiracy in 2008. This band – the long-awaited reunion of ex-Sepultura founder members Max and Igor Cavalera – released the 2008 album *Inflikted*, which received excellent reviews. With Deplantier in that band, and Gojira releasing the 2005 environmentally-concerned CD *From Mars To Sirius* as a new-for-2008 album (untitled as this book went to press), the focus on French extreme metal scene has never been greater. This is good news for a scene that in the past has been confined to the Osmose label and its roster of mostly black metal acts.

"
he operates at both underground and mainstream levels, working on solo, conventional, and supergroup projects, and all the while maintains a 'civilian' lifestyle.
"

> ▶▶| **Genius moment**
> Duplantier's excellent opening riff on Gojira's 2005 single 'To Sirius' is as good as any other player in this book for its superb precision and timing.

DAN SWANÖ
Edge Of Sanity, Bloodbath

Swedish death metal has been in a state of flux for some time. The old-school Stockholm metal made by Entombed, Dismember, and Grave was eclipsed by the more melodic variant that emerged from Gothenburg in the late 90s. Dan Swanö, whose talents encompass both clean and death vocals, guitar, bass, drums, and keyboards, has been in a host of bands of both styles. The best-known of these is probably Bloodbath (a brutal DM project featuring Mikael Åkerfeldt of Opeth), the progressive metal band Therion, and Edge Of Sanity (originally a collaborative act before it became Swanö's solo band).

A notable vehicle for Swanö's guitar work is Ribspreader, a band that performs Bloodbath-style music. He also runs the Unisound recording studio in his home, and allegedly holds down a sales assistant's post at a record store there, too.

94

Swanö is symptomatic of the modern extreme metal scene in that he operates at both underground and mainstream levels, working on solo, conventional, and supergroup projects, and all the while maintains a 'civilian' lifestyle – despite his fame as a musician and songwriter.

Although Swanö withdrew from Bloodbath when too many commitments made it impossible for him to contribute fully, his involvement in dozens of other acts over the years – let alone those he has produced or of which he has been a studio-only member – makes him one of the few musicians essential to the metal scene.

▶▶◀ Genius moment

In Swanö's solo band Edge Of Sanity, he uses the full range of textures to express himself, not merely metal sounds. Listen to the 2003 album *Crimson II* and, in particular, the controlled playing in the ten-minute prog-metal epic 'Passage Of Time'. The album is dedicated, appropriately, to a fallen hero of the guitar, Death's Chuck Schuldiner.

ROBB FLYNN
Machine Head

San Francisco quartet Machine Head was one of the few bands to play an updated form of thrash metal in the mid to late 90s, when the genre had fallen from fashion. The band was responsible, along with Pantera and Sepultura, for keeping thrash alive at a point when three of the Big Four Of Thrash had abandoned the style.

Metallica, Megadeth, and Anthrax had moved away from the fast-paced chugging of the original movement, leaving only Slayer to fly the thrash flag. Machine Head's espousal of the style was largely due to singer–guitarist Robb Flynn's earlier membership of Vio-Lence, a shortlived but much-respected thrash band from San Francisco's Bay Area.

Flynn immediately established a combination of groove-metal and thrash metal with Machine Head, alongside a variety of other styles, and at times came close to the rapcore sound played by Biohazard.

I've had a million injuries. I jumped off a drum riser and herniated a disc in my lower back. I've got permanent 'metal neck.

▶▶◀ Genius moment

'Imperium', from Machine Head's fifth album – 2003's *Through The Ashes Of Empires* – features a fast breakdown at 3:24 with a riff highly reminiscent of modern Swedish bands such as The Haunted. It is as good an illustration as any of Flynn's roots and his admirable picking precision.

Burn My Eyes, the highly successful 1994 debut album, was followed by a major tour with Slayer that gained the band international respect. The follow-up, *The Burning Red*, was less successful and the band effectively lost its way until the new

MANTAS

decade, when Flynn's old Vio-Lence bandmate Phil Demmel, a shredder of serious renown, joined the band. Machine Head then recorded fresher, harder material, culminating in 2007 with the excellent *The Blackening*. This led to a slew of industry awards and a Grammy nomination for the song 'Aesthetics Of Hate', written in the wake of the death of Dimebag Darrell Abbott.

Flynn on danger

"I've had a million injuries. I jumped off a drum riser and herniated a disc in my lower back. I've got permanent 'metal neck': I've got a 15-pound weight around my neck, I'm hunched over a microphone, and I'm headbanging – basically, I'm turning myself into a hunchback. My teeth have been chipped from people stage-diving and from slamming the microphone into my face. I've got a permanent upside-down U on my two front teeth. I sprained my wrist from smashing it into the corner of my guitar. I broke a rib from stage-diving off the PA – two or three times. I've given myself black eyes from headbanging into the microphone. I've smashed my nose into my guitar. Then there was this time that our bassist Adam Duce was playing a bass with a razor-sharp headstock, and he came flying past me, head down, not looking where he was going – and this headstock literally ploughed into my temple. I was pretty much unconscious for a second there."

MANTAS (Jeff Dunn)
Venom

Black metal (the term) was invented by Venom; black metal (the sound) was invented jointly by Venom, Bathory, Mercyful Fate, and Hellhammer. In the early days, this darkest of metal's many subgenres was essentially thrash metal with Satanic lyrics and imagery – light years away from the theatrical sophistication that the second wave of black metal had attained by the mid 90s.

However, that doesn't mean that the music was easy to play, and Venom guitarist Jeff 'Mantas' Dunn – an acolyte of Judas Priest and Kiss – was and remains a talented axeman, despite the now rather dated approach of his band.

After their first two albums – *Welcome To Hell* (1981) and *Black Metal* (1982) – Venom seemed set on an unstoppable trajectory, taking Metallica and Slayer on tour as support acts and introducing the extreme metal concept to the USA and Europe. Dunn's guitar riffage grew faster and more refined as the band, then still in their early twenties, expanded their ideas and approach.

But Venom's ambitions outgrew the possibilities offered by their place on a lowly indie label (Neat), and internal tensions between Dunn and singer Conrad 'Cronos' Lant were beginning to affect the band's performances. After two more studio albums and a live LP, Dunn quit and embarked on a sporadic solo career under his own name.

A 1988 solo record, *Winds Of Change*, showcased his interest in more melodic playing, while a much later album, *Zero Tolerance* (not released until 2004), revealed

> **" our bassist Adam Duce was playing a bass with a razor-sharp headstock, and he came flying past me, head down, not looking where he was going – and this headstock literally ploughed into my temple. "**

92/100

LEFT Jeff 'Mantas' Dunn was perhaps the very first thrash metal guitarist, pioneering the movement with the Newcastle, UK trio Venom.

how far his style had evolved in the 16-year gap. Between those releases, Dunn returned to Venom twice, but left on both occasions after further disputes. However, his relationship with Lant, who continues to front Venom with a variety of different musicians, remains strong enough for a Cronos–Mantas line-up to be a real possibility in the future. Dunn has expressed an interest in re-forming the band in order to play songs from the first two albums only, a sound suggestion in the light of today's nostalgic metal scene.

> ❝
> **look at the other side of the stage and you'll see a guitarist who, in my opinion, deserves far more recognition than he gets – Glenn Tipton.**
> ❞

> ▶▶❙ **Genius moment**
>
> The song that started thrash metal as we know it – 'Witching Hour' from the 1981 album *Welcome To Hell* – is full of punkish tremolo picking and a filthy attitude. It inspired a whole generation.

Dunn on the ultimate

"I first saw Priest on the *Killing Machine* tour. That one event really sealed my fate and made me determined to be in a band. K.K. Downing had it all – the look, the attitude, the performance, and *that* solo from 'Victim Of Changes'. If any single artist inspired me to play guitar, it would have to be K.K. Downing. But look at the other side of the stage and you'll see a guitarist who, in my opinion, deserves far more recognition than he gets – Glenn Tipton. His solos are memorable, they take the song to another level, and they aren't just there because the genre dictates the formula."

PAUL MASVIDAL
Cynic

The amazing Cynic was one of the first bands to fuse jazz with metal, and in particular death metal. Founder and frontman Paul Masvidal, a Florida-raised musician with a Latino background, applied complex riff patterns to the powerful groove supplied by second guitarist Jason Göbel, bassist Sean Malone, and drummer Sean Reinert on Cynic's sole album, *Focus*.

Released in 1993, that album came at a point when death metal had reached its commercial peak in its then-current form, a couple of years before the modern prog-metal wave was in full motion. The most successful album in this style was probably the breathtaking *Human* by Death, whose frontman Chuck Schuldiner invited Masvidal and Reinert to play on it. But *Focus* attracted the same fans and has kept its reputation equally well.

Masvidal was unusual among players of extreme metal at the time. On *Focus*, he employed a guitar synthesizer to achieve an unusual tone on some of the riff patterns. This was an instrument popular in the jazz-fusion field in the 70s and 80s but hardly common in extreme metal. Also, like many of the more accomplished prog-metal guitarists, his riffs and leads are not always distinct: he used the guitar's mid and high registers both for rhythm and for solos, for example. Elsewhere, his and Malone's guitar parts fuse with a degree of complexity that is seen in today's mathcore scene, but at the time this was not a common approach.

> ▶▶◀ **Genius moment**
> 'I'm But A Wave To…', from the 1993 album Focus, features a chord where Masvidal bends all the notes within it. This is not easy to achieve, even with the special vibrato system that Masvidal employed for the purpose.

PAUL ALLENDER
Cradle Of Filth

Cradle Of Filth's primary songwriter and rhythm guitarist Paul Allender is refreshingly free of pretensions and has a work ethic that seems very British in the face of the US-dominated metal scene. He plays a combination of old-style thrash, with symphonic influences, and traditional heavy metal.

The band originated in Suffolk, in eastern England, and began their career as a reasonable facsimile of a black metal band, although it's been some years since they invoked Satan lyrically or wore real badger-style corpsepaint. If anything, their infamous T-shirt slogan, 'Jesus Is A Cunt', was the reason they attracted the black-metal tag.

Allender, who has claimed that his favourite metal bands are Judas Priest and Destruction, reveals the influences of both bands in his guitar style. Straightforward thrash rhythms inform Cradle songs such as 'Her Ghost In The Fog', while the band's covers of Slayer and Sodom songs ('Hell Awaits' and 'Sodomy And Lust') are as fast and aggressive as the originals. However, the trad-metal Priest and Maiden sounds are all over later Cradle albums, such as 2006's *Thornography*, and their many fans, accrued over a decade and more of dedicated touring, have criticised non-extreme songs like 'No Time To Cry'. Meanwhile, the band simply go from strength to strength.

> ▶▶◀ **Genius moment**
> At 3:10 in 'Her Ghost In The Fog', from the 2000 album Midian, the band embarks on a gripping riff somewhere between classic heavy metal and the softer end of death metal.

Personally, I don't like any of that widdly shit. I don't really like Malmsteen and Vai.

Allender on shredders

"Personally, I don't like any of that widdly shit. I don't really like Malmsteen and Vai. For me, the best metal guitarists ever are Glenn Tipton and K.K. Downing – the best metal guitar duo that ever lived."

90/100

GALDER (Thomas Rune Andersen)
Dimmu Borgir, Old Man's Child

Now that Cradle Of Filth are no longer a truly extreme metal band and Emperor have split for the foreseeable future, the biggest band in black metal is undoubtedly Norway's Dimmu Borgir (it means 'dark fortress' in Icelandic). Thomas Rune Andersen, who defies black metal conventions in many ways – not least by shaving his head and sporting a neatly-trimmed moustache – plays guitar alongside Sven 'Silenoz' Kopperud of Dimmu Borgir, as well in his own band, Old Man's Child.

While Dimmu Borgir play deft, semi-extreme music with swathes of keyboards and orchestral parts – with more than a little in common with the aforementioned Cradle Of Filth – it is in Old Man's Child that Galder (as Andersen styles himself) exercises his considerable skills to most notable effect.

Melodic black metal is still a relatively uncommon subgenre of metal, and Old Man's Child are among its most accomplished exponents. Galder is the sole constant member, while other metal luminaries, such as drummers Nick Barker and Gene Hoglan, have passed through the band's ranks.

After an early demo, *In The Shades Of Life* (1994), Galder went on to record several highly-regarded albums with various line-ups, the most successful of which was probably 1998's *Ill-Natured Spiritual Invasion*. Although fans hoped for a tour to promote the record, Old Man's Child has remained a studio project, with Galder devoting most of his time to Dimmu Borgir.

> **Melodic black metal is still a relatively uncommon subgenre of metal.**

▶▶❘ **Genius moment**

'Obscure Divine Manifestation' from Revelation 666 – The Curse of Damnation (2000) is a perfect demonstration of Andersen's precise, eerie riffing.

STEFAN ELMGREN
Hammerfall

Hammerfall were formed by members of melodic death metal acts In Flames and Dark Tranquillity as a tribute to classic heavy metal acts such as Judas Priest and Iron Maiden. The band were surprised by the enormous enthusiasm with which they were received, and their popularity soon outstripped that of the parent bands. It was an about-face that highlights the retrogressive nature of the current heavy metal scene.

Guitarist Stefan Elmgren, accompanied by Oscar Dronjak, delivers straightforward heavy metal riffs in Hammerfall, with little of the excessive speed or aggressive nature of the extreme metal movement from which the band arose. Epic soundscapes are at the core of the band's sound, laced with the familiar heavy metal themes (true steel, burning hearts, standing as one, riding until victory, and so on).

RIGHT **Galder (left) plays double duties in Dimmu Borgir, now the world's biggest black metal band, and his own project Old Man's Child.**

GALDER

89/100

STEFAN ELMGREN

88/100

All is set under the Bruce Dickinson-like vibrato of vocalist Joacim Cans – and none of this relentlessly dated stuff is delivered ironically. That seems to be Hammerfall's secret: the fans love them for their unashamedly studs-and-leather approach.

There's certainly nothing ironic about Elmgren's virtuoso playing, whether as a rhythm or lead player. Although speed-picking isn't as prevalent in Hammerfall's songs as elsewhere in the metal world, the rapid downstrokes in songs such as 'Heeding The Call' require expert picking-hand precision. Stefan's leads, meanwhile, are clean and melodic: he rarely bothers to venture into shredding territory for its own sake, making frequent use of a harmoniser to deliver duelling guitars in a style indebted to Iron Maiden. There's speed and dexterity in his playing, but he is more to be admired for his restraint, economy, and melodic awareness.

> **▶▶⊦ Genius moment**
>
> In 'Never Ever', from Hammerfall's Chapter V: Unbent, Unbowed, Unbroken album from 2005, Elmgren displays his control of single and harmonised leads, clean arpeggiated chords, and straightforward downstrokes.

> **"**
>
> Even in Fate's early days, the insane speed and deliberately necro production of classic black metal was absent.
>
> **"**

MICHAEL DENNER
Mercyful Fate, Force Of Evil

Black metal was conceived by Venom with their album of the same name in 1982. Almost immediately came expansions on the idea by Sweden's Bathory, Switzerland's Hellhammer, and Denmark's Mercyful Fate. Of these four bands, the only really technically adept guitarists were in Mercyful Fate, a highly charismatic band fronted by the corpsepainted Satanist King Diamond (Kim Bendix Petersen, to you). Michael Denner, who had honed his chops in a rock band called Danger Zone, soon formed a guitar partnership with Fate's second axeman, Hank Shermann. They were noted for a fusion of Denner's melodic, Iron Maiden-style playing with Shermann's slightly more raw style.

Today, the music that Mercyful Fate recorded for their best-known albums – *Don't Break The Oath* (1984) and *In The Beginning* (1987) – would only be regarded superficially as black metal, thanks to Peterson's devilry-focused lyrics. The guitar work laid down by the Denner/Shermann team is much more akin to modern power metal, or even traditional heavy metal. Even in Fate's early days, the insane speed and deliberately necro production of classic black metal was absent.

Denner's proficiency on the guitar made his band a much more accomplished beast than contemporaries such as Thomas 'Quorthon' Forsberg of Bathory, for example, who focused on dark, atmospheric gloom rather than technical ability. The fact that Denner was a few years older than, say, Jeff 'Mantas' Dunn of Venom, a parallel pioneer on the scene, partly explains his greater instrumental skill at the time. To this day, he remains a much-respected guitarist, even though his association

LEFT Stefan Elmgren (far right) surprised many Hammerfall fans by quitting the band in 2008: his riffs were among the band's most obvious assets.

87/100

with Mercyful Fate is sporadic. You can hear his excellent riffage in Force Of Evil, a band he shares with Shermann.

> ▶▶◄ **Genius moment**
> For a fix of raw first-wave black metal, Don't Break The Oath from 1984 is still a must-have album. Denner is on particularly fine form on 'Come To The Sabbath'.

'FAST' EDDIE CLARKE
Motörhead, Fastway

Like so many bands, Motörhead have always suffered from 'classic first line-up' syndrome – which leads critics and fans to label any albums a band release in their later career as inferior to those they record in their honeymoon period. However, in this case it is largely justified: Motörhead's first four albums redefined the boundaries of British heavy metal to a degree that their later work couldn't hope to match.

They were driven by the raw, overdriven guitar riffs of Clarke and anchored by the rhythm section of Lemmy and Phil 'Philthy Animal' Taylor. The *Overkill* and *Ace Of Spades* LPs from 1979 and 1980 demonstrated the perfect marriage of Clarke's thick, deliberately imprecise Strat sound and Lemmy's famously overdriven Rickenbacker bass.

Clarke left Motörhead in 1982 after a row with Lemmy over a decision to release a duet single with US punk band The Plasmatics. He formed Fastway, a more melodic outfit. While he was supported with obvious affection by Motörhead's fans, Clarke never really regained the career highs that he had experienced alongside Lemmy and Taylor, and he has become relegated to the second tier of British metal guitarists. His enduring skills as a blues-rock player mean that he is a much-valued studio guest artist – including occasional appearances on Motörhead releases.

> ▶▶◄ **Genius moment**
> 'Ace Of Spades' from 1980 has it all: the solo, the single wailed note that accompanies the song's stop-start ending, and the frantic, imprecise riff itself.

" LPs from 1979 and 1980 demonstrated the perfect marriage of Clarke's thick, deliberately imprecise Strat sound and Lemmy's famously overdriven Rickenbacker bass. "

MAX CAVALERA
Soulfly, Sepultura

A pioneer in the field of metal guitar, Max Cavalera would have earned himself a place much higher in our ranking if he'd ever bothered to learn to play lead. He has

86/100

RIGHT The legendary 'Fast' Eddie Clarke, pictured at his peak.

'FAST' EDDIE CLARKE

86/100

> **"**
> I have a very strange relationship with my guitars — they're like weapons. I pick them up before a tour and say, 'Let's go to war!'
> **"**

admitted that his strengths lie elsewhere. The some-time Sepultura frontman has made a career-long point of removing the top E and B strings from his guitars, focusing on rhythm parts and experimental sounds with a range of effects.

Cavalera and his younger brother Igor founded Sepultura in 1983, inspired by the new wave of thrash metal coming from the USA. Max's guttural vocals and the ridiculous speed of the first Seps songs resulted later in them being credited as one of the first death metal bands, although a purer thrash metal sound became apparent when they signed to Roadrunner and were finally given a decent recording budget.

The band peaked with *Beneath The Remains* and *Arise* (1989, 1991) but, aware of the changes within the metal scene at the time, they slowed down for *Chaos AD* (1993) and again for *Roots* (1996), their first non-thrash album. Heaviness and groove had replaced speed in Sepultura, with Max's experimental side taking him as far as a collaboration with the Xavantes Indians on the song 'Itsári'.

A highly acrimonious split in 1996 led to Cavalera founding Soulfly and spending some years in the nu-metal doldrums before rediscovering his passion for extremity. He took the band back to fast, violent territory with their third and fourth albums, and finally, reunited with Igor in 2007 with a new band, Cavalera Conspiracy, Max released *Inflikted*, the most extreme album he has recorded since *Arise*.

▶▶❙ Genius moment

There are so many, but you'll appreciate Cavalera's speedy picking precision on 'Inner Self' and 'Slaves Of Pain' from 1989's Beneath The Remains, the punk attitude of 'Biotech Is Godzilla' from Chaos AD (1993), and the alternately clean and overdriven guitars on 'Tree Of Pain' from Soulfly's album 3 of 2002.

Max on weapons

"I have a very strange relationship with my guitars – they're like weapons. I pick them up before a tour and say, 'Let's go to war!' My signature ESP is very simple: I designed it with only one volume knob. I've had guitars in the past with four knobs, which I hate. I'm also in the process of designing my own body shape – I don't know what it is, but I want a guitar that actually hurts people when they play it."

MICHAEL WEIKATH
Helloween

Michael Weikath is the founder and primary songwriter of the German metal band Helloween, and he has a grasp of the power metal style that makes him one of the genre's true pioneers. Power metal is too pleasant and melodic to be truly extreme, but nonetheless it requires highly developed picking skills for the rhythm-guitar parts – which can be as fast or faster than that of power metal's evil cousin, thrash – and serious shredding ability. Weikath has all this and

84/100

more, making him the core of a band that has endured a revolving-door policy for personnel over the years.

Helloween began their career by signing to Germany's Noise label (responsible for Kreator, Sodom, Celtic Frost, and many more mid-European metal acts) and contributing a track to the 1984 *Death Metal* EP. In the mid 80s, the extreme metal scene had not yet separated fully from the mainstream, which explains the wholly inappropriate title of this collection of songs – including proto-black metal from Hellhammer.

Weikath and vocalist Kai Hansen, his main ally in Helloween had been labelled speed and thrash metal for the nippy pace of their music, but they forged a new sound based on anthemic choruses and uplifting solos, coining the power metal tag and establishing a new scene. This reached its peak with the two *Keeper Of The Seven Keys* albums, released in 1987 and '88. However, the band lost their way after this highpoint, releasing albums with 'amusing' titles like *Pink Bubbles Go Ape* (1991) and *Rabbit Don't Come Easy* (2003) and wasting too much time on cover versions and line-up reshuffles. The power metal movement, now a huge scene, owes Helloween an enormous debt, and Weikath continues to steer the band with his expert playing.

> **❝**
> they forged a new sound based on anthemic choruses and uplifting solos, coining the power metal tag and establishing a new scene.
> **❞**

▶▶❙ Genius moment

'Ride The Sky', from Helloween's 1985 debut album Walls Of Jericho, is an epic ditty in the power metal style, which would dominate German music in the following decade. Weikath's ferocious tremolo picking in the mid-section is as precise as anything that the parallel thrash metal movement had to offer.

DAVE SUZUKI
Vital Remains

The technical death metal scene has always been a fertile ground for young guitar talent. It requires an expert grasp of fast, precise riffs and solos of varying types – melodic (Death), atonal (Deicide), or downright experimental (Cynic, Atheist). A new wave of bands such as Nile, Behemoth, and Decapitated have surpassed the standards of old-school death metal pioneers like Massacre and Obituary, in complexity if not in overall power.

Among them is the underrated Vital Remains, from Rhode Island. Led by guitarist Tony Lazaro and featuring on recent albums the instantly recognisable vocals of Deicide's Glen Benton, the band also benefits from the serious guitar pyrotechnics of Dave Suzuki.

It's easy to see why Suzuki was recruited to Deicide upon the departure of the band's previous guitarists, brothers Eric and Brian Hoffman. Suzuki plays effortless swept and picked solos, has a machine-like rhythm technique, and is able to absorb and learn complex arrangements quickly. He is also a drummer, providing a complex blastbeat technique to the albums that Vital Remains have recorded for various

labels. The best of them is *Dechristianize*, the 2003 album that first featured Benton's vocals. Outside Vital Remains, Suzuki has been relatively quiet, making him something of an underrated musician on the metal scene.

▶▶∣ **Genius moment**

The title track of 2003's Dechristianize, a concept album that centres on the French Revolution, features excellent guitar playing from Suzuki as well as his performances on bass and drums. Just the three instruments, then, Dave?

CHRIS POLAND
Megadeth, Ohm

Apart from Megadeth's founder member and frontman Dave Mustaine, the band's first long-standing guitarist was Chris Poland, a jazz-trained player of astounding skill. He was a member of 'Deth from 1983 to '87, when a crippling heroin habit and a disagreement with the ever-mercurial Mustaine forced his departure.

During his time in the band, Poland provided an essential melodic counterfoil to his partner's much-admired technical riffing. It was the combination of the speed and prowess of these two gifted players that gave Megadeth's early albums their glittering, drug-fuelled charm. And while the band was always in Metallica's shadow, for many reasons, for a moment back then the two bands were neck and neck, critically and commercially.

In some ways the story of Poland is that of Megadeth, his finest hour. In turn, the tale of Megadeth is that of Dave Mustaine, whose personality drove the band but also hampered its progress. Mustaine was enraged when he was fired from Metallica in early 1983 for being a drunken idiot. He assembled the best thrash metal band available to compete with his erstwhile bandmates. Enter Poland, whose youthful desire to be the fastest and heaviest guitarist on the block meshed perfectly with Mustaine's own vengeful vision.

> **"**
> He assembled the best thrash metal band available to compete with his erstwhile bandmates.
> **"**

▶▶∣ **Genius moment**

Killing Is My Business from 1985 contains a song called 'Mechanix', written by Dave Mustaine while he was still in Metallica and, it seems, re-recorded by Megadeth just to irritate his old band. Listen out for Poland's nifty riffs on this ever-controversial song.

Their initial work together on the 1985 album *Killing is My Business … And Business Is Good* was far too ambitious for the production budget and Mustaine's limited vocal range. But it set out their stall in no uncertain terms, with both men delivering riffs of fearsome complexity for the era. Poland's work on 1986's *Peace Sells*

… But Who's Buying? was less self-consciously elaborate, better produced, and more economical, allowing song structures to settle at the forefront without obscuring the overall sound.

Poland was ejected from the band shortly before their masterpiece, *Rust In Peace*. He played with Damn The Machine and, later, the fusion act Ohm, as well as recording under his own name. In 2004, Mustaine surprised many fans by inviting Poland back to play on the latest Megadeth album, *The System Has Failed*. The record was an average one, but Poland's playing was as incendiary as ever.

DAN SPITZ
Anthrax

"I've been throwing Arabian scales at the riffs to see what happens," said Anthrax's lead guitarist Dan Spitz in 1988 as his band hit their commercial peak. This observation defined his approach and explained his eventual split from the band, correctly implying that he was something of a maverick when it came to the art of the lead guitar.

The Big Four Of Thrash Metal (Megadeth, Metallica, Anthrax, Slayer) each had something unusual that separated them from the rest of the thrash pack. In the case of Anthrax, it was the stunning precision of Scott Ian's rhythm parts and the insane leads of Dan Spitz.

Spitz is a highly trained musician on both acoustic and electric instruments, and the diminutive shredder – he stands at an inch over five feet – comes from a musical dynasty, with his brother Dave a some-time bassist with Black Sabbath. Dan is a multifaceted player. On Anthrax's breakthrough album, *Spreading The Disease* (1985), he performs a breathtaking classical piece, 'SSC', while his leads on later songs such as 'I Am The Law' and 'Indians' reveal the depths of his guitar study as a youth.

When Spitz left Anthrax after 1993's *Sound Of White Noise* album, it came as a surprise to many fans that he ended up as a Swiss master watchmaker, one of the very few Americans to do so. Today, he is acknowledged as an authority on the art, and apart from a two-year reunion from 2005 to '07 with the classic Anthrax line-up – Spitz, Ian, singer Joey Belladonna, bassist Frank Bello, and drummer Charlie Benante – he seems content to continue working as an expert watchmaker.

> **"** it came as a surprise to many fans that he ended up as a Swiss master watchmaker, one of the very few Americans to do so. **"**

▶▶❙ Genius moment
The fastest song Anthrax ever recorded, 'Gung-Ho', was a highlight of 1985's Spreading The Disease, with its ferocious double kick-drums and a rhythm guitar part that has to be heard to be believed. Now, who could pull off a solo over that? Dan could – and he did.

81/100

JANICK GERS
Iron Maiden

Janick Gers is perhaps the only guitarist from the New Wave Of British Heavy Metal to make a long-term career in music who wasn't in Iron Maiden or Def Leppard. He is also that rare thing – a third guitarist. He's been a permanent member of Iron Maiden since 1990, when that band's long-term guitarist Adrian Smith left for a brief solo career.

Gers remained with the band when Smith returned in 1999, to the surprise of many fans (and more than a few disapproving comments). However, the three-guitar attack seems to suit Maiden's music well, allowing songwriter and bassist Steve Harris to expand the band's already complex approach.

Gers is of Polish descent but was born and raised in Hartlepool, northern England. He plays a series of Fender Stratocasters in a highly melodic style derived from that of his major influence, Ritchie Blackmore of Deep Purple. This must have been useful in his pre-Maiden career when he was a member of Ian Gillan's band.

Gers also played in the NWOBHM act White Spirit, who never made it beyond the B-league of that influential scene but gained a reasonable amount of praise during their short career. However, Gers will probably be remembered most for his time in Maiden, where he exercises his on-stage flamboyance with evident enjoyment. Now in his early 50s, Gers may not have many years left at the frontline of heavy metal, but he has certainly made his mark.

> " Now in his early 50s, Gers may not have many years left at the frontline of heavy metal, but he has certainly made his mark. "

▶▶❙ Genius moment

White Spirit's NWOBHM anthem 'High Upon High' was included on the seminal Metal For Muthas compilation, released in 1980. Like the rest of that scene, it showcased a band whose youthful energy far outstripped their technical ability. Still, Gers' future skills were apparent, even at that early stage.

THOMAS FISCHER
Celtic Frost, Hellhammer

Thomas Gabriel Fischer is not a simple shredder by anyone's definition, but a guitarist who knows how to wring every drop of darkness out of the notes he plays on his Ibanez Iceman. Fischer, who in the early days of his career used the name Tom G. Warrior, takes an unorthodox approach when it comes to the tools of his trade. Buffeted by a loveless childhood and the ultra-conservative environs of rural Switzerland, he poured the agonies of his youth into the early black metal of his first band, Hellhammer, who were inspired – like so many others in his book – by the primitive rage of Venom.

80/100

LEFT Dan Spitz of Anthrax was one of the 1980s thrash scene's most inventive soloists – before departing to establish a career in watchmaking.

THOMAS FISCHER

Fischer realised at an early stage that slow music would be much heavier than faster material. He famously became aware of this when he accidentally played a 45rpm Venom vinyl single at 33rpm. So he wrote songs that were deadly slow, crushingly heavy – and very effective. Hellhammer recorded three demos (collated in 2008 as *Demon Entrails*) and an EP, *Apocalyptic Raids*, but never played live. They wound up in 1984 when Fischer and his co-writer Martin Eric Ain decided that the band had reached its limits. They were correct.

Their next project, Celtic Frost, was an avant-garde and highly influential metal band whose influence would resonate down the years. Although the band were most praised for the *To Mega Therion* and *Into The Pandemonium* albums (1985, 1987), their comeback album, *Monotheist* – released after an absence of almost 15 years – was a behemoth, a terrifyingly dark record of deep, gothic songs.

> ▶▶ **Genius moment**
> 'Circle Of The Tyrants' from To Mega Therion is a classic Fischer riffathon, but you may also derive profound pleasure from 'Drown In Ashes' from Monotheist (2006).

Fischer on gods

"My favourite metal guitarist is Tony Iommi. He plays like nobody else – or at least he used to. Nowadays, everybody copies him. Including me. When I first heard him play in the 70s, all heavy metal bands had the same logical way of resolving their riffs, and he had a disharmonic way of doing it, which gave his music an extreme darkness that at the time was completely unheard of. Discovering that was a defining moment in my life."

" My favourite metal guitarist is Tony Iommi. He plays like nobody else – or at least he used to. Nowadays, everybody copies him. Including me. "

KIRK WINDSTEIN
Down, Crowbar

Down, the supergroup of the moment, is composed of talents that make the band far more than the sum of its parts. Singer Philip Anselmo and bassist Rex Brown come from Pantera, the biggest metal band of the 90s apart from Metallica and Iron Maiden. Guitarists Kirk Windstein and Pepper Keenan served time in Crowbar and Corrosion Of Conformity. Drummer Jimmy Bower was in Crowbar, too, as well as the legendary New Orleans band Eyehategod. The combined sounds of all these bands make up Down, who play slow, super-heavy, stoner–sludge–doom metal of serious riff weight.

The combination of Windstein and Keenan is a major element of Down's memorable sound. Windstein is a lead guitarist influenced by Robin Trower and Frank Marino. He had a background in an underground thrash metal band that used to support Anselmo's pre-Pantera band, Razor White. His rhythm playing is highly evolved, too.

Windstein worked on a picking precision that served him well in his later career and developed a slow, measured approach with the doom metal band Crowbar,

78/100

adding to his all-round ability that he uses to the full with Down. On the other hand, Keenan's punk–country–stoner-metal background with Corrosion Of Conformity makes for a completely different guitar style that acts as a kind of counterpoint to the blues-rock influences of Windstein.

> ## ▶▶┃ Genius moment
> The whole of Over The Under, Down's third and most successful album, released in 2007, was a guitar marathon from both Windstein and Keenan, but 'I Scream' – the most evidently commercial song – contains a riff and solo that reveal the full extent of Windstein's ability.

Kirk on idols

"We're obviously heavily influenced by Sabbath, but I don't think we come across as one of the stoner bands which are blatantly trying to rip them off. Tony Iommi was one of my main idols, and Sabbath were one of my favourite bands ever. It was surreal to walk onto the plane when we were touring with them and see Geezer Butler and Tony Iommi, and hear them say 'Hi Kirk!' It was really weird. And I had some drinks with Ronnie James Dio at the airport. We were waiting all day for a delayed plane – so we tied one on."

> *We're obviously heavily influenced by Sabbath, but I don't think we come across as one of the stoner bands which are blatantly trying to rip them off.*

MATTHIAS JABS
Scorpions

Replacing the eerily talented Uli Jon Roth would be a challenge even for the most accomplished of heavy metal guitarists, but when Roth left the Scorpions in 1978, Matthias Jabs rose to the occasion. Then only 23 years old, Jabs had already played in an assortment of rock bands, learning his craft on a Fender Stratocaster before moving to a Gibson Explorer in the 80s.

Like many metal guitarists of his vintage – he was born in 1955 – Jabs was influenced heavily by Ritchie Blackmore and Jimmy Page, and he incorporated their heavily overdriven blues-rock styles into the albums he went on to make with the Scorps. As well as lending his guitar expertise to the band, Jabs made a visually arresting sight on stage, especially when combined with the extrovert guitar pyrotechnics of Rudolf Schenker, the moustachioed Viking of metal.

Although the Scorpions have maintained a successful career with Jabs and Schenker at the band's heart for over three decades, their fortunes have fluctuated, just like other classic metal bands of their era. In the 90s – the decade of dread for many established metal acts, when even Iron Maiden found it tough – the band's resolutely old-school approach to metal made them seem a little obsolete – not helped by their cringe-making 1990 ballad, 'Winds Of Change'. However, at the end of that decade there was a new audience for classic rock and metal, and they made it clear that they wanted Scorpions music. It was a welcome boost from which the band are still benefiting.

RIGHT Matt Tuck of Bullet For My Valentine has impressed many guitar fans with his James Hetfield-style speed-picking.

MATT TUCK

76/100

> **▶▶▋ Genius moment**
> 'Money And Fame' from 1990's Crazy World – the album that also gave us 'Winds Of Change' –
> features a rare Jabs songwriting credit. It is a useful reminder of his formidable guitar skills, so often
> overshadowed by the more flamboyant Schenker.

MATT TUCK
Bullet For My Valentine

Like Max Cavalera, Bullet For My Valentine's frontman Matt Tuck is more of a rhythm player than a soloist – although he also takes pleasure in delivering leads with big bends, tapping, and all the other 80s metal tricks that influenced him as a youth. As he once told me: "Speed picking is what I've been doing since I was 14 years old. I can play it with my fuckin' finger up my arse." His James Hetfield-style rapid-fire rhythm parts are indeed impressive for a relatively young player.

While Bullet For My Valentine's fans are mostly teenagers, this allows Tuck, the band's primary songwriter, to bring in influences from a disparate range of sounds – thrash metal, modern metalcore, classic galloping Iron Maiden riffs, big-hair Mötley Crüe-style rock, and whatever else he fancies. The band's followers then judge the results on their own merits rather than any existing prejudices.

Sharing a manager with Slayer has helped the band to ascend the metal ladder quickly, supporting Guns N' Roses in the USA and only missing a support slot with Metallica at London's Wembley Stadium in 2007 because Tuck was obliged to undergo an emergency tonsillectomy. And yet Bullet For My Valentine came from such humble, if fertile, roots: a small corner of Wales, near Bridgend, that has also produced the some-time nu-metal stars Lostprophets and the emo band Funeral For A Friend. There must be something in the water down there.

"
Speed picking is what I've been doing since I was 14 years old. I can play it with my fuckin' finger up my arse.
"

> **▶▶▋ Genius moment**
> Tuck's famous picking agility comes to the fore on 'All These Things I Hate (Revolve Around Me)', a
> single from Bullet For My Valentine's first album, 2005's The Poison.

SAM TOTMAN
Dragonforce

When the self-categorised 'extreme power metal' band Dragonforce first came to prominence in 2004 with their album *Sonic Firestorm*, many metal fans were gobsmacked. By simply amping up the speed of the songs, applying super-catchy singalong choruses, and delivering fearsome guitar solos, the band made the power metal genre their own.

Guitarists Sam Totman and Herman Li deliver an insanely rapid barrage of riffs and leads to the songs, all delivered at a thrash-metal tempo. The result is not far removed from happy hardcore, the briefly popular version of electronica that combined squeaky vocals with sugary high-speed beats a few years ago. Dragonforce's fans are rabid about the band, but more than a few established metalheads are still confused about what it all means.

Whatever the overall sound, the quality of the guitar playing is not in doubt. Li and Totman are accomplished players, although Li tends to express himself a little more flamboyantly. Totman's tone and style is slightly more raw than that of Herman, whose liquid-smooth lead lines flow from his instrument to contrast with his partner's abrasive sound. Totman's solos are entertaining, containing sweeps, multi-finger fretboard tapping, and wide string-bends on a signature Ibanez. His onstage persona – a beer-fuelled, anarchic rock monster – adds enormously to the Dragonforce experience.

> ▶▶▎ **Genius moment**
> The extensive duelling in the award-winning 'Through The Fire And Flames' solo is captured in an unforgettable video, currently viewable on YouTube, in which the guitarists watch each other's leads while drinking beer. Totman's contributions are a flurry of notes, legato and alternately picked, and show just how to cram a tasteful solo into a mere few seconds.

> " By simply amping up the speed of the songs, applying super-catchy singalong choruses, and delivering fearsome guitar solos, the band made the power metal genre their own. "

JACK OWEN
Deicide, Cannibal Corpse

Jack Owen is a founder member of the world's biggest-selling death metal band, Cannibal Corpse. He possesses incredibly precise picking abilities and a lead style that is atmospheric rather than technically eloquent. He lays down solos that don't attempt to out-shred the already complex rhythm guitar figures, but instead he likes to add feel and emotion. As with so many of the most extreme musicians, Owen is a calm, thoughtful figure off-stage, and was relatively restrained while performing with Cannibal Corpse, putting his creative energies into writing classic songs such as 'Gallery Of Suicide' and 'The Spine Splitter'.

Fans point to two different eras for the band, the first with frontman Chris Barnes, whose pioneering vocals pushed out the sonic boundaries, and then with George 'Corpsegrinder' Fisher, a more refined vocalist with enormous power. Owen was a crucial element in both line-ups, but he chose to leave in 2004 to concentrate on his heavy rock side project, Adrift.

Owen also plays with Deicide, another highly successful American death metal act. He joined them when their original guitarists, Eric and Brian Hoffman, departed

JACK OWEN

under acrimonious circumstances. He took over the guitar duties alongside Dave Suzuki of Vital Remains, staying on as a permanent member after Suzuki returned to his old band. Shredder extraordinaire Ralph Santolla was then recruited alongside him, and together they helped to record *The Stench Of Redemption* (2006), Deicide's best album in some years. The next album, 2008's *Till Death Do Us Part*, maintained the high quality level of the earlier record.

> ▶▶▎ **Genius moment**
> 'Nothing Left To Mutilate', from Cannibal Corpse's 2004 album The Wretched Spawn, features two solos from Owen that both are a step up from the usual atonal approach of pre-1995 death metal.

Jack on the best
"OK, it was a tough decision, but I would have to go with Dave Carlo from the Canadian thrash band Razor. Everything was great about this guy. Great tone, incredibly fast and tight picking, and aggressive and to-the-point leads. Nothing makes me more pissed off and angry than listening to a Razor record. If I play one in my car, I'm automatically driving faster and angrier, and whenever I get to where I'm going, I wanna punch somebody's face in."

> " If I play one in my car, I'm automatically driving faster and angrier, and whenever I get to where I'm going, I wanna punch somebody's face in. "

ZACKY VENGEANCE (Zachary Baker)
Avenged Sevenfold

Zachary Baker delivers a dose of melodic metal in Avenged Sevenfold alongside his guitar partner Brian 'Synyster Gates' Haner, mostly playing rhythm parts and allowing Haner full scope when it comes to the leads. A founder of the band, Baker chose his stage-name as a warning to those who doubted that he would make a career in music following the failure of his old band, MPA (Mad Porno Action).

Baker is an accomplished player – he started to play the instrument aged 13 years – and now delivers riffs that take in metalcore, mainstream heavy metal, and 80s-style hair-rock influences. Beyond his grasp of the guitar, he also plays a key role in the band's image. He invented the abbreviation of Avenged Sevenfold to A7X and pointed the direction of their albums toward a range of influences, peaking with 2005's *City Of Evil*.

As much as his more extrovert bandmate Haney, Baker gathered together a surprisingly wide range of sounds for their most recent album, 2007's self-titled release. Some critics thought that their songwriting ambitions went too far when the band moved into ballad territory with 'Afterlife' and other less-than-metallic tunes. But Baker's guitar work remains exemplary, even if his picking accuracy did remain untested in some of the softer songs.

73/100

LEFT **The unique Jack Owen, now with Deicide after many years with death metal's biggest-selling band, Cannibal Corpse.**

> **▶▶◄ Genius moment**
> The fast central riff in 'Beast And The Harlot' – featured in the video game Guitar Hero II and the song that opens City Of Evil – demonstrates well Baker's speedy and precise picking ability.

MARC RIZZO
Soulfly, Cavalera Conspiracy

Jazz and world influences permeate the expert guitar playing of Marc Rizzo, who used these styles to great effect in the Latino nu-metal band Ill Nino and, later, alongside Max Cavalera in Soulfly. He also plays in the newly-formed Cavalera Conspiracy, although this band requires his lead skills rather than any world-inflected riffage, because (famously) Cavalera can't play lead guitar.

Rizzo's rise to a prominent position in metal guitar is testimony to his all-round grasp of the instrument – even in a world hostile for some years to the art of the lead-guitar solo. Ill Nino adhered firmly to the nu-metal template of no solos and no dexterity – which seems like a terminally stupid approach today, five years after its peak. Riffs and breakbeats were what nu-metal was all about, until it imploded in about 2002, and Rizzo employed dazzling picking accuracy and invention within the constraints of the songwriting.

Although Soulfly, too, avoided solos for their first couple of albums, once leads had come back into vogue thanks to the new wave of metalcore and true metal acts, Rizzo was able to explore this area of the guitar once again. In fact, his career has been one of increasing extremity: Ill Nino made slightly dull nu-metal; then Soulfly did the same but gradually ramped it up to include thrash metal elements; and finally the Cavalera Conspiracy play metal that ranges from moderate hardcore to an all-out crossover of thrash and death metal.

" *Ill Nino adhered firmly to the nu-metal template of no solos and no dexterity – which seems like a terminally stupid approach today.* **"**

> **▶▶◄ Genius moment**
> 'I And I', from Soulfly's most recent album, 2005's Dark Ages, features an ambient mid-section that showcases Rizzo's experimental side. Elsewhere in the song, listen out for his more traditional but still impressive riffing.

JESSE PINTADO
Terrorizer, Napalm Death

The late Jesse Pintado, who died suddenly in 2006 for reasons thought to relate to an alcohol habit, was partly responsible for the rise of grindcore, one of the heaviest

RIGHT The great Jesse Pintado of Terrorizer and Napalm Death, pictured in the 1980s: his premature death deprived the scene of a great talent.

> *Another time, this girl came on stage and I thought she was gonna stage-dive. She grabbed my hair and so, not to be rude, I had to give her a little boot off.*

genres of music ever invented. His pioneering riffs with the band Terrorizer, a sporadic outfit that defined the new grind sound at the end of the 80s, will endure for a long time to come.

When Terrorizer's pioneering album *World Downfall* was released in 1989, there had already been moves toward a tougher, faster, politicised new brand of music within the hardcore and anarcho-punk scene. Napalm Death and Amebix were among the forward-thinking bands who fused punk and metal and accelerated the results with blastbeats and gruttural vocals, making a tangibly different sound to the more technical death metal movement, which was also in its infancy at the time.

World Downfall was one of the first albums to crystallise the new sound of grindcore. Among the members of Terrorizer, Pintado was the one most responsible for that sound. Drums and bass were provided by Pete Sandoval and David Vincent of Morbid Angel, a fearsome rhythm section that propelled Pintado's fast, low-register riffs at enormous speed, while the vocals came from the shredded throat of Oscar Garcia, later of Nausea. Solos were minimal and the focus remained on the main riff in almost every song. Pintado demonstrated a phenomenally tight precision, especially so given his age (a mere 20 at the time) and the lack of precedent for this kind of music.

Pintado spent many years in Napalm Death after Terrorizer folded, but always hinted that his first band might be resurrected. In 2005 a comeback album was announced, the presciently-titled *Darker Days Ahead*, featuring Sandoval once more. In an era when grindcore is omnipresent, it made much less impact than its predecessor, but the album was positively reviewed and makes a suitable epitaph for its primary creator.

▶▶| **Genius moment**
The strange, hooky main riff of 'Fear Of Napalm', one of the high points of World Downfall (1989).

Pintado on stage escapades

"I've had many. I had a bottle thrown at me in Texas, which scratched my guitar. Another time, this girl came on stage and I thought she was gonna stage-dive. She grabbed my hair and so, not to be rude, I had to give her a little boot off. Not harsh, just a little boot. Later on, I found out that she thought I was wearing a wig."

JASON MENDONÇA
Akercocke

'Progressive blackened death metal' may be a cumbersome tag for a genre, but it perfectly suits the complex, ever-shifting music made by the British band Akercocke. The unpredictable arrangements of the songs and the dozens of ideas that populate them are founded on the guitar riffs and leads of the band's co-founder Jason

Mendonça (the ç is pronounced as an s) and the relatively new recruit Matt Wilcock.

Akercocke was formed in 1997 by Mendonça and drummer David Gray after the collapse of their previous band Salem Orchid. They bring a wide range of sounds to their albums, including warp-speed tremolo picking ('Enraptured By Evil'), arpeggiated acoustic 12-string ('Axiom'), and atmospheric, semi-electronic ambience ('The Dark Inside'). This was not the approach of your average metal band. Add to this the suits the musicians wear on stage, the occult sentiments of the lyrics, and their predilection for matters psychosexual, and the Akercocke recipe is a potent one.

Where Mendonça and Wilcock excel is in their range of playing techniques and the apparently unlimited palette of ideas that they apply to the Akercocke sound. Key elements of the band's approach include extended instrumental introductions, riffs that change key and tempo every couple of bars, and the use of unusual instrumentation for added atmosphere.

However, Mendonça and his co-writer Gray make a point of writing actual songs, without taking the experimental approach too far, and the basis of their sound remains anchored to the extreme metal template. The backbone of the sound consists of very fast rhythm picking, complex unison riffs, and melodic solos, all inspired by the band's appreciation of classic metal, from 80s thrash to technical death metal. There is no other band quite like them.

> **"**
> **They bring a wide range of sounds to their albums, including warp-speed tremolo picking, arpeggiated acoustic 12-string, and atmospheric, semi-electronic ambience.**
> **"**

▶▶❙ Genius moment
Mendonça has described the riff in 'Eyes Of The Dawn' as one of the fastest ever written. He has good reason for this claim.

DALLAS TOLER-WADE
Nile

South Carolina has never been a hotbed for heavy metal, so when the most brutal and technical death metal band on the planet emerged from the city of Greenville in 1993, many metal fans were taken by surprise. Led by primary songwriter Karl Sanders, Nile plays a terrifying brand of music as a vehicle for Sanders' obsession with Egyptology. He has studied the ancient history and religion of Egypt and writes extensive, complex lyrics alongside comprehensive explanatory sleevenotes.

Sanders shares guitar parts and vocals with Dallas Toler-Wade. The two men play an intricate blend of unison and harmonised riffs, changing patterns every few bars and overlaying the rhythm parts with melodic solos. Their approach has been at the core of the Nile sound since the first album, *Amongst The Catacombs Of Nephren-Ka*, released in 1998. They peaked with *Black Seeds Of Vengeance* in 2000 and the stunning *In Their Darkened Shrines* two years later. Subsequent albums have included ever more complex guitar parts.

Unusually for any band, Sanders, Toler-Wade, and bassist Chris Lollis share the

69/100

JASON MENDONCA

Akercocke, probably the UK's best extreme metal band, relaxing at home. Guitarist/vocalist
Jason Mendonça is pictured far right.

vocals, all offering a death-metal grunt alternating with screams. Toler-Wade takes the mid-range vocals on renowned Nile songs such as 'Papyrus Containing The Spell To Preserve Its Possessor Against Attacks From He Who Is In The Water'. It was released as a single in 2007, typical of Nile's lyrical themes and Toler-Wade's stunning vocal malevolence. The song's central riff is a remarkably difficult one, making it all the more impressive when the two guitarists and bassist perform it in unison at very high speed.

> **▶▶ Genius moment**
> Listen out for Toler-Wade's stop-start punctuation of Sanders's fast solo riff in 'Black Seeds Of Vengeance', the title track of their 2000 album and Nile's most anthemic song so far.

PIOTR WIWCZAREK
Vader

Death metal bands tend to find it difficult to get off the ground. They get little mainstream exposure because of the extreme nature of the music and little money for equipment, recording, and touring – and that's in the supposedly enlightened West. Imagine what it must have been like in the 80s, when there was hardly any awareness of this music. Then, imagine how tough it must have been to do this behind the Iron Curtain in Poland. That's what Piotr (aka Peter) Wiwczarek did at the end of that decade when he formed Vader, naming his band for the Sith Lord from *Star Wars*. He faced severely limited access to instruments and recording gear, and an official disapproval of heavy metal.

However, Wiwczarek pulled it off. He formed one of the most enduring extreme metal bands in Europe and built a successful career based on endless touring and a well-received album every year or two. Inspiring a new Polish wave of death metal at the same time, Vader grew to rival the status of the old-school Swedish death metal bands (Entombed, Grave, Dismember), a respectable achievement for a band arising from such unfavourable circumstances.

As a guitar player, Wiwczarek is a powerhouse. He delivers remarkably fast and tight riffs and solos that strike the perfect balance of anarchy and harmony. From time to time, Vader stray into commercial metal territory, a usually unsuccessful indulgence, but one that their fans easily forgive after the band has worked so hard for two decades to push the extreme-metal envelope. On these occasions, Wiwczarek plays solos that demonstrate he has a perfectly intact grasp of melody.

"
He delivers remarkably fast and tight riffs and solos that strike the perfect balance of anarchy and harmony.
"

> **▶▶ Genius moment**
> Wiwczarek and band play a cover of Slayer's ineffable 'Raining Blood' from time to time in their live set. His delivery of the song's third riff – the unfeasibly fast one based on two hammer-ons – is like a machine.

68/100

RIGHT **Technical death metallers Nile, with Dallas Toler-Wade at the centre. Egyptology used to be much less scary than this.**

DALLAS TOLER-WADE

69/100

68/100

MATT HEAFY
Trivium

Florida quartet Trivium have reshaped the mainstream end of Metallica and added a dose of metalcore to create a sound that is dexterous if not particularly original. The band base their energetic sound on the guitars of frontman Matt Heafy and Corey Beaulieu. Born in 1986, Heafy – a cerebral individual whose drive to succeed has been largely responsible for the band's rise to prominence – spent years of his life practising the guitar.

Now an accomplished shredder along the lines of his heroes James Hetfield and Dave Mustaine, Heafy graduated from a Gibson Les Paul to a Dean Razorback as part of a general metalling-up of his image, adding tattoo sleeves and beefing up the band's sound and image at the same time.

It's easy to see why Trivium have been so successful. The band have the whole package: a reasonably heavy sound with properly-structured songs that their predominantly teenage fans adore; expert musicianship; the right look; and the right label, Roadrunner, behind them. Older metalheads tend to dismiss them as mere Metallica clones or metalcore dullards, but that's not entirely fair given that Heafy and the others are still at such an early stage in their careers.

> **"**
> For warming up my fingers, I have John Petrucci's Rock Discipline. I memorised the book.
> **"**

▶▶▌ Genius moment

Heafy's solo in the Trivium song 'Detonation' (from their 2006 album The Crusade) features breathtaking sweep picking. Could you do that when you were 20?

Heafy on ritual

"An hour before show time I change and stretch. Two hours before show time I warm up my fingers and then I do my vocals. Three hours before I eat dinner, and four hours before the show I work out. For warming up my fingers, I have John Petrucci's *Rock Discipline*. I memorised the book. First I do the weird-sounding exercises without a metronome, then I do chords, and then I pretty much go through the whole book with a metronome. Then I do some sweeps."

SYNYSTER GATES (Brian Haner, Jr)
Avenged Sevenfold

Trivium, Bullet For My Valentine, and Avenged Sevenfold are the best-known bands of the newest wave of youthful heavy metal. They bring expert guitar skills and a blend of classic and modern metal sounds to the table. Of the three, Avenged Sevenfold (usually referred to as A7X) are the most poppy. They play hooky and often deliberately lightweight songs with extended solos and instrumental passages.

LEFT Polish quartet Vader, who spearheaded the Eastern European extreme metal wave in the early 1990s. Piotr 'Peter' Wiwczarek appears second from right.

Guitarists Brian Haner and Zachary Baker – who play with the stage-names Synyster Gates and Zacky Vengeance – offer a breathtaking mixture of melodic shredding and a barrage of riffs, even if their production doesn't allow the songs to be truly heavy. With enormous record sales and concert attendances, A7X have hit a winning formula, and Gates has contributed to this with a lead style that combines the most memorable elements of 80s hair-metal with vintage thrash.

Gates's studies of jazz guitar and his piano work on some A7X songs provide him with the classic multi-instrumentalist's ability to see the entire shape of a song rather than merely one facet of it. His playing chops were encouraged by his father, a professional musician who has played acoustic guitar on Avenged Sevenfold albums, and Gates has been recognised with awards from *Metal Hammer* and *Total Guitar* magazines among others. Whatever you may think of his band's songs, there's no denying his talent.

> **Power metal as it was defined in the 80s and early 90s was an enjoyable if unsophisticated beast.**

> ▶▶▮ **Genius moment**
> City Of Evil's 'Blinded In Chains' from 2005 features plenty of examples of the Gates guitar genius, even though the emo influences on the rest of the album at times threaten to become overpowering.

JON SCHAFFER
Iced Earth

Power metal as it was defined in the 80s and early 90s was an enjoyable if unsophisticated beast, with Helloween, Gamma Ray, and the rest of the European pack flaunting their influences with a little too much reckless abandon in the early years of the movement. But when American power metal began to gain significance a few years later, it was a tougher, more credible take on the old amped-up, sped-up-Iron-Maiden style. Iced Earth kickstarted the movement and remained more or less at its commercial peak in the decade since then.

Thanks to the transformation of the American metal scene in the mid to late 80s by the Big Four Of Thrash, US musicians had rather more to live up to, in particular a fearsome legacy of dexterous guitar-playing. This explains the rise of guitarists such as Jon Schaffer, a player whose awareness of vintage thrash tempers and informs the less extreme but equally technical music he makes with Iced Earth.

Schaffer is at the core of the band alongside his brother-in-law, singer Matt Barlow. He plays powerfully and accurately, adding sophisticated leads to the songs he writes according to his interests, which include the American Civil War and specifically the Battle of Gettysburg. As power metal fans will appreciate, military history is a good source of gripping, imagery-rich storylines and is particularly suited to the Iced Earth approach.

Schaffer never sacrifices warmth and feel for mere technical mastery, instead contributing guitar parts of great dexterity to the band, of which he is the sole remaining founder member and undoubted leader. He also plays alongside Blind

65/100

ANDRE OLBRICH

64/100

Guardian singer Hansi Kürsch in a more melodic, European-sounding band, Demons And Wizards, who are successful in their own right.

> ▶▶ **Genius moment**
>
> The 32 minutes of 'Gettysburg (1863)' from the 2004 album The Glorious Burden shows every facet of Schaffer's guitar virtuosity as well as his broad ambition.

ANDRE OLBRICH
Blind Guardian

Germany is the home of European power metal. There are notable exceptions, such as Dragonforce from the UK, but ever since Helloween first established the fast, clean, melodic style of power metal in the 80s, the bands have tended to a Teutonic polish. The current commercial leaders of that pack are Blind Guardian, who have been defining the scene since their foundation by frontman Hansi Kürsch and lead guitarist Andre Olbrich as long ago as the mid 80s.

Power metal requires immense picking precision from its rhythm guitarists if their parts are to be distinguishable and, indeed, listenable. The staccato crunch of thrash metal, particularly the Bay Area variant, is regarded as too dry for the true power-metal player, who applies enough palm muting so that some strings ring briefly outside the I+V power chord. This leads to a warmer sound, and Olbrich is an expert in this area. He is also an expert when it comes to recording blistering solos. His playing has contributed directly to Blind Guardian's rise to international prominence, with a rabid fanbase following their every move.

> **"**
> Power metal requires immense picking precision from its rhythm guitarists if their parts are to be distinguishable and, indeed, listenable.
> **"**

> ▶▶ **Genius moment**
>
> The 1998 album Nightfall In Middle-earth is typical of Blind Guardian's fantasy approach, and Olbrich's blistering solos throughout are a great showcase for his style. Listen out for his shredding on the single 'Mirror Mirror'.

NIKLAS SUNDIN
Dark Tranquillity

Melodic death metal was something of an oddity when it first made its presence felt in the mid 90s. Many fans of extreme metal felt that the combination of Iron Maiden-style duelling guitars with the brutality of death metal was an incongruous one. However, the early albums by At The Gates, In Flames, and Dark Tranquillity simply

RIGHT Progressive metal would never have come to pass without bands such as Queensryche and guitarists like Chris DeGarmo (left).

CHRIS DEGARMO

62/100

could not be dismissed, and the style gained a foothold very rapidly. A decade later, and MDM (as the cognoscenti refer to it) vastly outsells the older, more aggressive style.

Sweden's death metal scene is now split along stylistic and geographical lines, with Gothenburg the home of the newer sound, while old-school death is Stockholm-based. This is thanks to the pioneering guitar work of a few key individuals, and Dark Tranquillity's Niklas Sundin is one of them. His blistering leads, influenced heavily by the classic Maiden–Priest sound, combine with fast, powerful rhythm parts that require extreme accuracy.

Sundin is something of an everyman. He contributes to the band Laethora as well as Dark Tranquillity, guests as lead guitarist with the Japanese avant-garde metal band Sigh, and runs a graphics company, Cabin Fever Media, which has designed jackets for dozens of metal albums, mostly by Scandinavian bands. A one-man industry, Sundin is responsible for much of the currently healthy state of Swedish metal. (This is a subject worthy of its own book: *Swedish Death Metal*, written by Insision bassist Daniel Ekeroth).

> **Most of the typical shredders or guitar heroes aren't interesting to me, and there's also the whole ego-elevation context that I dislike. That whole wind-in-the-hair, foot-on-the-monitor thing is off-putting.**

▶▶| **Genius moment**

'Inside The Particle Storm' from Dark Tranquillity's 2007 Fiction album is as violent as the title sounds, and it is based on a superb guitar riff from Niklas.

Sundin on idols

"Most of the typical shredders or guitar heroes aren't interesting to me, and there's also the whole ego-elevation context that I dislike. That whole wind-in-the-hair, foot-on-the-monitor thing is off-putting. I admire creativity and a strong artistic vision, so if I had to pick one person, I'd chose Snorre Ruch of Thorns, whose dissonant and eerie riffing really was unique for its time and really made a mark on black metal riffing as we know it today."

CHRIS DEGARMO
Queensryche

Chris DeGarmo was a founder member of the Seattle-based progressive metal band Queensryche. He helped the band move quickly to a respected position in the metal field thanks to his excellent, inventive playing and two classic albums that fuelled the rise of the prog-metal genre. Without Queensryche, modern prog-metal giants such as Dream Theater might well not exist.

Queensryche's first major impact came with *Rage For Order* in 1986, an album prominently displaying the guitar interplay between DeGarmo and Michael Wilton, the operatic wails of frontman Geoff Tate, and the ambitious scope of the band's songwriting. Critics and fans noted the clean, precise picking of DeGarmo, who wrote or co-wrote most of the songs.

62/100

His contribution was also at the forefront of the band's huge-selling concept record *Operation: Mindcrime*, the 1988 album that defined the progressive-metal genre and made the band a big name for the first time. With his measured, economical solos and riffs that relied as much on atmosphere as attack, DeGarmo was a revelation at the time, his playing influenced by the prog-rock greats of the 70s as well as the metal pioneers.

However, Queensryche hit hard times in the late 90s. Like so many other classic metal bands, they were swamped by the nu-metal wave and deprived of a large chunk of their audience. DeGarmo quit in 1998, marking the end of a remarkable 17-year stint with the band.

Although DeGarmo now enjoys a second career as a commercial pilot, he may have chosen the wrong time to leave the band, who recorded *Operation: Mindcrime II* in 2006, toured both *Mindcrime* albums with Ronnie James Dio singing the part of the album's villainous Dr X, and regained a great deal of popularity as a result. DeGarmo's two guest appearances with them in recent years indicate that relationships with his ex-bandmembers are healthy, and it is to be hoped that he re-applies his considerable talents with them again.

> ▶▶ **Genius moment**
> DeGarmo wrote 'The Mission', from the original 1988 Mindcrime, and to this day it's clear that he was a songwriter and arranger ahead of his time. His melodic solos and complex rhythm parts made him one of the first virtuoso prog-metallers.

> "
> His contribution was also at the forefront of the band's huge-selling concept record Operation: Mindcrime, the 1988 album that defined the progressive-metal genre.
> "

MARTIN LARSSON
At The Gates

At The Gates were nothing less than pioneers on the European metal scene, fusing classic metal melodies – specifically in the lead guitars – with old-school death metal to create a new, radio-friendly version of the ol' death beast. Guitarist Anders Björler is perhaps better known than his axe-slinging partner Martin Larsson, because he went on to found the successful neo-thrash band The Haunted, but Larsson's contribution was certainly important. Björler himself made a point of commending his skills on the guitar, and Larsson remains one of the more underrated guitarists on the Scandinavian metal scene.

Larsson has an all-round style, as with the other guitarists in this book from the melodic death metal scene – and believe me, it would have been possible to completely populate our Top 100 with musicians from that movement. He has a flawless grasp of classic harmonised solos, playing both the upper and lower parts as required, and a perfect instinct for when to apply restraint to his solos and when to shred at full speed.

Similarly, the riffs that he and Björler used in ATG require an innate, near-

61/100

> **He has a flawless grasp of classic harmonised solos, playing both the upper and lower parts as required, and a perfect instinct for when to apply restraint to his solos and when to shred at full speed.**

telepathic awareness between the two men, each knowing when to accent a particular stroke during fast tremolo picking. This is essential to the success of all the best guitar teams – among them Adrian Smith and Dave Murray, Kerry King and Jeff Hanneman, James Hetfield and Kirk Hammett.

▶▶❘ Genius moment

The 1994 and '95 At The Gates albums Terminal Spirit Disease and Slaughter Of The Soul are stuffed full of essential guitar moments – but Slaughter's opening track 'Blinded By Fear' contains a millimetre-perfect core riff, which the Björler and Larsson team execute with stunning precision.

ANDY LA ROCQUE
King Diamond, Death

Swedish musician Andy La Rocque (yes, another Swedish metal man) is an accomplished guitarist, songwriter, and producer, and a guest artist on a stack of metal albums. He's best known for his deeply melodic European-style soloing, using wide string-bends and slides, delivered in the open, expressive style that evolved in the 70s with Scorpions and UFO and refined and beefed up by Metallica and others.

Today, a couple of decades after La Rocque began his career as a professional guitarist, there are identifiable differences between the lead styles of black and death metal – harmonised lines do not exist in old-school black metal, for example – but this has never stopped La Rocque from applying his skills in both subgenres.

He is best known for his playing and songwriting in King Diamond, the spinoff band from Danish black metallers Mercyful Fate named after their singer, but he also made a prestigious guest appearance on Death's superb, progressive 1993 album *Individual Thought Patterns*. For anyone unfamiliar with La Rocque, the fact that Chuck Schuldiner invited to him to play on the album and then found himself challenged to new heights of technicality by his guest should be enough to convince them of his skills. *ITP*'s closing song, 'The Philosopher', remains one of Death's best-known compositions.

▶▶❘ Genius moment

'The 7th Day Of July 1777' from King Diamond's classic 1987 concept album Abigail is ludicrously over-the-top in concept and lyrics, in perfect synch with Diamond's fantastical stage act. Guitar-wise, it's much more subtle, with a marvellous cluster of riffs.

La Rocque also contributed a solo to 'Cold' from At The Gates' classic 1995 album *Slaughter Of The Soul*. To this day, that band's primary songwriter, Anders Björler, a highly technical guitarist himself, admits that reproducing it on stage is something he could never easily do.

60/100

TIMO TOLKKI
Stratovarius

Timo Tolkki is the principal driving force behind Finnish power metal band Stratovarius – a band that, as their name would suggest, have a neo-classical and symphonic focus. Tolkki is a singer, bassist, producer, and songwriter as well as a remarkably literate guitarist. Over the 17 Stratovarius albums released so far, spanning close to two decades, he has evolved his style to achieve a state-of-the-art grasp of melodic soloing, while his rhythm parts – always a demanding task in the power metal field – are awe-inspiringly tight.

Along with Blind Guardian and Helloween, Stratovarius head up the European power metal movement, thanks not only to the unearthly playing skills of the guitarists but also to the songwriting abilities of Tolkki and his counterparts in the other acts. During breaks from his main band, he has contributed guest parts to other albums and found the time to record and release two records of his own, each of which explore an area that would not be wholly suited to the Stratovarius sound.

On his most recent solo album, 2002's *Hymn To Life*, Tolkki wrote intensely personal songs addressing family bereavements and religion, while back in 1994 he recorded *Classical Themes And Variations*, which was an exercise in adapting classical music for guitar. With a prodigious work rate and a band whose popularity has been in the ascendant for decades, Tolkki will no doubt be advancing the role of the heavy metal guitar for years to come.

> ▶▶◀ **Genius moment**
> 'A Million Light Years Away' from 2000's Infinite album demonstrates Tolkki's lyrical approach and his atmospheric guitar talents.

SCOTT IAN
Anthrax, Stormtroopers Of Death

The Big Four Of Thrash Metal had many similarities, but perhaps the one common strand that most strongly unites them is the ability of their guitarists to deliver a rhythm part of astonishing precision. Thrash – the term was defined by approximately 1987 – was all about the crunch, and often the 'Bay Area crunch', although none of the four came originally from the San Francisco Bay. This supertight, super-damped speed-picking style, achieved by extremely fast strumming of a power chord or a single string with judicious palm-muting, characterised the entire scene and continues to be the core sound of all extreme metal to this day.

Some bands couldn't do it, and sounded terrible at high speed as a result. Those

> "
> The Big Four Of Thrash Metal had many similarities, but perhaps the one common strand that most strongly unites them is the ability of their guitarists to deliver a rhythm part of astonishing precision.
> "

59/100

SCOTT IAN

that could, however, stood a chance of making it – and Anthrax combined this sound (courtesy of Ian, born Scott Ian Rosenfeld) with excellent songwriting. As a result they became one of the biggest extreme metal bands of the 80s.

Ian was influenced by Kiss, the New Wave Of British Heavy Metal, and one or two older acts, such as Ted Nugent. He has always been a flamboyant stage performer, growing a beard and spending much of the 80s with the word 'Not' shaved into his chest hair. His lead guitar skills have always been adequate rather than stunning, but his partners in Anthrax (first Dan Spitz and then Rob Caggiano) made up for that.

Ian's love of US hardcore punk informs his rhythm technique, and combined with the more extrovert influences already listed this makes for a style of unique power and strength. Although Metallica and Megadeth play more melodically and Slayer with more devoted aggression, Anthrax were the tightest band – or at least they were at their peak. In recent years, their place in the sun has been dimmed by too many line-up changes, record company problems, and an apparent inability to hold on to the songwriting genius that made their best albums – *Spreading The Disease* (1985) and *Among The Living* (1987) – so good and so popular.

> "
> He has always been a flamboyant stage performer, growing a beard and spending much of the 80s with the word 'Not' shaved into his chest hair.
> "

▶▍ Genius moment

The unbelievably precise and speedy rhythm picking of 'Gung-Ho'. The unbelievably precise and speedy rhythm picking of 'I Am The Law'. The unbelievably precise and speedy picking of 'Got The Time'. I could go on.

MILLE PETROZZA
Kreator

Let's face it, German thrash metal was mostly unglamorous compared to its American counterpart. Where Slayer were malevolent, Sodom were lumpen; where Metallica were sophisticated, Destruction were merely aggressive; and where Megadeth offered heroin chic, Tankard merely soundtracked a hangover.

But Kreator were different. Not only did they offer insane levels of speed for thrash-obsessed fans, they balanced it out with heaviness, actual songwriting skills, superb picking accuracy, and an aura of vitriol that came largely from the hissing vocal style of frontman Mille Petrozza and the apocalyptic subject matter of the songs. The combination of those vocals and the maddened sonic attack even briefly earned Kreator the sobriquet of 'hate metal' – a genre tag that didn't last long.

Petrozza in particular was the focal point of the band, boosted by the powerful drumming of Jürgen 'Ventor' Reil, the only other member who has stayed the distance over the band's 25-year career. Reil's dedication to the cause of numbingly violent thrash metal stemmed from a pivotal experience he had in 1981. His band,

57/100

MILLE PETROZZA

57/100

Tyrant, were playing average heavy metal at the time, but all that changed when he first heard a Venom single played at a nightclub. Upping the velocities of the songs and adopting a much more threatening lyrical stance, Tyrant became Kreator and the die was cast.

The band progressed rapidly: too rapidly for some. Although Kreator's 80s albums were all about incredible speed and intensity – *Pleasure To Kill* and *Extreme Aggression* are among the best – Petrozza explored other territory in the next decade, replacing gothic rock with experimental imagery. This didn't sit well with the fans, although a return to the thrash sound with 2001's *Violent Revolution* brought Kreator back to the top of the German thrash scene once again.

▶▶ **Genius moment**

It's only available on the Past Life Trauma (1985-1992) compilation released in 2000, but the demo track 'After The Attack' boasts a sickeningly visceral opening riff that hooks-in the dedicated Kreator fan every time. Otherwise, get Pleasure To Kill and listen to it – all of it.

RAND BURKEY
Atheist

Like Cynic, their closest contemporaries in style, Atheist played dense, layered death metal with elements of jazz, world music, and progressive rock. Guitarists Rand Burkey and Kelly Shaefer exchanged riffs with a deft interplay that earned them much respect, while bassist Roger Patterson and a succession of drummers backed them up with equally technical playing.

Sadly, Patterson died in a car accident in 1991, just before the band released their masterpiece, *Unquestionable Presence*. He wrote the bass parts for the album but never had the chance to record them. Tony Choy was his successor and the album went down in history as one of the best technical death metal records ever released, alongside Death's *Human*.

Burkey's guitar playing was incandescent, combining his love of classical and jazz with fearsome metal riffing. He claims that his influences were traditional metal acts such as Judas Priest and Black Sabbath and thrashers like Venom and Kreator – but at the same time Yes, Rush, Al Dimeola, and even Elvis Presley figured in there. This claim makes absolute sense given the multifaceted nature of his playing, which was much missed when Atheist took a seven-year hiatus due to business and personal pressures.

The band reformed in the early years of the new decade and again in 2006 for a well-attended and presumably lucrative tour. In the interim, prog-metal has become a popular form of music, perhaps proving all along that Atheist were simply ahead of their time.

> **Burkey's guitar playing was incandescent, combining his love of classical and jazz with fearsome metal riffing.**

LEFT **Mille Petrozza (front), whose raw guitar style on Kreator's early records has gained enormous power and fluidity over the years.**

GARY HOLT

55/100

▶▶| **Genius moment**
The entire Unquestionable Presence album of 1991 is a guitar workout for Burkey and Schaefer, but try 'Enthralled In Essence' for an eye-opening experience. (And look out for the 2005 reissue on Relapse that includes the demo featuring the late Roger Patterson.)

GARY HOLT
Exodus

In a way, 'the Big Four Of Thrash Metal' was an unfortunate phrase, because it excluded the next two bands in commercial terms, Testament and Exodus. Testament's guitarist and founder member Eric Peterson has expressed some dissatisfaction with the term, reasonably enough; to his credit, Exodus founder member Gary Holt appears to be happy with his lot as leader of a legendary band, and doesn't complain.

For many fans, Exodus defined the San Francisco Bay Area thrash sound, despite the importance of other local bands such as Death Angel, Forbidden, Possessed, Vio-Lence, and Testament. Metallica, who moved to San Fran in 1982, when they recruited their second bassist, Cliff Burton, established the city's first extreme metal scene. Their LA neighbours Slayer were hot on their heels, but after Slayer it was Exodus who trod the thrash metal path, releasing a demo of their gobsmackingly violent debut album *Bonded By Blood* long before the finished product was recorded.

That tape attracted metalheads by the thousand to Exodus's early shows, and the 1985 Combat Tour – on which they supported Slayer and Venom – was a crucial one. Holt's youthful shredding and a powerfully tight rhythm style, alongside the slightly less evolved playing of second guitarist Rick Hunolt, was a blast of energy that defied many other band's attempts to match Exodus.

It's interesting to note that Holt's original guitar partner in Exodus before Hunolt was Kirk Hammett, who helped to found the band and write some early songs but departed to join Metallica in early 1983 after they fired Dave Mustaine. It was an incestuous scene, then, but one in which Exodus played a major part. Why they never made it as big as the Big Four is a mystery to this day.

" Gary Holt appears to be happy with his lot as leader of a legendary band, and doesn't complain. "

▶▶| **Genius moment**
Bonded By Blood (1985) is a near-perfect thrash metal album. Choose any track for evidence of Holt's playing skills, but the classic 'A Lesson In Violence' still stands tall after all these years.

LEFT Exodus were the original Bay Area thrashers, even before Metallica — and Gary Holt (far left) was their most consistently impressive member.

55/100

MATT BACHAND
Shadows Fall

> **Guitarist Matt Bachand is among the most gifted of a young and necessarily hardworking new breed of axemen.**

Heading up the so-called New Wave Of American Heavy Metal (NWOAHM), Massachusetts band Shadows Fall enjoyed a rapid rise to prominence as the nu-metal movement breathed its last in the early years of the new century. Their ascent may have levelled off a little in recent years, but that's to be expected – the NWOAHM reached its natural level quickly, and the stronger bands will be all that remain a couple of years from now.

Whether or not Shadows Fall will be among the survivors when the dust settles is open to conjecture, but it certainly won't be down to any lack of technical skill among the musicians. Guitarist Matt Bachand is among the most gifted of a young and necessarily hardworking new breed of axemen. He is one of a small number of players whose abilities became in demand relatively suddenly, once it was clear that guitar solos were cool again.

Having worked his way through a succession of death metal bands, Bachand was a natural choice for Shadows Fall when they formed in the mid 90s, as he offered phenomenal ability on rhythm and lead parts. The band's third album, *The Art Of Balance* (2002), marked their international breakthrough and featured a cover of Pink Floyd's 'Welcome To The Machine' – a sign that Bachand and his bandmates have musical interests outside the usual box. When the NWOAHM is no more and he does something new, it will be fascinating to see where he takes his expertise.

▶▶❘ Genius moment

The War Within (2004) revealed that Shadows Fall were slowing down and giving some thought to their music. 'The Power Of I And I' has Bachand playing expert riffs and leads that serve the song rather than merely showcase his technical skills.

COREY BEAULIEU
Trivium

The Florida quartet Trivium had an unprepossessing metalcore approach in their earliest days, moved to a more thrash-based sound on their ascent to the major leagues, and today embrace 80s hair-metal, the classic metal acts of the previous decade, and (at last) a sound that is more or less their own. Guitarist Corey Beaulieu alternates leads with co-guitarist Matt Heafy, taking a slightly more complex route with the rhythm parts as Heafy is also handling vocals.

Beaulieu's sweep-picking and tapping are especially evolved features of his style, which is surprisingly technical for such a relatively young musician (he was born in

RIGHT **Corey Beaulieu, the youngest guitarist in this book, brings fast alternate picking and sweeps to the Florida quartet Trivium.**

COREY BEALIEU

53/100

1983). He cites Dave Mustaine and Dimebag Darrell Abbott as influences, and in recent years has added a Dean Razorback Flying V to his many Jackson guitars.

Beaulieu has many years left in him as a guitarist, so it will be interesting to see where he takes Trivium next. He clearly has the full range of tricks at his disposal, acquired over many years of practice. As he once told me: "If you're serious about making it in the music business, you need to apply some time management and pursue a real practice plan." This reveals much about Trivium, who have made serious progress in a serious, even slightly humourless way. Hard work and practice has certainly paid off.

> "If you're serious about making it in the music business, you need to apply some time management and pursue a real practice plan."

> ▶▶❘ **Genius moment**
>
> The 2005 single 'Pull Harder On The Strings Of Your Martyr' features supremely dexterous soloing from Beaulieu – and some impressive windmilling (in other words, headbanging in a circular motion rather than just back and forth).

KARL SANDERS
Nile

South Carolina quartet Nile are perhaps the world's most technical death metal band. They make complex, aggressive music that takes months to compose, arrange, and record – even years, in the case of one particularly demanding solo. Guitarists Dallas Toler-Wade and founder member and primary songwriter Karl Sanders are at the peak of their profession. Not only do they have the fearsome ability required to conceive and play the material, but also they manage to remember the arrangements of the songs.

Sanders is that rare thing in heavy metal – an educated intellectual. His guitar playing is rivalled in its central place in the Nile concept only by his lyric-writing, which comes from his academic interest in the history of ancient Egypt. The gods, wars, aristocracy, and occult magic of this long-gone era populate Nile's songs in intricate detail, matching the fine detail of the arrangements and solos. Sanders also supplies lengthy and exhaustive explanatory liner notes to his albums.

This intricate approach extends too Sanders' equipment. He currently plays an unbranded custom twin-neck guitar (with headstocks that are so sharp that playing near him must be dangerous), and he channels the sound through a variety of synth software, using a computer on stage to manipulate the various choral, ambient, and orchestral sounds for Nile's song introductions and between-song segments. Sanders loves this area of music-making so much that he released a solo album, *Saurian Meditation*, in 2004, which consisted of the atmospheric sounds that accompany the brutal grind of Nile's songs. In recognition of his impact on the international death metal scene, Sanders has been asked to supply guest solos to songs by Behemoth and Morbid Angel. He is one of a kind, and so is his band.

52/100

> **▶▶▎ Genius moment**
> The extended intro (super-heavy) and main riff breakdown (super-fast) in 'Divine Intent', a demo track released on In The Beginning, a 1999 collection reissued at least twice since then. And that's just a demo track.

JAMES ROOT
Slipknot, Stone Sour

James Root is one of the few musicians in this book to have survived the death of nu-metal – now possibly the most unfashionable musical genre on the planet – and also one of the small number who operate in two almost equally successful bands. Root has been a member of the Iowa nine-piece band Slipknot since 1999, when he replaced Josh Brainard in time for the release of their self-titled debut album – but not in time to get his masked face on the cover: that's Brainard in the gimp mask.

Root went unmasked for Stone Sour's eponymous first record in 2002. Slipknot were an established brand by then, and Stone Sour – a bunch of old friends from Slipknot's pre-fame days on the club scene in Des Moines – were only supposed to be a side project that needed a little helping hand from Root and Slipknot frontman Corey Taylor. No one was as surprised as Root when that band also hit the big time.

> **▶▶▎ Genius moment**
> Watch the 2002 DVD Disasterpieces and find the backstage footage of Root, evil mask leering into the camera, churning out the deathly heavy opening riff from Holocaust's 'The Small Hours' – an old NWOBHM tune made famous by Metallica on their 1987 Garage Days Re-Revisited EP – and adding some gut-wrenching pinch harmonics.

Root and his guitar partner in Slipknot, Mick Thomson, had a frustrating time in the early days of the band. Neither the debut record nor 2001's *Iowa* featured a single guitar solo. Why? The reasons are manifold. The band trusted producer Ross Robinson, but maybe he didn't think that solos suited the songs? Maybe the band themselves were labouring under the thou-shalt-not-shred credo of nu-metal? Who knows: maybe the record company thought solos were a bad idea?

All we really know is that by the time *Volume III: The Subliminal Verses* came out in 2003, the gloves were off. Robinson had been replaced by Rick Rubin, a producer from an older generation, and Root and Thomson were playing fast, malevolent guitar solos all over the songs, from atonal, Slayer-style squeals to melodic, even neo-classical figures. Talent will out, it seems.

Root and Thomson were playing fast, malevolent guitar solos all over the songs, from atonal, Slayer-style squeals to melodic, even neo-classical figures.

51/100

DEVIN TOWNSEND

DEVIN TOWNSEND
Strapping Young Lad

The Canadian singer-songwriter Devin Townsend is a law unto himself, combining death metal, traditional heavy metal, and epic atmospherics to create music unlike any other. He admits to experiencing a nervous breakdown after making every record (of which there have been many, issued under various guises) and has a habit of mocking his own receding hairline. Townsend is a bit like a mad professor of metal, channelling his eccentric worldview into albums by Strapping Young Lad, his own Devin Townsend Band, and the records he has released under his own name. After a decade of frantic activity, he announced in 2007 that he would no longer tour or release albums as a band, preferring to record as a solo artist and spend more time with his young family. Heavy Devy, as he would be nicknamed, was born in 1972 and has enjoyed a long and fruitful career both in his own right and as a guest musician with other artists. His roots on the Vancouver music scene may explain some of his slightly skewed approach to the guitar. Having learned to play the banjo at the age of five and developing a love of stage musicals, he switched to the guitar at 12 and began an exhausting practice schedule of up to ten hours a day.

His big break came in 1991 when he signed to Relativity Records, the Californian label responsible alongside Shrapnel for the rise of the 80s shredder. He was introduced to Steve Vai, who was looking for a singer. Townsend, also an accomplished vocalist, sang on Vai's *Sex And Religion* album and toured with him and his some-time support act The Wildhearts for the next three years.

A period followed in which Townsend applied his many talents to unrealised projects, such as the demo band IR8 with Metallica bassist Jason Newsted and Exodus drummer Tom Hunting. The recordings – not officially released until 2002, when Newsted had left Metallica – led to a deal with the Century Media label, who offered Townsend a five-album deal. This was the moment he'd been waiting for, and he embarked on a frenzy of activity with various incarnations until that retreat in 2007.

True to his nature, he recorded the first album for his new label almost entirely by himself and gave it a silly name, *Heavy As A Really Heavy Thing*. It's interesting to speculate how many more fans Townsend might have attracted to his fantastic music if he hadn't chosen the deliberately mystifying band-name Strapping Young Lad or persisted in choosing quirky album titles.

Never content to sit back in one musical style, Townsend then formed the first of many side projects, Punky Brüster, in which he performed joke punk songs. A second project was Ocean Machine, recording a 1997 album in Japan and avidly received there, although so far it appears to have been a one-off.

Strapping Young Lad released a live EP in 1998 called *No Sleep 'Til Bedtime* (a title that mocked the Beastie Boys and Motörhead simultaneously – quite an achievement). It was the first album to show what an accomplished guitarist he had become. Although lead guitar isn't as prominent a feature of his music as it is for most metal bands, Townsend's breathtaking rhythm playing is notable for its precision and range of textures.

> **Having learned to play the banjo at the age of five and developing a love of stage musicals, he switched to the guitar at 12 and began an exhausting practice schedule of up to ten hours a day.**

LEFT All hail Devin Townsend, the mad professor of extreme metal.

50/100

A man of considerable songwriting vision, Townsend had evolved a signature sound with many multilayered guitar tracks and a vast soundscape somehow fuller and more epic than the usual tightly-controlled metal sound. He smothers his vocals in reverb and occupies a wide range of frequencies with the guitar – and the bass guitar is reduced to a background rumble – in the process creating something genuinely new in heavy metal. This was all audible on *No Sleep 'Til Bedtime* and peaked on the next album, 2002's *City*, which has since achieved classic status.

A series of albums, by Strapping Young Lad and The Devin Townsend, has continued to attract new fans to his excellent, always unpredictable songwriting. The cult of Devin Townsend continues to grow thanks to his eccentric persona, which he projects in interviews. There's no one quite like him, in metal or elsewhere.

> ▶▶ **Genius moment**
> There are so many! However, the brutal opening riff in 'Relentless' from Strapping Young Lad's self-titled album of 2003 has it all – incredible speed, violence, and precision, and all propelled by the still-stunning drums of Gene Hoglan.

" One day I was fuckin' around at my house and I came across this setting that I just pissed around with. Now I've been using it for so many years that I can't hear myself without it. "

Townsend on sound

"I have a Roland GP-100, an obsolete guitar processor which lets you do 15 effects in a row. One day I was fuckin' around at my house and I came across this setting that I just pissed around with. Now I've been using it for so many years that I can't hear myself without it. It's a really saturated, solid-state guitar tone with tons of echo and tons of stereo delay and a pitchshifter. I only use one sound really, for lead and rhythm. The dynamics are in the pick."

ANDREAS KISSER
Sepultura

Brazilian band Sepultura are the best non-American thrash metal act ever. They emerged in 1983 from decidedly metal-unfriendly circumstances: the mean streets of São Paolo. Their frontman, Max Cavalera, played guitar alongside second guitarist Jairo Guedz, until Andreas Kisser was drafted in to replace Guedz in 1986. A far superior musician than his predecessor, Kisser had studied classical guitar as a teenager and brought a degree of skill to the band that neither Guedz nor Cavalera could match. Cavalera concentrated on rhythm guitar – he famously removes the top B and E strings from his guitars as a consequence – leaving Kisser free to add his superb leads to the songs.

Kisser played Charvel and Jackson guitars in his early career but moved to Fender Stratocasters in recent years – an unusual choice given that the tremolo picking he employed in Sepultura's early days required a scooped tone and a compressed frequency range, neither of which are typical of the Strat's classic sound. However,

Sepultura's more recent work is perfect for the warm, rounded Strat tone, an unexpected benefit of the fact that the band's career effectively falls into two halves.

Until 1991, Sepultura pursued thrash metal, as pioneered by Slayer, Kreator, and Possessed, bands that valued brutal riffs and incredible picking speed rather than the melodic songwriting of, say, Metallica or Megadeth. Adhering to the style with some panache, Sepultura blasted through four albums of increasing sophistication. *Morbid Visions* and *Schizophrenia* weren't much more than extremely fast thrash-by-numbers, but *Beneath The Remains* (1989) and *Arise* ('91) were breathtaking landmarks of the genre. Kisser's dexterous leads, Cavalera's icy picking-hand control, and the ability of both men to mesh with each other's unison and harmony riffs all became identifiable trademarks. Cavalera's brother Igor was the band's drummer and the two seemed to share a telepathic bond: the band played at a thrash speed that was "neither fast nor very fast, but somewhere in between" as Max told me in 2008.

However, by the time *Chaos AD* appeared in 1993 there had been a slightly depressing development in the band's sound. The album contained only one truly thrash metal track – the superb 'Biotech Is Godzilla', with lyrics written by Dead Kennedys frontman Jello Biafra. Although the song is fast and aggressive, the rhythm part executed by Cavalera and Kisser is punkish and sloppy, with none of the razor-sharp precision that Sepultura had displayed on earlier albums. The rest of the album showed the same movement away from extreme metal to more of a punk sound. Feel and groove were more of a focus for the writers now than tight delivery. In fact, *Chaos AD* showed the first signs of the groove-metal approach that Pantera and Korn would make their own and which Sepultura embraced by the middle of the decade.

A few years later, many extreme metal fans regretted this change in direction. The groove approach led to the nu-metal wave that dominated the scene for some years in the early 2000s and caused serious problems for many thrash and death metal bands. And all because a few key guitarists abandoned their grasp of picking-hand precision.

Kisser continued to add excellent leads to Cavalera's rhythm parts, which (depending on your point of view) either became more and more groove-oriented and experimental or just deteriorated from the former highs. When Max Cavalera quit the band in 1996 after their last album together, *Roots*, Kisser became the band's sole guitarist – a position he has apparently relished in the years since then.

Now, Sepultura have been a one-guitar band for as long as they were a twin-guitar band, and although Kisser's guitar playing has remained exemplary, the band's popularity has dimmed since Cavalera's departure. Examine Kisser's playing on 'Come Back Alive' from 2003's *Roorback* album, for instance, and you'll hear that it still bears the groove-metal hallmarks: a combination of up and downstrokes across a power chord; the polar opposite of the hardened, more challenging downstroke-only approach, or indeed of single-string tremolo picking. 'Leech' offers similar evidence, although the ferocious pace of both songs and the clarity of the production make them much better than average.

Furthermore, Sepultura with Kisser at the helm have always been criticised by their fans as inferior to the Cavalera line-up. This is perhaps inevitable given the success of Cavalera's post-Seps band, Soulfly, who became popular quickly. Although the output

> **They emerged in 1983 from decidedly metal-unfriendly circumstances: the mean streets of São Paolo.**

49/100

ANDREAS KISSER

Sepultura's post-Max Cavalera line-up features at its core guitarist Andreas Kisser (second left), whose warp-speed riffs and Latin influences make his hand one of a kind.

> **Kisser had studied classical guitar as a teenager and brought a degree of skill to the band that neither Guedz nor Cavalera could match.**

of both bands has been patchy since the great schism of 1996, Soulfly took the lead (after two depressingly modish records) when their third album, *3* (2002), and fourth, *Dark Ages* (2005), boasted some songs of blistering speed and violence.

The downward trend of Sepultura's career was emphasised further in 2007 when Igor Cavalera quit the band to join his brother in The Cavalera Conspiracy, whose debut album *Inflikted* received mostly positive reviews. Perhaps Kisser – a veteran of over two decades in metal – will trigger Sepultura's final demise when he releases his forthcoming solo album, rumoured at the time of writing to be titled *Hubris*. Another, less likely development is the full re-formation of the Max and Igor Cavalera line-up, although as The Cavalera Conspiracy gains momentum this looks more and more doubtful.

▶▶▌ **Genius moment**

The frantic but melodic solos all over Sepultura's 1989 album Beneath The Remains marked Kisser forever as one of the most talented guitarists in thrash. Much respect is due.

KAI HANSEN
Gamma Ray, Helloween

Power metal as we recognise it today was pioneered by Helloween, as you'll recall from the Michael Weikath entry. Combining the picking speed of thrash metal with the melodic elements and fantasy themes of traditional heavy metal, power metal sells a huge number of records – and it is the friendly face of metal for those who find the malevolence and sonic attack of death and black metal too unsettling.

Helloween were fronted for some years after their formation by Kai Hansen, a singer and rhythm guitarist from Hamburg who had honed his metal skills in a band called Gentry. He met Weikath, who played rhythm and lead guitar alongside him, and co-founded Helloween. The band recorded a self-titled album and two EPs before it became apparent that Hansen couldn't simultaneously play and sing to the best of his abilities. Fans of this early, raw line-up admired Hansen's alto voice – a nasal but melodic style that suited the music perfectly – as well as his extremely powerful rhythm guitar, and regarded this configuration as the 'classic' Helloween, despite the commercial success of later albums.

However, Hansen's playing was certainly boosted when he quit the microphone stand to be replaced by the teenage singer Michael Kiske, whose vocal style emulated that of Iron Maiden's Bruce Dickinson. Helloween's two *Keeper Of The Seven Keys* albums (1987 and '88) were enormously popular among European and American metal fans, and they were the first major hits of power metal.

Although the members of Helloween didn't know it, the *Keeper* albums would turn out to be the best they ever did commercially before an ill-advised sequence of records that included forays into mainstream rock, covers, and idiotic comedy titles. This made Hansen's decision to quit the band in 1989 seem wise, in retrospect. Tired of the endless touring required to promote the *Keeper* albums and seeking more control over his career, he formed a new act, Gamma Ray. This band enjoyed a reasonable degree of success for almost two decades, primarily in central Europe, the homeland of power metal.

For most of his career Hansen has played ESP instruments, primarily a couple of Flying Vs and a Randy Rhoads-style V. His picking style is tight and precise, exactly as is required for the power metal style to be appreciated, and his leads are dexterous and melodic. Although Gamma Ray's music has much in common with that of Helloween, the new band is no mere clone of his previous act, and they have done much to advance the cause of the genre in Germany and elsewhere. This is due to the expertise of the musicians, Hansen's knack for uplifting, anthemic choruses, and their relentless tour schedule.

Hansen's popularity has led to many invitations to guest on other groups' albums, including releases by Blind Guardian, Hammerfall (with whom he recorded a version of Helloween's 'I Want Out'), and Stormwarrior. Perhaps due to his diminutive stature and moustache, Hansen pulled off a convincing turn as a dwarf in *Avantasia*, a 1999 opera written by Edguy keyboardist Tobias Sammet.

Gamma Ray remain unofficially affiliated with Helloween among Hansen's many fans, not least because of the musical similarities between the two bands. Although the group's first album, 1990's *Heading For Tomorrow*, didn't make an enormous impact, *Sigh No More* from the following year was more developed – with lyrics inspired by Gulf War I – and was followed by a world tour.

After some personnel shuffles, the band embarked on a series of albums that have been popular enough to place them for the rest of their career on an equal commercial footing with Helloween (and, indeed, the rest of the power metal movement). Singer Ralf Scheepers eventually departed to found the very successful Primal Fear (after a failed to attempt to join Judas Priest) and Hansen returned to guitar and vocals once more. A compilation, *Blast From The Past*, consisted of re-recorded versions of old Gamma Ray songs as well as remixes. As we go to press, Gamma Ray are scheduled to tour as special guests with Helloween – quite a spectacle for fans of melodic metal guitar.

> **"**
> Combining the picking speed of thrash metal with the melodic elements and fantasy themes of traditional heavy metal, power metal sells a huge number of records.
> **"**

▶▶┃ Genius moment
If you can track down the long-lost Helloween track 'Ride The Sky' (it was on the ancient vinyl compilation Speed Kills II), you'll marvel at Hansen's remarkable picking speed and precision.

DAVE MURRAY
Iron Maiden

The concept of the solo-trading guitar duo finds its natural home in heavy metal, and what a beautiful thing it is. The duelling harmonies; the epic soundscapes; the

47/100

counterpoint parts weaving in and out of the unison lines with to-the-millimetre precision; the excitement as each player takes over from the other, building on what went before. It's all made for metal. Jazz musicians had of course established the idea of call-and-response decades before metal was even invented, but the metallers' modern version is just bigger, heavier, and more intricate.

Judas Priest were the first guitar team to define the image of a heavy metal band, even if hard rock acts such as Wishbone Ash and Kiss had pioneered the style before them. In the wake of Priest came Iron Maiden, whose ascent to popularity in 1979 was five years behind Downing, Tipton, and the others. While it took three years for the definitive Maiden line-up to stabilise, once it was in place it was immediately clear that something very special lay at its heart.

This was the Genius Moment of Dave Murray and Adrian Smith, whose interplay on stage was at times nothing short of telepathic. Complementing the unearthly vocals of Bruce Dickinson, the driving bass of Steve Harris, and Nicko McBrain's pounding percussion, the Murray–Smith partnership has become one of the most fêted in heavy metal, and for good reason.

Murray, who was born in 1956 in London, is one of the older guitarists in this book. He reached his mid teens as Black Sabbath first made heavy metal popular. Famously inspired toward the guitar after hearing Jimi Hendrix in the early 70s, Murray formed a band called Stone Free (named after the Hendrix's celebrated song) and began to pursue a career in music after sport had previously dominated his time. The band also included future Iron Maiden guitarist Adrian Smith, but the path towards the classic line-up was rocky – as anyone who has seen Maiden's *The Early Years* documentary will agree.

Murray briefly joined Maiden in 1976, while they were still making a name for themselves in London's East End nightclubs, trying to settle on a firm line-up. An argument with Maiden's vocalist of the time, Dennis Wilcock, caused Murray to leave the band. He joined Smith's new band, Urchin, and recorded a single, 'Black Leather Fantasy', according to the heavy metal conventions of the day. He returned to Iron Maiden once Wilcock had left.

Murray brought a proficiency and swagger to Iron Maiden, two key elements that have been central to the band's sound for over three decades. His value to the band is enormous, which perhaps helps to explain why he has appeared on every Maiden album recorded so far.

In the early days, he played a Fender Stratocaster through a Marshall amp, swapping the Fender's pickups for higher-output models by DiMarzio and other manufacturers across the band's career, creating a warmer, bigger sound. His tone range extends from a fragile, icy sound to a warmer, neck-pickup blues that complemented the earthy, analogue sound of the early Maiden songs such as 'Phantom Of The Opera'. His solos have a strong legato style and have always possessed a fluid quality that perfectly meshes with the harmony lines of Adrian Smith. On 'The Trooper', for example, the unforgettable looping harmony line makes it one of the most anthemic metal songs of the 80s. Murray's rhythm playing is exemplary, too, with the trademark galloping sound of Maiden (for example 'Run To The Hills') achieved by his precisely-accented tremolo picking.

> **"** His value to the band is enormous, which perhaps helps to explain why he has appeared on every Maiden album recorded so far. **"**

47/100

RIGHT Iron Maiden's longest-serving guitarist Dave Murray (pictured here with bassist Steve Harris) is one of the most respected British musicians of all time.

DAVE MURRAY

47/100

> *Murray's remarkable guitar skills are, as ever, at the forefront of Maiden's often-mimicked but never-equalled sound.*

As Maiden's career entered the digital age in the early 90s, the studio requirements for Murray's guitar meant that he had to retire his original 1967 Strat in favour of custom-shop models equipped with Floyd Rose vibrato systems. His effects set-up isn't complex: it centres on a Marshall JFX-1 unit and a rackmounted Dunlop Crybaby wah. This relatively simple signal path allows him to wring warmth from his Stratocasters, lending Maiden's songs a depth and clarity that only 35 years as a musician can bring. However, what fans love Murray and Smith for most is their unearthly ability to mesh with each other and third guitarist Janick Gers, synching to form an almost telepathic guitar team.

Although the members of Iron Maiden are all approaching their mid fifties, their commercial appeal remains strong. This is not because of their new albums, which are well executed and competent rather than groundbreaking. It's because of their incredible live shows, the quality of their back catalogue (and therefore their live set), and their work ethic, which takes them around the world – currently in a Boeing 747 piloted by Dickinson. Murray's remarkable guitar skills are, as ever, at the forefront of Maiden's often-mimicked but never-equalled sound.

▶▶| Genius moment

'Wrathchild', from Iron Maiden's 1981 album Killers, features a solo from Murray at about 1:00 into the song that still chills spines to this day.

ROB BARRETT
Cannibal Corpse, Malevolent Creation

The biggest-selling death metal band in the world, according to a Soundscan report published a couple of years ago, is Cannibal Corpse. Although the band are often erroneously associated with the Florida death metal movement that arose in the early 90s, they in fact originated in Buffalo, New York, and only relocated to Florida some years later, in order to join the scene led by Deicide, Morbid Angel, Obituary, Monstrosity, and Death.

Rob Barrett was the rhythm guitarist in Malevolent Creation who, like Cannibal Corpse, play super-fast, super-aggressive death metal. Barrett is a highly accomplished musician whose grasp of riff-writing has served his bands well. From 1989 – when Malevolent Creation formed and signed to the Roadrunner label – until his departure to join Cannibal Corpse in 1993, he was a key member of the band, creating and playing riffs of increasing complexity and brutality.

Barrett replaced Cannibal's founder member Bob Rusay, who went on to become a golf instructor, and appeared on the albums *The Bleeding* (1994) and *Vile* (1996). So it was that Barrett played an integral part in the evolution of Cannibal Corpse, from the old-style brutal death metal they played in their early days to the supremely technical beast of today.

46/100

Vile was the first CC album to feature new vocalist George 'Corpsegrinder' Fisher, whose vocals were more focused and precise than those of his predecessor, Chris Barnes (who went on to form Six Feet Under). The sound and style of *Vile* were enough to gain the album mainstream attention – it became the first death metal release to enter the Billboard Top 200 – but the principal reason for its performance was the controversy that had erupted around Cannibal Corpse's previous album, *Tomb Of The Mutilated*.

It was a horrific record that had offended more or less everyone. For its cover art, *Tomb* depicted a decaying corpse performing oral sex on another. The album included 'Hammer Smashed Face', 'Addicted To Vaginal Skin', 'I Cum Blood', and 'Necropedophile'. While many authorities made clear their disgust, leading to the banning of the record in some countries, 'Hammer Smashed Face' became a de facto death metal anthem, performed by the band in the 1994 Jim Carrey film *Ace Ventura: Pet Detective* (at Carrey's personal request) and a standout song in Cannibal Corpse's live set to this day. The following year, Senator Bob Dole referred to them in a speech, accusing them of violating human decency – although he later admitted that he'd never heard their music.

All this fervour contributed to the success of *Vile*, a fact that Barrett and his colleagues in the band must have noted with satisfaction.

The controversy continued, despite explanations by Fisher. "All our songs are short stories that, if anyone would so choose, they could convert into a horror movie," he told journalist Mark Prindle. "Really, that's all it is. We like gruesome, scary movies, and we want the lyrics to be like that. Yeah, it's about killing people, but it's not promoting it at all. Basically these are fictional stories, and that's it. And anyone who gets upset about it is ridiculous."

Whatever your view on the band's horrific lyrics, there is no denying the nimble-fingered skills of Barrett on guitar (usually a Dean Caddy or a Gibson Les Paul played through a Mesa/Boogie Dual Rectifier). By the time he returned to Malevolent Creation in 1997, Barrett and fellow Corpse guitarist Jack Owen had developed a style that centred on lightning-fast downstroking of surprisingly melodic riffs, millisecond-accurate pinch harmonics (the main riff of 'Hammer Smashed Face' is a perfect example), and soloing influenced by the atonal Slayer school.

Barrett's return to Malevolent Creation sparked a particularly prolific period for the band. They embarked on a run of albums that were received with critical praise but which remained modest sellers. Like Cannibal Corpse, Malevolent Creation benefited immensely from the late-90s rise of death metal überproducers such as Colin Richardson, Erik Rutan (also a guitarist), and Neil Kernon, who use digital recording technology well to create albums of glittering perfection. The unforgivingly clear reproduction of these albums mean that extreme metal guitarists now have to play with world-class accuracy if their songs are to sound good. (Either that, or make a lot of corrections with Pro-Tools.)

Barrett is known for his precise playing and, when he returned to Cannibal Corpse in 2005 for one of their finest and most technically complex albums, his found his skills were challenged to the maximum. *Kill* disposed of the usual graphic cover art and focused on blinding speed and intricacy, earning itself the title of

"

The sound and style of Vile were enough to gain the album mainstream attention – it became the first death metal release to enter the Billboard Top 200.

"

46/100

45/100

Cannibal Corpse's best album ever in *Kerrang!* magazine. Cannibal Corpse remain at the very top of their game, touring often and occasionally releasing new and retrospective albums. Barrett and Owen's replacement, Pat O'Brien, are one of the most formidable guitar teams in heavy metal as a whole, not just the death metal subgenre.

▶▶| Genius moment

Listen to Barrett's execution of the central riff in Malevolent Creation's 'All That Remains' from the 2002 album The Will To Kill. It's a combination of fast tremolo picking and palm-muted downstrokes that requires serious skill to execute with this level of precision.

JENSEN (Patrik Jensen)
The Haunted

Thrash metal was an underground phenomenon in the late 90s, with only Slayer playing the music at a mainstream level. The enveloping wave of nu-metal had swamped the extreme metal scene. However, when the Björler brothers from the esteemed Swedish metal band At The Gates formed a new act, The Haunted, they played vintage thrash metal with a modern twist. Guitarist Anders Björler had worked on his skills as a melodic death metal player in At The Gates and retained those elements in the more straightforward music he played alongside fellow guitarist Jensen in the new band. Patrik Jensen, usually referred to simply as Jensen, was a founder member of The Haunted when they were first formed in 1996. He has applied devastating speed and power to his playing with the band across their five studio albums so far. While the sudden tempo and key changes that made the first wave of thrash so exhilarating were present in almost every Haunted song on the 1998 self-titled album, the band brought an indefinably new awareness to the music, perhaps thanks to the slick production and their ability to stop and start with ultra-tight precision.

By the time of *The Haunted Made Me Do It* (2001), the band had developed a fantastic command of thrash that, enhanced by the throaty roar of singer Marco Aro, bordered on death metal. Listen to the unfeasibly violent 'Silencer', written by Jensen, on which he and Björler execute a series of complex riffs that demand a near-telepathic synergy.

As Jensen explained to me in 2005, extremely fast tremolo-picked riffs in thrash metal can consist either of simple, equal strokes (such as the fast breakdown in Anthrax's 'I Am The Law') or of patterns broken down into triplets or other clusters of notes with accents of varying complexity (of which there are hundreds of examples, but Slayer's 'Necrophobic' main riff is as good an example as any). Getting this right when two guitarists are executing a fast, complex line is crucial in thrash metal, and The Haunted exemplify the very highest skills in this respect.

The Haunted Made Me Do It was followed by an in-concert album, *Live Rounds In*

> "We never set out to play thrash metal. It's the press who need to pigeonhole everything. My initial plan was to play Chris Isaak mixed with metal."

45/100

Tokyo, which demonstrated the expertise of the Jensen–Björler guitar team beyond any reasonable doubt. *One Kill Wonder* (2004) and the following year's *rEVOLVEr* retained the blistering speed and aggression, but The Haunted took a left turn with 2007's *The Dead Eye*, which slowed down to focus more on Black Sabbath-style heaviness than the thrashed-up speed of before. Fans were taken aback, but the guitar playing was as dexterous as ever, and those who appreciated the melodic solos and hard-edged riffs for which Jensen had become well known were not disappointed.

Jensen also leads the band Witchery, a blackened thrash metal act that includes Sharlee D'Angelo of Arch Enemy, one of the most successful Swedish death metal bands. Although the riffs are slower and the aggression taken down a notch compared to The Haunted, Jensen's playing in Witchery is melodic and beautifully executed, allowing listeners access to both sides of his playing ability.

> ▶▶∣ **Genius moment**
> We know how well Jensen can execute thrash metal, so for a different vibe try 'Dark Intentions', the short instrumental piece that he wrote for the band's best album to date, The Haunted Made Me Do It.

Jensen on genres

"We never set out to play thrash metal. It's the press who need to pigeonhole everything. My initial plan was to play Chris Isaak mixed with metal – it never happened, though. ... After playing together for so many years, we mould together somehow. We know when to be slightly on the beat or off it. It's funny: thrash metal is almost like surf-rock. It's like Dick Dale."

> **"** It's funny: thrash metal is almost like surf-rock. It's like Dick Dale. **"**

WACŁAW 'VOGG' KIEŁTYKA
Decapitated

In the olden days, say about 1992, death metal was largely an American phenomenon. Thrash metal had evolved into this faster, more guttural, more graphic genre in the late 80s, with early albums by Possessed, Death, and Massacre establishing the cookie-monster-vocal-and-blastbeat formula. A particularly fertile centre for death metal had arisen in Florida. Granted, Swedish death metal bands such as Entombed were doing well by the early 90s, but in critical and commercial terms the new music was all about Morbid Angel, Deicide, Obituary, Malevolent Creation, Cannibal Corpse, and the aforementioned Death – all of whom originated in or moved to Florida. Things stayed this way until the end of the 90s.

To everyone's surprise, as the commercial fortunes of the Florida death league levelled or, in some cases, waned, a new death metal movement emerged from Poland, a country until then largely disregarded for heavy metal. The scene was spearheaded by Vader (guitarist Piotr Wiwczarek) but was followed rapidly by the bands Yattering, Behemoth, and Decapitated. Of these, Decapitated are the most technically-minded of them all, thanks largely to the phenomenal guitar skills of Wacław Kiełtyka, nicknamed Vogg.

The fiendishly intricate riff patterns that populate Decapitated's songs are matched only by the dexterity of Kiełtyka's soloing. Unusually for this genre, he is the band's sole guitarist, a measure of his frequency-spanning solos and his confidence in the strength of the songs, which do not lose power as he moves from rhythm to lead playing.

Like many metal guitarists, Kiełtyka took his first musical steps on a different instrument – in his case the accordion. Metalheads might snigger, but as anyone who has actually seen an accordion player in full flow will testify, the instrument requires incredible speed and accuracy with both hands – a roots equivalent of shred guitar. He graduated from the Academy Of Music in Krakow before joining a series of bands. The best-known is Decapitated, but others include Lux Occulta and Sceptic.

Kiełtyka settled into a complex, fast style – using ESP and Ran guitars through Line 6 heads and Randall cabs. He debuted his band with the 1997 demo *Cemeterial Gardens* before Decapitated signed to the British extreme metal label Earache, releasing a full-length album, *Winds Of Creation*, in 2000. A vast achievement for such a young band, *Winds* was stuffed full of complex arrangements, thick layers of riffs, and a clean tone that gave the songs clarity despite their immense power. The album was rewarded with a Best Newcomer award in the 2000 readers poll in *Terrorizer* magazine.

Subsequent albums – *The Negation* (2004) and *Organic Hallucinosis* (2006) – maintained Decapitated's progress, despite a change of vocalist in '05 when frontman Sauron quit and was replaced by Covan. However, the progress of the band was put in serious jeopardy in late 2007 when their tour bus was involved in an accident in Belarus. Covan and Kiełtyka's brother Witold (nicknamed Vitek), the drummer, were admitted to a local hospital; Covan remains in a coma at the time of writing; Witold died of his injuries in November '07. It is to be hoped that Kiełtyka continues to employ his considerable skills in Decapitated, or – if that band is no more – in another equally uncompromising outfit.

> **To everyone's surprise, as the commercial fortunes of the Florida death league levelled or, in some cases, waned, a new death metal movement emerged from Poland.**

▶▶┃ Genius moment

The thick, detailed layers of riffs that typify Kiełtyka's songwriting can be heard to intense effect on the grinding 'Eye Of Horus' from Winds Of Change. Kiełtyka also produced the album, placing guitars and drums high in the mix. Listen out for Decapitated's cover of Slayer's 'Mandatory Suicide' on the same album – it's a slower song that demands and receives precise downstrokes.

DINO CAZARES
Divine Heresy, Fear Factory

As the American death metal scene was beginning to crystallise in the early 90s, the LA-based Fear Factory was among the first bands to attempt to take it into a more

43/100

mainstream direction. Although some might argue that Fear Factory took it too far – becoming effectively a nu-metal band by the end of the decade before re-introducing some elements of extremity into their sound – Dino Cazares's guitar-playing was always vibrant and exploratory in nature.

Cazares, a US-born musician of Latino parentage, first developed his guitar style in the grindcore band Excruciating Terror after spending his teenage years on the nascent Californian thrash and death metal scene. Together with drummer Raymond Herrera, Cazares co-founded Ulceration before renaming the band Fear Factory. After a couple of shuffles the line-up stabilised to Herrera and Cazares plus vocalist Burton C. Bell and bassist Christian Olde Wolbers.

The early Fear Factory music was heavy but unrefined, although from the start it showed that a certain synergy existed between the members. This became especially obvious with the tight interaction between Cazares's picking hand and Herrera's double kick-drums, leading to a triple-picked style that, it later emerged, Fear Factory's Texan contemporaries Pantera were also working on at the same time.

Fear Factory's first significant success came in 1995 with the *Demanufacture* album, released by the influential Roadrunner label, whose espousal of the alternative metal wave in the mid 90s led directly to the rise of nu-metal a few years later. The album marked giant step away from the extreme sounds that had typified Fear Factory's earlier material – whether up or down depended on your point of view. The record contained groove-metal and industrial-metal elements as well as plenty of electronic samples, and it was among the first of its kind. Cazares played bass on some of the songs as well as Ibanez seven-string guitars, tuned down a whole step for extra weight to the riffs. His fast split-second-accurate picking on both instruments was made all the more remarkable by the necessarily heavy gauge of the strings.

Demanufacture was such a success that a remix album based on it, *Remanufacture – Cloning Technology*, was issued in 1997. Drawing upon hardcore techno with some token guitar samples, the album divided the fans and stressed the fact that Fear Factory's songs featured electronica and metal in more or less equal measures. This was particularly so with Bell's lyrics, which focused on then-current cyber themes such as the rise of artificial intelligence.

This all reached a peak (or nadir) on 2001's *Digimortal*, whose lead single 'Linchpin' included such a processed central riff that it sounded as if it had been created by a computer. *Digimortal* was a fully nu-metal album thanks to its synthetic sound and the semi-hip-hop song 'Back The Fuck Up' but now sounds somewhat dated. It was the last to feature Cazares, who left apparently because he was disgusted by the direction that the music had taken. Ironically, when Fear Factory regrouped without him – with Olde Wolbers on guitar and Strapping Young Lad's Byron Stroud on bass – the music they made was much heavier and arguably marked a return to old-school form.

However, Cazares had other things on his mind. There was a side-project, Asesino, with Static-X bassist Tony Campos, who like Cazares, an extreme metal player at heart whose main band played unsatisfyingly mainstream music. But that wasn't enough to sustain him. Similarly, his membership of Brujeria was sporadic at most, even though this well-known Mexican grindcore band's masked identity

> **"** the music they made was much heavier and arguably marked a return to old-school form. **"**

43/100

43/100

42/100

concealed ex-members of Faith No More as well as Cazares. What he wanted was a new band, and this came in the form of Divine Heresy, whose music had the brutal heaviness of early Fear Factory but none of the dated themes or poppy hooks that had blighted that band's later material.

After working on a song for the *Roadrunner United* compilation in 2005, Cazares signed his new band to Roadrunner. *Bleed The Fifth* was released in 2007 and featured the Nile and Hate Eternal drummer Tim Yeung along with singer Tommy Vext. A year's worth of touring consolidated the new band, hindered slightly by Vext's sudden departure after an argument with Cazares.

Since the *Roadrunner United* project, Cazares has been playing an Ibanez eight-string guitar of the type pioneered by Meshuggah. Its lowest string is a whopping .085 gauge – similar in size to the A-string of a bass guitar. These days Cazares plays the scooped sound he's delivered since Fear Factory's earliest recordings through Ibanez Toneblaster amps. It's a modern sound that gives huge weight to Divine Heresy's recordings, and fans hope that there will be many more of these.

> ▶▶▮ **Genius moment**
> Depending on your point of view (whether your taste in metal is extreme or classic), try Fear Factory's 'Invisible Wounds (Dark Bodies)' for its icy, futuristic clean-picked sound (from 2001's Digimortal) or Divine Heresy's 'Bleed The Fifth' from the 2007 album of the same name.

Cazares on the future

"When Dimebag Darrell passed away, I went to his funeral, and Zakk Wylde said to me, 'Dimebag passed the torch to us. It's up to us to keep the legacy of metal going.' That's how I feel about the metal scene."

> "
> When Dimebag Darrell passed away, I went to his funeral, and Zakk Wylde said to me, 'Dimebag passed the torch to us. It's up to us to keep the legacy of metal going.'
> "

MICHAEL SCHENKER
Michael Schenker Group, Scorpions

Brothers Michael and Rudolf Schenker were influential in the rise of German heavy metal in the 70s and 80s, establishing themselves as master musicians within the genre at a time when very few precedents for this type of music existed in their country. While Rudolf has enjoyed a long and profitable career with Germany's biggest-selling metal act, the Scorpions, his younger and less flamboyant brother Michael has played in several different bands.

Born in 1955, Schenker was ideally placed to take advantage of the new heavy metal sound when it spread from the UK to Germany in the early 70s. After bands such as Black Sabbath had debuted their down-tuned, doom-laden music in Europe, especially a notable residency at Hamburg's Star-Club in their early incarnation as Earth, the German music scene was gripped by a feverish desire to create heavy music.

LEFT The one and only Michael Schenker, an inspiration for Michael Amott, Kirk Hammett, and many other metal guitarists.

42/100

Ozzy told Hit Parader magazine in 1982: "It so happens I did contact Michael Schenker, but he wanted a king's ransom before he'd do anything. ... I don't need that annoyance."

One of the first bands to make any significant impact with the new style was the Scorpions, whose 1972 debut album *Lonesome Crow* featured both the Schenker brothers on guitar. Although the Scorps' patented over-the-top riffage had yet to come to full maturity, the guitarists' excellent command of their instruments was remarkable for such a young pair of performers – all the more so for Michael, who played a form of melodic, bluesy lead while Rudolf handled rhythm.

However, Michael's career in the band did not last. After a one-off gig with British heavy metallers UFO where he stood in for that band's guitarist Bernie Marsden, he was asked to join them full-time. After consulting Rudolf, who thought it would be a good idea, Michael accepted the offer, although his girlfriend at the time was obliged to translate between band and guitarist until he learned English. He spent the next five years with UFO, although a certain degree of intra-band friction meant that it was far from an easy ride. He finally left in 1978 to rejoin the Scorpions.

UFO's best-known albums to this day are the first and last which Michael recorded with them: *Phenomenon* (1974) and *Obsession* (1978). It was Schenker's melodic, clear playing that attracted most attention. He valued precise enunciation of his flurries of notes and applied great clarity to their execution. His choice of weapon, the Gibson Flying V, has become iconic, even more so thanks to Rudolf's use of the same instrument. After playing on the Scorpions' much-praised *Lovedrive*, Michael left the band after a series of uneven performances, allegedly because of a dependency on alcohol. Matthias Jabs replaced him.

Meanwhile, Michael was offered a place in Aerosmith and with Ozzy Osbourne. Ozzy told *Hit Parader* magazine in 1982: "It so happens I did contact Michael Schenker, but he wanted a king's ransom before he'd do anything. ... I don't need that annoyance." At this point Michael launched his own band, The Michael Schenker Group (universally referred to as MSG), an outfit that has continued with a variety of line-ups. As with UFO, it hasn't always been a smooth ride: clashes between Schenker, his first singer Gary Barden, and his successor Graham Bonnet led to hirings and firings every couple of albums or so. Stability was only attained after vocalist Robin McAuley was recruited, leading to a subtle rebranding of the band as The McAuley Schenker Group.

In the 90s, as the modern heavy metal movement and its myriad subgenres expanded in range and technicality, Schenker found himself on unsteady ground – joining, leaving, and rejoining UFO (punctuated by arguments with bassist Phil Mogg, which sometimes escalated into violence) – and faced with financial problems at the end of the decade. However, he returned with new music and a new band in 2005, taking advantage of MSG's silver anniversary and playing with all his previous singers on an album called *Tales Of Rock'N'Roll*.

His current touring band, Michael Schenker And Friends, goes some way toward rebuilding his reputation. They released a decent, guitar-heavy album, *In The Midst Of Beauty*, as this book went to press. Michael's fans were elated recently when he announced a new endorsement deal with Dean Guitars, who now manufacture a signature Flying V-type model. Let us hope he continues to wield it for many years to come.

42/100

▶▶▌ **Genius moment**

Try the bombastic 'Into The Arena' from The Michael Schenker Group's self-titled debut album from 1980 for a perfect example of Schenker's lean, melodic guitar style.

Schenker on favourites

"The best doesn't exist for me: it's just a question of taste. It's a matter of playing things in a different way. But in terms of the notes he puts together and how he expresses emotion with them, I'll say Eddie Van Halen. I like Yngwie Malmsteen's playing on his first album, too, although I didn't hear anything new after that."

ADRIAN SMITH
Iron Maiden

Adrian Smith and Dave Murray are the quintessential guitar partnership in heavy metal and the best-known axe duo in the world (apart from Keef and Ronnie). They are the powerhouse riff-and-lead team that propels Iron Maiden, year in and year out. And the duo is now a trio, thanks to the fluctuations of the Maiden line-up over the years, with Janick Gers filling out the sound and allowing the band's primary songwriter, Steve Harris, to compose complex guitar parts for three instruments.

Born in 1957, Smith became friends with Murray as a schoolboy and bought his first electric guitar from his mate. The pair later played together in a heavy rock act, Urchin, which has some cult cachet nowadays – but back then the band seemed destined to remain in obscurity. When Murray left Urchin to play with the brand-new Iron Maiden in the late 70s, Smith remained with Urchin until the departure of the other Maiden guitarist, Dennis Stratton, provided him with a clear opportunity to rejoin Murray.

Smith joined up in time for Maiden's second album, *Killers*, in other words just before the huge leap in popularity that followed its release, along with the replacement of original frontman Paul Di'Anno with Bruce Dickinson and a support tour with Kiss.

It was during the 80s that Smith and Murray fully evolved their duelling-guitar style, most notably on 'Phantom Of The Opera' from *Killers*. Just listen to the superb clarity and melodic beauty of the harmony lines immediately after Harris's ethereal triads-based bass solo, or the fast and aggressive '2 Minutes To Midnight' from the *Powerslave* album, and the band's most expansive (not to say pretentious) song, 'Rime Of The Ancient Mariner', also from *Powerslave*.

Smith's solos can be heard all over Maiden's catalogue, with expert leads on 'Stranger In A Strange Land', 'Wasted Years', and many others. He has a bluesy, legato style, rather than any speedy alternate picking or sweeps, which is in line with Maiden's 'vintage' status that commenced before the heyday of the modern, übertechnical shredder.

It was during the 80s that Smith and Murray fully evolved their duelling-guitar style.

Fans mourned when the classic Dickinson–Murray–Smith–Harris–McBrain line-up split in 1990. Smith had recorded a solo album the previous year as ASAP (it means Adrian Smith And Project) and chose to pursue the project full-time. His replacement was Janick Gers. But the band seemed to have lost some momentum as they entered the 90s, which would be a difficult decade for them.

As Maiden floundered, losing their key member Dickinson in 1993, Smith played on Helloween singer Michael Kiske's solo record _Instant Clarity_ – ironically, as Kiske had been suggested as a replacement for Dickinson – and then formed Psycho Motel. That band released two albums, _State Of Mind_ (1996) and _Welcome To The World_ ('97), which were moderately well-received rather than praised, and contained unchallenging, lightweight heavy metal that didn't engage too many listeners.

Iron Maiden's fortunes recovered a little with the emergence of a new classic-rock-loving audience. After guesting on Dickinson's albums _Accident Of Birth_ and _The Chemical Wedding_, Smith made the clever decision to rejoin Maiden in 1999. Dickinson followed suit, telling the press later that he wouldn't have done so had Smith not re-enlisted before him. The new three-guitar line-up moved forward.

Their albums since then – _Brave New World, Dance Of Death_, and _A Matter Of Life And Death_ – have not matched the quality of classic 80s records such as _Powerslave_ and _Seventh Son Of A Seventh Son_. But Maiden's real strength has turned out to be their immense live show. After a series of increasingly ambitious tours in the new millennium that took the band to six continents, the ultimate Maiden jaunt was in progress as this book went to press. The band, piloted by singer Dickinson in a Boeing 747, are playing vast stadium shows with 12 tons of equipment.

Among this equipment is, of course, a significant number of guitars belonging to Smith. Although he is a long-time player of Fender Stratocasters, which helped him to deliver Maiden's essentially bluesy solos with great panache in the 80s, the demands of modern heavy metal have required that he use alternative axes. His current Strat includes a DiMarzio humbucker at the bridge, which issues a hot signal and complements the other guitarists' tones perfectly – in particular the Seymour Duncan pickups preferred by Gers. Smith has also been known to use a double-neck Jackson model with six-string and twelve-string necks along with Deans, Ibanez Destroyers, and a whole range of Gibsons (and he still plays the first Les Paul Goldtop that he bought aged 17). Hamers, Charvels, Lados, and ESPs also feature in his collection, and he uses them regularly, despite the fact that his current endorsement deal is with Jackson. All this weaponry goes through a series of Marshall heads and cabs to produce a smooth, heavy tone, which has been much copied but remains part of Smith's unique sound.

▶▎ Genius moment

Smith's work in Iron Maiden is deservedly popular. On almost every song from their 80s albums there is a solo or riff played by him that stands out for its clarity and dexterous execution. However, let's look outside the Maiden box and recommend an ASAP track: 'You Could Be A King' from 1989's Silver & Gold. It's not as fast, heavy, or technical as Iron Maiden's music, but it's got all the right ingredients.

41/100

ANDERS BJÖRLER

ANDERS BJÖRLER
The Haunted, At The Gates

As we noted in Patrik Jensen's entry, thrash metal as we used to know it was effectively a one-horse outfit by 1997, the name of the nag in question being Slayer. The other members of the Big Four Of Thrash were either too big (Metallica), too interested in being as big as Metallica (Megadeth), or just too confused to play fast any more (Anthrax). Meanwhile, the melodic death metal scene that had risen in Sweden had gained many new fans for whom thrash was now old-fashioned – and in the midst of that scene stood the remarkable At The Gates.

The band was formed in Gothenburg by the Björler twins, Anders (guitar) and Jonas (bass), and filled out by singer Tomas Lindberg, drummer Adrian Erlandsson and guitarist Alf Svensson. They were the founders of Gothenburg death metal, which differed radically from the Stockholm variant played by Dismember and Entombed, who focused on raw textures and blistering aggression. The Björlers and their band played fast and hard, for sure, but applied exquisitely-gauged melodic solos to their songs, the whole benefitting from flawless production. The template was Iron Maiden meets Autopsy, and At The Gates used it with great success.

The scintillating solos that Björler and Svensson played over supertight, superfast riffs, over a pounding rhythm section and the shredded roars of Lindberg, made them a gradual if not an instant hit. At The Gates soon expanded from humble origins to form a whole melodic death metal scene as other bands signed up to their sound.

Björler was the primary songwriter, taking his influences from classic thrash and death metal and adding his love of harmonious, clear soloing to the mixture, creating a wholly new sound. After issuing a series of albums to great acclaim, the band called it a day in 1996, citing a weariness with the endless album–tour–album grind and looking for different musical paths. The two brothers decided to form a new band with a greater focus on the speed and pure sound of classic thrash, and they returned the following year with The Haunted.

The Haunted, issued in 1998, was a revelation. The Björlers had retained drummer Erlandsson and put together an album of supremely speedy and precise songs, laced with venomous vocals from ex-Mary Beats Jane singer Peter Dolving. Patrik Jensen replaced Alf Svensson in the new band, and the guitar team clicked immediately, combining their speed-picking skills for some fearsome rhythm parts. However, the solos were less melodic than they had been on the At The Gates albums, with a greater emphasis on atonal patterns – Slayer was the obvious influence – and mid-song breakdowns with acute, sudden tempo changes, tricks nicked from classic thrash. This refinement of thrash metal continued with the band's masterpiece, *The Haunted Made Me Do It*, released in 2000, and the rather less impressive *One Kill Wonder* three years later.

Since then the band has toured incessantly, releasing albums that have not matched *The Haunted Made Me Do It* but still contain elements of the best thrash metal released anywhere. The neo-thrash wave that arose in The Haunted's wake is now split into two factions – the party-metal of Municipal Waste, Gama Bomb, and

> From the beginning, we had a lot of folk and classical influences, which made the music very dark and gloomy.

their ilk, and the more serious bands such as fellow Swedes Carnal Forge, Hypnosia, and Corporation 187. Without the Björlers, the re-emergence of thrash metal might have been a slower and more arduous process.

Anders, now one of the Swedish metal scene's elder statesmen, delivers his crushing riffs these days from a series of Caparison guitars. Like Jensen, he has used Les Pauls, in The Haunted, as well as several Ibanez and ESP models, and plays these instruments through Engl heads and cabs. In his earlier career he was a devotee of Peavey amps, specifically the classic 5150 and 5150 II models. These set-ups give him a tight, crisp sound, which he distorts without overdoing the gain for maximum clarity and accuracy.

With all the retrogressive nostalgia for thrash metal, At The Gates announced a brief re-formation between Haunted albums. Melodic death metal, the genre that they effectively founded before bands such as In Flames made it their own, is still a much-respected area of music – and it will be interesting to see if a decade of playing thrash has left an impression on the band's phenomenal musicianship.

> ▶▶| **Genius moment**
> The mid-section of 'Victim Iced' from The Haunted Made Me Do It, tucked in between the second chorus and the impossibly exhilarating tempo leap that accompanies the soaring guitar solo, is a good example of Björler's guitar and songwriting skills. OK, so 'Victim' sounds a lot like Slayer's 'Necrophobic' in parts. But there are worse sources to plunder.

" I used to play along with Metallica's Ride The Lightning and Master Of Puppets albums, but I used to fool around with Bach and Vivaldi as well, because I liked the gloomy, depressing atmospheres. "

Björler on technique

"From the beginning, we had a lot of folk and classical influences, which made the music very dark and gloomy. I used to play along with Metallica's *Ride The Lightning* and *Master Of Puppets* albums, but I used to fool around with Bach and Vivaldi as well, because I liked the gloomy, depressing atmospheres. … It doesn't matter how fast you can play arpeggios – listen to Ritchie Blackmore or Tony Iommi. I admired Yngwie Malmsteen, because he's not one hundred percent technical. He has the right feeling. If you don't have the feeling, it sounds boring."

FREDRIK ÅKESSON
Opeth

Swedish guitarist Fredrik Åkesson has applied incredible lead and rhythm guitar playing to the various metal bands with whom he has played, and he is now a member of the much-praised progressive death metal band Opeth. He joined that band when their long-time guitarist Peter Lindgren departed after many years of recording and touring.

As a creative foil to Opeth frontman Mikael Åkerfeldt (also an accomplished guitarist), Åkesson is a perfect fit. Åkerfeldt's songwriting is usually complex and

39/100

never predictable, so a full range of instrumental ability is required across a wide range of musical styles – and Åkesson is a master of them all.

Åkesson first came to the guitar-playing limelight in 2005, although he had been studying the instrument for many years before. Arch Enemy was probably the most commercially successful Swedish band, alongside In Flames, and when they lost their guitarist, Chris Amott, who decided to take a break from the music business, Åkesson was asked to step in. This he did, adding a deft melodic touch to Arch Enemy's blend of traditional heavy metal and death metal vocals and drums. He left when Amott returned to the band in 2007.

By a fortunate coincidence, Peter Lindgren was on the point of leaving Opeth and, with communication moving quickly between the bands on the incestuous Swedish metal scene, Åkesson was offered a place alongside Åkerfeldt, where he remains to this day.

So far, Åkesson has contributed to just one Opeth album, but it happens to be one of the best they've ever released. *Watershed*, issued in 2008, is a fiendishly intricate album on which Åkesson and Åkerfeldt not only perform their most complex, atmospheric material so far but also investigate styles of music at which they have only hinted on previous albums.

Åkesson's contributions vary from smooth, bluesy soloing over Åkerfeldt's mellow acoustic passages to raging shreds delivered over the death metal riffage for which the band first became known. Åkesson came up with the idea of slowly untuning (not detuning, but taking out of tune) the acoustic guitar on which Åkerfeldt plays the long, pastoral outro of the song 'Burden'. He untuned each string, one after the other, and then tripped over when he turned to return to the studio control room, causing Åkerfeldt to laugh. The laughter was sampled and looped to create an eerie postscript to the acoustic part.

> **"**
> I used to play Metallica songs in a covers band, and learning 'Master Of Puppets' was a very good way of learning that downstrokes style.
> **"**

> ▶▶ **Genius moment**
> Over his varied and fascinating career, Åkesson has played some amazing solos. One recent piece of work that shred fans are advised to check out is 'Heir Apparent' on Opeth's 2008 album Watershed. It's a long, frantic, and beautifully melodic lead, and one that Mikael Åkerfeldt admits he couldn't have played.

Åkesson has enjoyed a recent and varied career as an in-demand session guitarist. He has contributed to the second album by heavy metal act Krux and is a sporadic member of Talisman. Opeth is his full-time occupation, but he still finds time within that band to teach his bandmates: as Åkerfeldt told me, Åkesson spent time in 2007 helping him to improve some of his right-hand technique.

Åkesson used ESP guitars for some years before switching over to Paul Reed Smith upon joining Opeth. The fluidity of his legato playing and the accuracy of his alternate picking have always been exemplary. Within Opeth, however, technical brilliance is a lower priority than feel and texture, so his most dazzlingly technical playing is only occasionally required.

In many ways, Åkesson is a perfect example of the modern metal guitarist who you'd want in *your* band: he's adaptable, a state-of-the-art player for hire in many musical styles, and easy to get along with. The American and British metal scenes – and it is only players from those two countries who match or exceed the number of Swedes in this book – would do well to take notice.

Åkesson on genius

"This is a difficult question. One of the best rhythm players is definitely James Hetfield. His stamina for playing downstrokes is very good, especially on the classic early Metallica albums. I used to play Metallica songs in a covers band, and learning 'Master Of Puppets' was a very good way of learning that downstrokes style. For lead guitar, it's probably Dimebag. When he played solos, you could tell it was for real – it was so full of emotion. He had good vibrato, good tone, and of course good technique as well."

JEFF LOOMIS
Nevermore

As we've already seen with Michael Weikath and Kai Hansen, the modern version of power metal – as opposed to the earlier Judas Priest-alike style – was effectively invented by Helloween in the mid 80s. Germany dominated the movement until the 90s, when three American bands – Iced Earth, Jag Panzer, and Nevermore – retaliated with a sound of their own, which placed equal value on shredding ability, chunky riffs, and epic lyrical themes.

The shredder movement of the previous decade – Satriani, Vai, Malmsteen, and others – had made a serious impression on this new breed of guitarists, who noted that earlier generation's devotion to developing outrageous flamboyance in their solos within ice-cold picking of split-second accuracy. Applying these skills to bone-solid riffs derived from classic heavy metal, the new breed of power metallers recorded albums of serious weight and credibility.

Nevermore are among the most commercially successful American heavy and power metal bands of the new breed, at least in part because of the breathtaking guitar skills of Jeff Loomis. A relative latecomer to the world of metal – he didn't start practising guitar with any degree of seriousness until his mid teens – Loomis played in a few low-key acts before scoring the remarkable coup of an audition with Megadeth. After the try-out he was informed by 'Deth's frontman Dave Mustaine that at only 16 years old he was too young for the job, but also that he had great potential as a guitarist. As legend has it, Loomis later saw Marty Friedman's band Cacophony on tour and told him that Megadeth were auditioning new guitarists – prompting Friedman to go for and secure the position.

Loomis's first successful band was Sanctuary, who were about to change their style from metal to grunge. They didn't remain together for long, due to disputes over the wisdom of that switch. Loomis, bassist Jim Sheppard, and vocalist Warrel Dane went on to form Nevermore.

> **Applying these skills to bone-solid riffs derived from classic heavy metal, the new breed of power metallers recorded albums of serious weight and credibility.**

38/100

> **"**
> Recognition of Loomis's guitar skills went so far as Guitar World magazine offering him a monthly column.
> **"**

With Loomis the primary songwriter and most expert player – his sweep picking is among the most advanced anywhere – the band have issued several successful albums that hover at the edge of mainstream heavy metal and power/thrash metal. Recognition of Loomis's guitar skills went so far as *Guitar World* magazine offering him a monthly column, 'The Merchant Of Menace', in which he chooses a riff or solo from Nevermore's large catalogue and explains in detail how to play it.

In common with many modern shredders, Loomis has successfully explored the world of the seven-string guitar, using a series of models for maximum range in his solos, both picked and swept, and for the requisite heaviness in the rhythm parts. He remains among the most revered guitarists on the American non-extreme metal scene.

▶▶ Genius moment

Nevermore's many fans will tell you that every song on every one of their albums is the essence of guitar mastery, but for one standout track we recommend 'The River Dragon Has Come' from the 2000 album Dead Heart In A Dead World. Produced by Andy Sneap, fader-tweaker on many of the current metal scene's best albums, the record sounds clean, bass-heavy, and atmospheric, the perfect vehicle for Loomis's unearthly talents.

RUDOLF SCHENKER
Scorpions

Rudolf Schenker is the most iconic of the heavy metal guitarists of mainland Europe thanks to his exuberant stage presence, his identification with the even more iconic Gibson Flying V, and a droopy blonde moustache that made him look like some kind of crazed Viking. He is a legend in guitar circles – even to people who aren't into heavy metal. Of course, this may in part be because the 1990 power ballad 'Wind Of Change' was such a vast worldwide hit, pulling in fans who had never heard of Schenker and his band, the Scorpions.

But we're jumping ahead of ourselves. Schenker was born in August 1948 – six months too late to qualify as the oldest guitarist in this book; that honour goes to Tony Iommi, born in February that year. Schenker began his guitar career on a Fender Stratocaster before becoming hooked on the V when it re-appeared in the early 60s. Although he learned to play lead guitar, he has always specialised in rhythm, developing a choppy, flamboyant technique and composing riffs that have endured for decades.

By the time Schenker was accomplished enough to form a band, the beat boom of the mid 60s was in full swing, and the first incarnation of the Scorpions played music similar to the stuff played by the many English bands who had residencies at Hamburg's Star-Club. You may recall that in the classic mockumentary *Spinal Tap* the eponymous band begin life Beatles-style, all chirpy falsettos and sharp suits, before discovering overdrive and switching to heavy metal. Well, the Scorpions were an obvious inspiration for this.

Taking note of the heavier, more expansive sound of late-60s and early-70s rock, the Scorpions settled on a steady line-up featuring Schenker's younger brother Michael and vocalist Klaus Meine, who took over the singing from Rudolf. In 1972 they recorded a debut album, *Lonesome Crow*. The heavy metal template that the band applied from that point had been established, although the immediate departure of Michael to UFO led to a hiatus of a couple of years in the band's activities.

Some of the later Scorpions albums became infamous for their jacket designs, in particular *Virgin Killer* (with its unpleasant artwork depicting a young girl, naked and covered in shards of broken glass) and *Lovedrive* (which featured a more palatable depiction of a woman's breast, albeit with a nipple stretched out like bubblegum). But most of the songs within attracted a great deal of respect for the band's songwriting and playing skills.

Rudolf, like his brother Michael, believed in enunciating his rhythm parts with great clarity and precision, as well as the occasional solo, such as in 'Wind Of Change', for instance. His picking-hand accuracy was exemplary and became an influence on the guitarists growing up in the 70s who would go on to found the first thrash metal bands in the following decade.

Fans have always wondered why Schenker doesn't play more leads, especially as he uses one of the most solo-friendly instruments available. One answer may be that he prefers to think of himself more as a songwriter than a performer, and another must surely be that the Scorpions' lead guitarists – from Michael Schenker to Uli Jon Roth to their current soloist, the underrated Matthias Jabs – have all performed the job with such extreme talent that Schenker has been able to focus on his strengths: writing songs and performing riffs. Indeed, some of the songs that he has composed have become metal classics, 'Rock You Like A Hurricane' and 'Big City Nights' among them.

Like so many classic metal bands whose commercial peak came and went in the late 70s and early 80s, Judas Priest and Motörhead among them, the Scorps had a difficult 90s as metal became less fashionable and grunge and nu-metal sounds dominated the charts. Schenker had difficulty finding a modern sound for his band, which wavered from Def Leppard-style pop-metal to a kind of metal-electronica hybrid that sounded immediately dated. Line-up shuffles and an inability to settle on a permanent producer also dogged the band's progress, and it took the rise of the classic rock generation in the late 90s to restore the Scorps to a respectable place in the metal firmament.

In 2000, Schenker's band released *Moment Of Glory*, a collaboration with the Berlin Philharmonic. While the music was generally well-received by the fans and his excellent solos stood out from the mix with great panache, critics accused them of having jumped on board the Metallica bandwagon. The San Francisco ex-thrashers had done something similar the previous year with a semi-orchestral album, *S&M*. Although it emerged that a project with the Berlin Philharmonic had been under discussion for the previous five years, when the Scorps released an acoustic album in 2001 titled *Acoustica* it seemed as if they had lost their way completely. (Guitar fans will be interested to hear that Rudolf played a specially-built acoustic Flying V made by Dommenget.)

"

Rudolf Schenker is the most iconic of the heavy metal guitarists of mainland Europe thanks to his exuberant stage presence, his identification with the even more iconic Gibson Flying V.

"

37/100

ERIC PETERSON

The reformation of Testament's classic line-up, pictured here, accompanied some of their best performances in years. Eric Peterson, pictured far right, is their primary songwriter and an immensely talented guitarist.

The Scorpions did not remain in the commercial doldrums. Like his brother Michael, Rudolf Schenker became a Dean guitar endorser in 2006 and, with the release of a couple of gripping albums in the new millennium, the band appear to be ageing gracefully.

> ▶▌ **Genius moment**
> 'Still Loving You' and 'Big City Nights' showcase the now 60-year-old Schenker's way with a solo, and both songs also demonstrate how precise his riffing can be. His moustache, now downgraded to a polite upper-lip fuzz, deserves its own reward for perseverance.

ERIC PETERSON
Testament

"If you ask me," Testament guitarist Eric Peterson told me in 2003, "the term 'The Big Four Of Thrash' is meaningless. We sold millions of records too. It should have been a Big Five!" He's not just complaining: he has a reasonable point here. After all, Testament may not have sold out stadiums like Metallica or retained the extreme edge of Slayer – but in terms of songwriting and sheer guitar chops, they equalled or bettered the albums made by Anthrax and Megadeth throughout the 90s.

Much of Testament's edge comes from Peterson, their primary songwriter. Raised in San Francisco during a key period in metal history, he soaked up the music around him and emerged as one of the prime movers on that small but vibrant scene. In 1982, when Metallica, the first American thrash metal band, were issuing their initial demos, Peterson was a young guitarist in the process of putting together his own band, Legacy. Preferring Gibsons from the start of his career for their fat tone and easy playability, Peterson has used Explorers and SGs for much of his career, although he has been spotted with an Ibanez Iceman at times. Like so many other musicians in this book, he now endorses Dean and plays an ML model.

> **"** I think that the greatest heavy metal guitar comes from team players. That's kind of what I do. **"**

As the band's line-up stabilised, it soon became clear that the focal point of the band would be the interplay between Peterson and the band's other guitarist, Alex Skolnick, a talented musician who had taken lessons from shredder extraordinaire Joe Satriani. He brought a wide awareness of all genres of music to the band, including a penchant for jazz and Latin folk.

Legacy lost their singer Steve Souza to another rising Bay Area band, Exodus, and replaced him with the hulking Chuck Billy. After threats from a local jazz act called The Legacy, they changed their name to Testament and signed to Metallica's previous record label, Megaforce, performing their audition for label owner John Zazula on the day that he heard of the death of Metallica bassist Cliff Burton, in September 1986 – a miserable experience for all concerned.

When Megaforce released Testament's debut album, *The Legacy*, fans and critics pointed to its similarity to Metallica's first three albums. The speed and vitriol of early thrash metal combined with a big-studio polish and complex arrangements did indeed resemble the Metallica recipe, but this didn't hinder Peterson and his band, who developed their own sound – in fact, the essence of the Bay Area thrash tone – over the next couple of releases.

Skolnick and Peterson evolved a complex, melodic rhythm style overlaid with clear, expressive solos, all the while maintaining the speedy thrash-based approach that marked their origins. The peak of this songwriting style came with their third album, *Practice What You Preach*, released in 1989 to major acclaim and thought likely by critics at the time to elevate the band to a position alongside The Big Four Of Thrash. The 1990 'Clash Of The Titans' tour, which featured a thrash metal line-up to die for – Slayer, Megadeth, Anthrax, and Suicidal Tendencies in the US, with Testament replacing Anthrax in the UK –seemed to confirm this perception.

However, next came a downward spiral – commercially, at least. In the wake of Metallica's metal-redefining *'Black Album'* in 1991, it seemed that Testament tried to make their music more mainstream – a move the fans resented. When Skolnick and Peterson clashed over songwriting preferences, because the former wanted to soften up the sound, the band fragmented. Skolnick left in 1993, and the end of their deal with major label Atlantic reduced their exposure.

Over subsequent albums, Testament were never as popular as in the *Practice* era, but in some ways this freed Peterson – now the main songwriter – to exercise his more extreme songwriting skills. As thrash metal faded away, he took the wise decision not to relax the band's aggression levels but to amp them up. They approached a death metal sound on the *Low* and *The Gathering* albums, recorded with a stellar cast including ex-Slayer drummer Dave Lombardo. Peterson's solos remained melodic and precise, and the downtuned, bass-heavy tone of his riffs, and Billy's vocals, which had evolved from a high-pitched bark to a guttural roar, revealed a new extremity behind his recent songwriting.

> **"**
> As thrash metal faded away, he took the wise decision not to relax the band's aggression levels but to amp them up.
> **"**

> ▶▶ **Genius moment**
> When Testament play heavy, they don't do it by halves – and the super-twisty introductory riff in 'Legions Of The Dead' from their masterpiece, The Gathering, reveals the extent of Peterson's mastery of the death metal idiom as well as the more expected thrash metal sound.

In the last decade, Testament have endured enormous trials – which have led to unexpected benefits. Billy suffered from germ cell seminoma, a rare form of testicular cancer, which led to a spectacular fundraiser called Thrash Of The Titans, held in August 2001 in San Francisco. This sole show led directly to the revival of several classic thrash bands, including Death Angel and Forbidden – and stated to the world's media with great emphasis that thrash metal was back and was very popular.

Testament themselves rebounded with an excellent album of reworkings of their classic tunes in their newfound more powerful style (*First Strike Still Deadly*) and a new album in 2008, *The Formation Of Damnation*, that kept the melodic thrash flag flying. Skolnick returned in time to play on that record and to participate in several high-profile tours fronted by the now-healthy Billy – all of which adds up to a band again

36/100

in the ascendant. Long may Testament continue – and if people don't understand why they never became part of a Big Five, they're missing an important point.

Peterson on duos

"I think that the greatest heavy metal guitar comes from team players. That's kind of what I do, with Alex. I'm gonna say that the best duo is K.K. Downing and Glenn Tipton of Judas Priest, and then Adrian Smith and Dave Murray of Iron Maiden. The greatest individual player is Tony Iommi, though – he invented the darkness."

ERIK RUTAN
Hate Eternal, Morbid Angel

Many fans of American death metal regard Morbid Angel as the ultimate expression of the genre, thanks to the jaw-dropping guitar feats of Trey Azagthoth. But the band were supported through a significant chunk of their career so far by guitarist Erik Rutan, who played on three of their albums. With his parallel band Hate Eternal, which became a full-time project when he left Morbid Angel, Rutan played a slightly different form of death metal, which was rather more intense than Morbid's sometimes atmospheric music and more focused on blastbeats. He excelled in both bands and has also built a reputation as a producer in recent years.

Ripping Corpse was Rutan's first band, formed in 1987 when he was 16. They played primitive and raw music, like most of the first wave of death metal. However, their sole album, 1991's *Dreaming With The Dead*, contained strong hints of the innovation to come, with three members going on to form Dim Mak, and Rutan joining Morbid Angel at their commercial peak in 1994.

In Morbid Angel, Rutan and Azagthoth (real name George Emmanuel III) often exchanged riffs and leads of brain-frying dexterity, bolstered by vocalist–bassist David Vincent and drummer Pete Sandoval. This rhythm section powerhouse had provided much of the drive to grindcore band Terrorizer on their debut album, the classic *World Downfall*, in 1988.

Morbid Angel were the most prestigious death metal band in the world when Rutan joined them in 1994. They had just come to the end of a deal with Sony subsidiary Giant Records as the first band of their style to sign to a major. Their new album was *Domination*, on which Rutan provided expert playing alongside Azagthoth. It was followed by a huge world tour. A major upheaval was to come, however: David Vincent had personal issues which he wished to resolve – nothing to do with the other members, he announced – and he left after the next release, the live album *Entangled In Chaos* (you'll note that Morbid Angel title their albums in alphabetical order).

Although Azagthoth recruited the capable bassist–vocalist Steve Tucker in Vincent's place, some of the charisma had left the Morbid Angel line-up, it seemed, and the next album – *Formulas Fatal To The Flesh* – was a little disappointing after the occult majesty of *Domination* and its three prequels. Rutan contributed to this

"
Truly this is a death metal everyman.
"

35/100

ERIK RUTAN

35/100

and the following album, *Gateways To Annihilation*, but Morbid Angel's music now seemed generic rather than groundbreaking. The post-Vincent albums were harsher, faster, and less intelligible than before. You might think that in the extreme environment of death metal this could have been a benefit, but the new music lacked a certain evil nonchalance or contemplative arrogance.

How much of this was down to Rutan is impossible to say. Morbid Angel's primary songwriter was still Trey Azagthoth, after all. Still, when Rutan bid an amicable farewell to Tucker, Azagthoth, and Sandoval in 2002, his many fans were pleased to see him strike out on his own in a band that might be better suited to his songwriting.

Rutan's guitar playing on all four Hate Eternal albums so far – *Conquering The Throne*, *King Of Kings*, *I, Monarch*, and *Fury And Flames* – has been deeply technical. The complex riffs are a match for the flurries of notes that make up the solos by Rutan and his second guitarist, Doug Cerrito of the legendary Suffocation. Hate Eternal have accumulated a wealth of tour anecdotes during their 11 years as a band – it's no picnic working your way up the extreme metal ladder, and the band have had their share of personnel shuffles, equipment nightmares, and all kinds of logistical problems.

It was little wonder that Rutan took time out from the band in 2006 for a tour with Morbid Angel once again, just after David Vincent rejoined the fold after a decade's absence. The press noted that the *Domination* line-up was back together, albeit briefly, and audiences flocked to the shows as a result.

Alongside his parallel careers in Morbid Angel and Hate Eternal, Rutan has played in a band called Alas with a female singer, Martina Astner. They perform melodic, orchestral metal almost completely opposed to that of his other groups, and he plays gentle, harmonious leads with perfect precision. It's a sign of Rutan's ability that he pulls it off. He's also a renowned producer in the death metal field, buffing up Cannibal Corpse's most recent album *Kill* to a polished sheen and manning the consoles for Six Feet Under, Goatwhore, Vital Remains, and others. Truly this is a death metal everyman.

> "You might think that in the extreme environment of death metal this could have been a benefit, but the new music lacked a certain evil nonchalance or contemplative arrogance."

▶▶▌ **Genius moment**

'Servants Of The Gods' is a song best seen performed on Hate Eternal's In The Perilous Flight DVD from 2006, with Rutan powering through a ridiculously complex riff while windmilling and singing at the same time. Elsewhere on the DVD there's a look at his Florida studio: the guitars and amps will be a visual feast for any metal freak.

BJÖRN GELOTTE
In Flames

As we've seen in earlier entries, melodic death metal is now a thriving movement composed of harmonious guitar parts juxtaposed with the fast beats and brutal

34/100

vocals of traditional (or old-school) death. The biggest MDM band in the world is the Gothenburg quintet In Flames, who are now reaping rewards after a decade and more of hard work – a period in which they often struggled to be taken seriously by those who believed that melodious dexterity and extreme metal do not go together.

Björn Gelotte was a drummer and guitarist with a history in a metal band called Sights before he was asked to join In Flames, the new project of Jesper Stromblad. Initally, Gelotte joined the band to play drums, before a line-up change made it advisable for him to switch to guitar.

He doesn't regard himself as a great player. He told me in 2008: "I don't know any scales apart from the E minor and the pentatonic. We just play whatever sounds good along with the rhythm part. When it comes to solos, I'm not very spontaneous, because I have to think it through and arrange it. Even though it might sound improvised sometimes, it's not. I'm not Chris Amott or Alexei Laiho or Zakk Wylde, who can just wing it and it will always rock – I have to think about it and write it down."

He added, "Jesper's got a beautiful sense for melodies, and it's insane the way he can rearrange rhythm parts. He knows even less about theory than me, and I know basically nothing. He almost can't tune a guitar – and I know how to do that. I've had to develop some speed and technique, having done the solos on the last few records, but Jesper never had to – so he didn't. We're just not the most technical or progressive guitarists out there, although we like it when it sounds progressive."

This more or less sums up the In Flames approach – which is that there is no consistent approach. Gelotte and Stromblad like to push the musical envelope a little with every release. The fact that they are at heart a death metal act is irrelevant, and they can choose to go in any direction they prefer. Gelotte doesn't possess much technical knowledge, but his ability to execute a smooth solo is evident, helped along by his weapon of choice, a Gibson Les Paul Custom with EMG 85 active humbucking pickups. This guitar gives him a warm but focused sound that provides enough delicacy for the harmony leads he executes with Stromblad and a sufficiently powerful output for the heads-down riffing sections.

>
>
> **melodic death metal is now a thriving movement composed of harmonious guitar parts juxtaposed with the fast beats and brutal vocals of traditional (or old-school) death.**

▶▶◀ Genius moment

Try one of the "heavy metal hits" by In Flames, as singer Anders Friden once put it – in this case 'Cloud Connected' from their 2002 album Reroute To Remain. Duelling harmonies, wide-open soundscapes – what's not to like?

After several years of hard slog and an apparently constant barrage of criticism from the press with every new album they make – the three stock responses are "It's too mainstream," "It's the same as the last one," and "It's weird" – In Flames are now on the cover of every metal magazine on the planet alongside Opeth, their fellow Swedes with a similar career trajectory (although the music bears only a passing resemblance).

34/100

CHRISTOPHER AMOTT

33/100

The new metalcore bands – Trivium, Still Remains, and so on – line up in interviews to pay their dues to In Flames, and the industry in Sweden has come to recognise them as an asset rather than a liability. On presenting In Flames with the Export Award, a category in the 2006 Swedish Grammys, the country's minister for the economy said in his speech: "Thanks to In Flames, Sweden now has a metal band in the absolute world elite." And he spoke as if he really knew what he was talking about. This is at least partly down to the songwriting of Gelotte and the guitar parts which he writes and delivers. Now there's justice at last.

Gelotte on allergies

"I have a nickel allergy, which is a stupid thing to have if you play the electric guitar. Basically you get blisters, which crack open and bleed, so you're playing with the flesh of your fingers. It really fuckin' hurts. Coins and keys and belt-buckles cause it too. Funnily enough, it's not the pain which is the problem, because you're full of adrenaline when you play live and you don't really feel it – the problem is the blood, which gets sticky! You can't slide or anything. In the end I found a brand of string which doesn't contain nickel, but before that I used to stick contact lenses on my fingertips with superglue. It worked, too. The only problem was that it took two fuckin' months to get them off afterwards."

> **Basically you get blisters, which crack open and bleed, so you're playing with the flesh of your fingers.**

CHRISTOPHER AMOTT
Arch Enemy

Brothers in metal are always bankable. Think Dimebag and Vinnie Paul Abbott; Michael and Rudolf Schenker; the Grover brothers in Megadeth; Tom Araya of Slayer and his brother Johnny in Thine Eyes Bleed; drummers Adrian and Daniel Erlandsson. But surely none more so than Swedes Chris and Michael Amott, both currently of Arch Enemy.

Mike is the elder by six years, and he was already a successful musician by the time Chris became aware of metal music. The senior Amott made a name for himself in the British grindcore band Carcass, helping to pilot them through a radical style change toward the first melodic death metal sound.

Chris was fuelled by a desire to do what his brother had done, and started to learn to play the guitar as a young teenager. After working on an impressive technique at music college, he was asked by Mike to contribute solos to the first recordings of the melodic death metal band Arch Enemy. These leads owed much to classic European guitar pioneers such as John Sykes of Thin Lizzy and John Norum of Europe, both of whom play rock rather than metal but whose shadows loomed long on the nascent MDM movement, indebted as it is to classic rock melodicism as much as metal riffage.

The Arch Enemy album, *Black Earth*, was a hit in Japan. While he played there as a full member of the band, Amott was able to snag a record deal for his own side project, Armageddon. This act has released three albums so far, the second of which – *Embrace This Mystery* – was the first to reveal Amott's interest in power metal and traditional heavy metal as much as the death metal in which Arch Enemy was rooted.

Arch Enemy might seem from the outside to have enjoyed a long and smooth ascent to prominence alongside fellow Swedish acts such as In Flames, but there have been more than a few hitches along the way. It seemed at one point that Amott's expertise in the art of the metal guitar was greater than his interest in the band's incessant touring. After the band had been rejuvenated by a new singer, Angela Gossow, and released their most successful album, *Anthems Of Rebellion* in 2005, he quit, stating that he had lost interest in playing with them.

A two-year break from the music industry followed for Amott, although he did teach and study music. Armageddon appeared to be on hold, and he even told the press in one interview that he might choose to play non-metal music if he ever returned to the business. In Amott's absence, his place was filled by the formidable Fredrik Åkesson, now of Opeth. But in 2007 Amott returned to the band, where he remains to this day.

Recently he has been using a brand new signature guitar from the Japanese luthier Caparison, the Dellinger Christopher Amott Signature model, as well as various other models from the same manufacturer. This high-end guitar, with its perfect set-up for sweep picking, tapping, and the aggressive vibrato that typifies Chris's playing, complements the fast riffage in which Arch Enemy specialise. Little wonder that Caparisons are the guitars of choice for more than a few extreme metal acts, The Haunted among them.

> ""
> Bending and vibrato are also important if you want to play melodic lines and harmonies nicely. They're more important than speed.
> ""

▶▶▎ Genius moment

If you can find Armageddon's Embrace The Mystery album from Japan, listen to the whole record – it's Amott exploring the world of power metal and, perhaps, asking himself if extreme metal is really all there is.

Amott on greats

"The late Criss Oliva of Savatage had an original riffing style and frantic yet tasteful lead playing. Definitely an underrated guy. The main riff of 'Heaven And Hell' by Black Sabbath is the biggest and most epic ever – simple and effective. Song? 'Neon Knights' by Black Sabbath: *Live Evil* was the first Sabbath album I heard. A guy at school lent it to me one day. When that song kicked in... man, I was hooked! Dio's voice, the magical lyrics, and the guitar solo that's so long. For me, the best metal album has to be Metallica's *Ride The Lightning*. Great songs and a super-heavy production, for the time. Every song is a classic. As for technique – you need tight, solid downpicking, of course. Without that there is no metal. Bending and vibrato are also important if you want to play melodic lines and harmonies nicely. They're more important than speed."

33/100

32/100

RON JARZOMBEK
Watchtower, Blotted Science

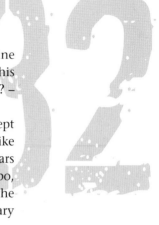

Progressive metal isn't usually very extreme, and vice versa, so when a genuine progressive extreme metal band comes along, it's worth listening. What is more, this PEM act, as we'll call it – why not coin a phrase when the opportunity comes up? – formed after many years of work in other bands. Let me explain.

Texan guitarist Ron Jarzombek is everything a metal guitarist should be, except incredibly famous. His band Watchtower made exhilarating music and had chops like very few other musicians on the metal scene of the day – but they were several years ahead of their time. Today, progressive metal with numerous changes of key, tempo, and even mode is far from uncommon, with bands such as Dream Theater leading the way when it comes to sheer compositional complexity, and bringing the necessary playing skills along with it.

Back in the 80s, however, even a slightly unorthodox album such as Metallica's sprawling, bassless 1988 record ...*And Justice For All* caused brows to furrow and a certain breed of unreconstructed metalhead to complain that the solos sounded out of tune. What chance did Watchtower have when their *Energetic Disassembly* and *Control And Resistance* albums sounded as if they'd landed from another planet?

Jarzombek, who had honed his style in San Antonio Slayer until 1984, is a ferocious guitarist, applying razor-sharp playing precision to riffs that stop and start on a dime and come with tricky time signatures attached – and that's before we even address the song arrangements, which are unpredictable, unorthodox, and (for most of us) unplayable. Years of playing in Watchtower and other projects such as Spastic Ink (where he played with brother and drummer Bobby Jarzombek) left him in a position in 2006 to write and record the awe-inspiring *Machinations Of Dementia* with his new band, Blotted Science.

This was a complex, epic album stuffed full of time-changes, atmospheric guitar parts, high-speed riff workouts of great extremity, and arrangements that seem near-impossible to produce. *Machinations* is one of the best prog-metal albums in years. Jarzombek is accompanied by two other virtuoso players, Alex Webster of Cannibal Corpse (who would easily make the Top 10 in a book devoted to metal bass players) and drummer Charlie Zeleny. He powers through death metal, straightahead heavy metal, and ridiculously intricate prog to make an album with few equals. The music has been labelled math-metal or mathcore, thanks to its wild, unpredictable complexity, but there's also a certain sense of humour in his lyrics and in some of the more unexpected textural changes in his songs.

Technically speaking, Jarzombek has all the weapons in the shredder's arsenal at his disposal – tapping, sweeps, and alternate picking par excellence – but he tends to focus more on an incredibly tight rhythm technique with a thick, crunchy sound. He has a penchant for soundscapes composed of single-note wails or otherwise simple figures, showing that he is aware of the key 'less-is-more' mantra that almost all modern shredders have forgotten to observe. Jarzombek only breaks into a full solo

> **He powers through death metal, straightahead heavy metal, and ridiculously intricate prog to make an album with few equals.**

LEFT The phenomenally talented Ron Jarzombek, whose warp-speed picking and unpredictable soloing give his current project Blotted Science a unique edge.

32/100

when a song requires one. He usually seems to have too many ideas to solo for its own sake – an attitude that will serve him well. Let's hope for more material from Blotted Science before too long.

▶▶❙ **Genius moment**

All of the Blotted Science album Machinations Of Dementia. Don't argue: just go and buy it.

Jarzombek on the ultimate

"Glenn Tipton, to me, is the epitome of what a metal guitarist should be. He is a riffmaster supreme, and he also writes solos that are perfect for the song. I probably played my *Sad Wings Of Destiny* album literally thousands of times when I was a kid. No slight to Black Sabbath, but classic Judas Priest is the ultimate definition of a heavy metal band – and Tipton was, and is, the man in charge."

ALEX AUBURN
Cryptopsy

Canadian extreme metal has been a potent force since the 80s, when Razor and Annihilator dominated the thrash metal scene in that country. Today Canada is known for technical death metal bands, specifically Kataklysm and the more extreme, less commercially successful Cryptopsy, which began life as Necrosis in the late 80s.

The band immediately made an impact due to the vastly technical nature of their riffs and drums and the insane vocals of Dan 'Lord Worm' Greening. Crytopsy made a series of albums that gradually decreased in venom but improved in production and performance. The first three – *Blasphemy Made Flesh*, *None So Vile* (a title cunningly reworked as *None So Live* for a later in-concert release), and *Whisper Supremacy* (1994, '96 and '98) – were fast, almost impossible to emulate, and largely buried in a thick sound that did the intricate riffs no favours.

Alex Auburn, who sings backing vocals in the band with drummer extraordinaire Flo Mounier, joined Cryptopsy in 1999 and first appeared on their *...And Then You'll Beg* album the following year. Auburn is a guitarist of remarkable skill, and his razor-sharp picking on the subtly detailed riffs of songs such as 'My Prodigal Sun' and 'Back To The Worms' satisfied fans of the band's renowned technicality. But this less extreme album compared to the earlier material was not welcomed by many long-time followers.

The band had certainly stepped down a little from the levels of attack that had so enthralled listeners of their first two albums – records that allegedly had been supported by shows in which Lord Worm chewed up handfuls of, yes, worms (whether real or otherwise is not known).

Auburn's predecessors, Steve Thibault and Miguel Roy, as well as his current guitar partner Jon Levasseur, delivered blindingly powerful contributions to the

" Auburn is a guitarist of remarkable skill, and his razor-sharp picking on the subtly detailed riffs of songs. **"**

31/100

ALEX AUBURN

31/100

> **Auburn is famed for possession of a 'skullet' (a mullet balding from the front, like that of Devin Townsend, Dallas Toler-Wade of Nile, and indeed Worf the Klingon).**

songs – but they were masked in that foggy production and pushed along at tempos that smothered them. All this was smoothed over a little for *...And Then You'll Beg* – which may explain why the band sounded less extreme.

Subsequent albums have continued this gentle slide away from total sonic extremity, with the band recruiting a keyboard player and performing riffs of perceptibly mainstream nature. Cryptopsy have never stinted for their live shows, with Auburn delivering rapid-fire riffs and leads on their old and new material, but on the albums themselves the old ear-bleeding material is but a distant memory.

▶▶▮ Genius moment

Auburn is famed for possession of a 'skullet' (a mullet balding from the front, like that of Devin Townsend, Dallas Toler-Wade of Nile, and indeed Worf the Klingon) but he is also known for the vast proficiency he displays on songs such as 'Slit Your Guts'. This song, recorded before he joined the band, takes on new life on None So Live from 2003.

Auburn on key shredder

"I'll go with Marty Friedman. There is a lot of stuff by him that I haven't heard, but the stuff he did with Megadeth is enough. There is so much feeling and precision in his solos, it's just incredible – he's so good. When he plays, he's happy and laughing, and everything seems so easy."

MÅRTEN HAGSTRÖM
Meshuggah

Complex metal for demanding people, Meshuggah's music is unpredictable, unorthodox, and headspinningly technical, performed by world-class virtuoso musicians whose grasp of their instruments is so far ahead of most of us that it's almost impossible to grasp. Guitarists Mårten Hagström and Fredrik Thordendal interchange riffs and textures with blinding speed. The difficult riffs mean that the distinction between rhythm (Hagström) and lead (Thordendal) playing is almost unimportant. It's sometimes hard to tell to the difference.

All this tricky stuff has led to Meshuggah (Yiddish for 'mad') being labelled variously as prog-metal, math-metal, and progressive death metal. True, death metal is the template, but like their countrymen Opeth, Hagström and Thordendal have introduced so many elements of jazz, prog-rock, ambient electronica, and other more obscure sources that labels have effectively become meaningless. It's best just to enjoy the music, and specifically the twisting, restless riffs from Hagström, whose command of his Nevborn and Ibanez eight-string guitars is remarkable.

Hagström abandons lead parts for the endless chordal possibilities of the eight-string, which might appear at first to be an unwieldy instrument. But he plays it with great delicacy and power, adapting the techniques of his primary influence – Alex

Lifeson of Rush – to the heavy metal environment, using expert palm-muting, speed-picking, and string bends.

Jazz is a major interest of Hagström, notably on the song 'Acrid Placidity' on Meshuggah's 1995 album *Destroy Erase Improve*, but elsewhere he delivers huge, grinding riffs straight from the Carcass old school, with no obvious departure from the death metal template. This taste for a monstrous sonic attack may explain two eminently quotable facts about Meshuggah: one, none other than axe-wielding madman Zakk Wylde, he of Ozzy Osbourne's band (and a high-roller in this book) works out to their music; and two, one of their albums was played by Osbourne's son Jack to intimidate the neighbours in an episode of the MTV show devoted to his erratic family.

It's refreshing that a guitarist can make as powerful an impact on the metal world these days without being known for soloing skills alone. Hagström does play the occasional solo (or solo-like piece) and obviously has much to offer in the field. But, simply, he sees more opportunities for expression in playing rhythm parts. To support this view, he has developed a wide palette of sounds, valuing tone and texture as much as the chord sequences themselves. Surprisingly, he manages this without a huge range of effects, sending his eight-string through a TC Electronics preamp and a Line 6 head.

Perhaps the most interesting aspect of the Meshuggah phenomenon, fuelled by Hagström's dense, ever-changing rhythm guitar, is that so many people are willing to invest the considerable time necessary to appreciate their music. Prog-metal's time is now, with audiences prepared to devote serious energy to digesting the often-difficult songs that emerge from its progenitors. And thank god for that. It's a great time to be interested in the heavy metal guitar.

> " It's the best fucking guitar I ever had. The attack is very solid, working the fretboard is easy, and the intonation is very smooth. For such a big guitar, playing it is effortless. "

▶▶❙ Genius moment
Anything from ObZen, the 2008 album that propelled Meshuggah forward another step into the math-metal limelight and is a workout for Hagström's ridiculously evolved skills.

Mårten on eight-string

"The eighth string is a .070, as thick as a bass guitar second string. In fact, if you're not careful, it just sounds like a bass. We could simply have tuned down a seven-string, but we wanted to try this and see if it gave us a different texture. In fact, we even tune down the eight-string: it would normally be tuned to F-sharp if the guitar was tuned to standard A440, but we go down half a step to F.

"With the first prototypes, which were made by Nevborn, there was a problem at the nut because the string was so thick, but that's been fixed now on the Ibanez models. It's got a 30-inch scale and it needs a reinforced neck to handle the extra tension – so it's very heavy. Sometimes on stage you really feel it, but you know what? It's the best fucking guitar I ever had. The attack is very solid, working the fretboard is easy, and the intonation is very smooth. For such a big guitar, playing it is effortless."

30/100

K. K. DOWNING

K.K. DOWNING
Judas Priest

Kenneth Downing, as he is probably never known these days, is said to have been rechristened K.K. when a resident of Denmark found his given name impossible to pronounce. He has been an iconic member of the heavy metal scene for four decades under that name. Born in 1951 and playing the guitar by the end of the 60s, Downing left school early with little focus in life until his love of the guitar gave him a goal for the first time. Forming Judas Priest with bassist Ian Hill, Downing set out on a path that has lasted close to four decades – and which, despite various ups and downs along the way, has never lost momentum.

Like so many guitarists of his vintage, Downing began his career playing clear, melodic solos with a focus on clarity and bluesy emotion. Since then his style has reflected the evolution of heavy metal itself, maturing and becoming more aggressive as the years have passed. When Judas Priest released their first album, 1974's mostly ignored *Rocka Rolla*, Downing's leads (and those of his fellow guitarist Glen Tipton) were similar in style to those of contemporaries such as Michael Schenker – expressive and extravagant rather than technical and aggressive.

In the 80s, as the extreme metal virus spread, metal guitarists such as Downing were obliged to include more technical devices in their playing, and he stepped up to a faster, more virulent style of shredding. Tapping and sweep-picking became more obvious in his solos. Downing's current style also incorporates highly expressive techniques such as pinch harmonics and whammy-bar dives, as well as the usual fast alternate picking.

A Judas Priest trademark since their earliest work has been Downing and Tipton's harmonised leads, a style perfected a couple of years later by Iron Maiden and which has since become a staple of heavy metal. The device characterised many of Priest's earlier songs to such a degree that the Downing/Tipton partnership has itself become iconic, the first of many guitar duos in metal – followed by Maiden's Smith and Murray and Slayer's King and Hanneman, for example. Guitarists who do not interact with each other so intimately aren't usually regarded as 'guitar duos' – Metallica's James Hetfield and Kirk Hammett, for example, who only occasionally harmonise leads and never partake in the call-and-response technique pioneered by Downing and Tipton.

Priest's career has been a revealing microcosm of the commercial fortunes of heavy metal. Rarely bothering to take note of what more extreme bands were up to, Downing and Tipton – the band's primary songwriters, along with vocalist Rob Halford – have ploughed a persistent furrow that is recognisably their own, even when traditional heavy metal fell from fashion in the early 90s. Thanks to the rise of grunge and alternative rock in 1992, when the metal-loving legions of the previous decade suddenly discovered Nirvana's *Nevermind* and the Red Hot Chili Peppers' *Blood Sugar Sex Magik*, bands such as Judas Priest found many of their commercial opportunities falling away.

Heavy metal as it had been previously understood – mid-tempo or faster anthems

> "Downing set out on a path that has lasted close to four decades – and which, despite various ups and downs along the way, has never lost momentum."

29/100

LEFT One of the original metal shredders and still a force to be reckoned with – K.K. Downing of Judas Priest.

(but not thrash-speed) with slablike riffs and extended melodic shredding – now only existed on a commercial plane with Metallica and a small number of new bands such as Pantera. Priest wavered for a few years when Halford left to pursue a more modern, slightly more extreme approach, as did the only other British metal band to match them commercially, Iron Maiden, also rocked by personnel shuffles.

In the 90s, the decade when Priest struggled the most, Downing's guitar style remained solid, but something of the malevolent essence of his songs seemed to be missing. Worse still, while we were all listening to Pearl Jam and Smashing Pumpkins, the leather-and-studs image that he shared with the rest of the band seemed a bit old-fashioned. Halford was working with Trent Reznor of Nine Inch Nails on industrial metal, which seemed like the future at the time (even though we know now that it was nothing of the sort), and for a while it even seemed that Priest might fold.

However, the recruitment of ex-Winter's Bane singer Tim Owens – nicknamed 'Ripper' for his note-perfect Halford impressions – saved the band from complete extinction, even though the albums the band recorded with him (1997's *Jugulator* and 2001's *Demolition*) were adequate rather than essential. Those records are more notable for the range of guitar styles that Downing experimented with than their musical content, and also because they're now regarded as stepping stones between the early and later Halford periods. Halford returned to the band in 2003.

At the time of writing, Judas Priest have regained critical kudos with two recent albums, *Angel Of Retribution* (2005) and *Nostradamus* (2008). The latest in particular has been hailed as a masterpiece by many, thanks to its courageous change of direction from much of Priest's previous output. Composed primarily of slow, doomy, operatic songs – in stark opposition to the biker-metal anthems of yore – the album is expansive, atmospheric, pretentious, and very enjoyable. Downing contributes with a guitar synthesiser as well as a conventional guitar, further adding to the sense of the epic that Priest have always delivered so well.

> "
> his style has reflected the evolution of heavy metal itself, maturing and becoming more aggressive as the years have passed.
> "

▶▶| Genius moment
Check Downing's sweep-picking in 'Painkiller' from the 1990 album of the same name. The technique was less common then than it is today, and it lent his solo a burbling, rolling quality of great dexterity.

MICHAEL AMOTT
Arch Enemy, Carcass

Born in the UK and raised in Sweden, Michael Amott and his younger brother Chris have defined a particular slice of extreme metal, building the profile of their current band Arch Enemy to its status today as one of Europe's best-known and biggest-selling metal bands. Before Arch Enemy, Michael had come to prominence as part of the legendary extreme metal band Carcass – a genuine reason for hailing him as one of his generation's most influential musicians.

28/100

RIGHT Older brother of Chris Amott – also a formidable musician – Michael Amott was among the first guitarists to fuse classic melodies with death metal riffs in Carcass.

MICHAEL AMOTT

Amott began his guitar-playing career as a teenager, although he had been listening to extreme metal and hardcore punk since he was 11. His early guitar heroes were blues-influenced melodic players such as Michael Schenker and Frank Marino. Schenker's expansive lines, delivered with great clarity and emotion, impressed him as much as Marino's penchant for pentatonic-scale solos executed at great speed. He took violence and speed from thrash metal, after it first penetrated Europe (Slayer in particular were a great influence on him), and his guitar style soon encompassed both extreme and mainstream metal.

After forming a shortlived death metal band called Carnage with vocalist Johan Liiva, which split in 1990 after releasing the *Dark Recollections* album on the Necrosis label, the 16-year-old Amott travelled to the UK and met members of Napalm Death at various gigs. He was a big fan of the punk scene that had spawned Napalm's grindcore sound and became friends with Jeff Walker and Bill Steer of Carcass, which operated in similar musical territory. In due course he was asked to join them for their next album, set for release by Earache in 1991. This record, 1991's now-classic *Necroticism – Descanting The Insalubrious*, was a great stylistic leap forward for Carcass, due in part to the recruitment of Amott, whose expertly melodic soloing added a touch of class to the band's grind grooves.

The importance of this change in style is almost impossible to exaggerate. Before Amott's arrival, Carcass had released two seminal but indigestible records, *Reek Of Putrefaction* (1988) and *Symphonies Of Sickness* ('89), with their trademark low-frequency, high-velocity grindcore featuring gruesome lyrics focusing on matters intestinal. Although the albums set a new benchmark for lyrical extremity – song titles included 'Carbonized Eye Sockets', 'Embryonic Necropsy And Devourment', and 'Crepitating Bowel Erosion' – the music itself was under-produced, perhaps the inevitable result of being several years ahead of its time.

> **Amott began his guitar-playing career as a teenager, although he had been listening to extreme metal and hardcore punk since he was 11.**

All that changed with *Necroticism – Descanting The Insalubrious*, which contained just as much thematic violence ('Lavaging Expectorate Of Lysergide Composition' and so on) but contained within songs of much greater melodic content. The music was now a form of technical extreme metal that is instantly recognisable today, now that we have a commercially viable melodic death metal scene.

This process was refined further on the excellent *Heartwork*, released in 1993 and now regarded as the pinnacle of Carcass's creative skills. The album contained harmony lead lines delivered by Amott and Steer and became one of the first records in death metal to acknowledge the influence of classic heavy metal in this way. Amott regards Steer to this day as one of the prime movers in modern death metal, a superb guitarist in his own right, and a highly underrated musician.

To the surprise of many fans, Amott quit Carcass after *Heartwork*, citing the usual musical differences while evidently maintaining a good relationship with the other musicians. Within months he had formed a new band, Spiritual Beggars, playing classic rock and metal with little hint of the extremity that had characterised his old band. They self-released an eponymous debut album in 1994, and Music For Nations released a follow-up, *Another Way To Shine*, two years later – although by then Amott was involved in a more ambitious project.

28 / 100

The concept of melodic death metal had been firmly established by *Heartwork*, but very little else like this was about in 1996, apart from At The Gates and In Flames, both Swedish acts. A new label from that country, WAR, asked Amott if he would be interested in founding another band in the melodic death metal vein. He obliged, forming Arch Enemy with his old singer Liiva, guitarist Chris Amott (then a music student), and drummer Daniel Erlandsson, brother of Adrian, the drummer in At The Gates.

After recording *Black Earth* (1996), the band were surprised to discover an instant fanbase in Japan, where they enjoyed much early success. A series of albums followed, with major international acclaim in 2001 when Amott recruited a new singer, Angela Gossow, whose death metal vocals are terrifying. That year's *Wages Of Sin* album was followed by *Anthems Of Rebellion* two years later, *Doomsday Machine* in 2005, and *Rise Of The Tyrant* in '07, all of which were followed by extensive tours.

Arch Enemy are currently Sweden's biggest-selling metal band alongside Opeth and In Flames – no mean feat for a band whose selling point is the simple fusion of classic death metal riffage with old-school melodic solos.

Amott executes his vision today with a signature ESP guitar with Seymour Duncan pickups through a signature Randall head, the Ninja V2. He announced the reformation of the *Heartwork*-era line-up of Carcass in 2007, to the delight of a generation of headbangers. Touring the band through the European festival circuit to enormous acclaim, Amott has not placed a limit on how far the reunion might go – although, of course, Arch Enemy will require his services again before too long. After all, he is a man with much to do, having played guest slots with Kreator and The Haunted and performed occasionally with Spiritual Beggars again in recent years.

> " their trademark low-frequency, high-velocity grindcore featuring gruesome lyrics focusing on matters intestinal. "

▶▶| Genius moment

There are doezns of examples of incredible guitar dexterity throughout Amott's career, but let's go back to the old school and nominate 'Incarnate Solvent Abuse' from Necroticism (1991). He composed the song in its entirety.

Amott on melody

"Michael Schenker is my favourite. When he was in his golden years, so to speak – 1974 to '84 – his composition style, his riff playing, and his melodic solos were unparalleled, I think. He's been a big influence on me. My tone is a lot heavier and deeper than his, and more extreme, I guess, but when it comes to solos I always think that players like him are the benchmark: as good as it gets. I loved the way that his solos were often like a song with the song. They were like a little piece of music in themselves. I've definitely adopted that. He's not just using the background – the riffs were sometimes different from what he was playing. It was very orgasmic, if you know what I mean. I can't really breathe when I listen to them, they're so intense. Him and Frank Marino, John Sykes, John Norum of Europe, and Gary Moore – they all have that melodic side when they're tearing it up."

28/100

JAMES MURPHY
Death, Testament

James Murphy is one of a small number of in-demand journeyman metal guitarists and has lent his skills to many distinguished heavy metal bands over the years, both as a full member and as a guest musician. He is known for extremely fast and melodic soloing skills, often using harmonised lines, and for his production work and songwriting. A longtime user of Ibanez guitars, he recently switched to Caparison instruments, like many of his extreme metal contemporaries.

Murphy's CV reads like a list of the great and the good of extreme metal. His own band, Disincarnate, released the excellent technical death metal album *Dreams Of The Carrion Kind* in 1993 on Roadrunner, who were releasing similar albums at the time by Deicide and Malevolent Creation.

Murphy guested on the *Spiritual Healing*, the classic third album by Death, and the record elevated the band to a new level of prestige. Death mainman Chuck Schuldiner was a mercurial character of great talent whose band was a revolving door of the best musicians available to him. He required a fellow shredder of serious ability – and the collaboration with Murphy was a marvel, all ice-cold riffing precision and warm, spiralling solos.

Before forming Disincarnate, Murphy performed with Obituary, whose swampy death metal was even heavier than Death's. His work on *Cause Of Death* (1990) lent the band's guttural, relentless grooves a touch of class with his expert, clear expression. The same was true of British death metallers Cancer, on whose *Death Shall Rise* album (1991) Murphy supplied his most exhilarating work to date.

But Murphy found a true vehicle for his talents in the veteran Bay Area thrash act Testament, with whom he played for three albums. It was a crucial combination, because Murphy's role demanded a player of incredible power and talent. Testament's long-time guitarist Alex Skolnick is one of the metal scene's most accomplished guitarists, but he had just left the band to pursue jazz-fusion, a path that so many musicians follow when their technique passes a certain point. It is, perhaps, the ultimate musical challenge.

> **He is known for extremely fast and melodic soloing skills, often using harmonised lines, and for his production work and songwriting.**

Forbidden guitarist Glen Alvelais had filled in briefly, but Testament's choice to recruit Murphy was wise: he is one of the few guitarists whose playing can equal that of Skolnick. Their 1994 album *Low* was the first to feature Murphy and was hailed by existing fans as a solid extension of the brand that had made them famous. So too was the following year's *Live At The Fillmore*, which also featured three studio tracks.

But most fans would agree that *The Gathering* (1999) was the finest work of the Murphy line-up Testament, especially as the drums were handled by Dave Lombardo, the ex-Slayer musician regarded by many as the best metal drummer of all. The album was a ferocious set of songs that marked Testament's step up from thrash metal to melodic death metal, with sterling guitar parts from Murphy and the band's primary songwriter Eric Peterson.

After a three-album stint with Danish metallers Konkhra and two albums issued under his own name, Murphy has become a prominent name in metal circles. He lays down guest solos with a whole array of bands such as Artension, Agent Steel, Malevolent Creation, Enforsaken, Gorguts, and Daath. But his presence hasn't been confined to the extreme metal field: he also played a solo on Steve Morse's *Prime Cuts* and on a Rush tribute album, *Working Man*, where he also played keyboards. Despite a brush with cancer in 2001, Murphy has also become a much sought-after producer, manning the console for Daath and others and founding a studio, Safehouse Production.

▶▶ Genius moment

Murphy's section in the long and ferocious guitar solo on Death's 'Defensive Personalities', from 1990's Spiritual Healing album, is like a song in itself, all dizzying climbs, razor-sharp alternate picking, super-smooth legato, and the occasional pinch harmonic.

Murphy on class

"I enjoy very much the work of Jonas and Per of Scar Symmetry, Gus G of Firewind, Mike and Chris Amott of Arch Enemy, Alexei and Roope of Children Of Bodom, and Michael Åkerfeldt of Opeth. Each of those players is very talented and plays things that move me. Åkerfeldt isn't nearly as technically adroit, but he plays so tastefully and with such feeling that you don't even notice the lack of shred. I usually prefer that over flash playing. It's the same with Mike Amott: the others I mentioned are guys that play a lot of flashy, technical things, but always very musically, and they can also phrase quite well and it never loses emotional impact. That pretty much sums up my standards for greatness in guitar playing ... or any instrument for that matter."

> **"**
> He is a man for all seasons, renowned for his expert shredding in any context, whether rock, metal, or the Japanese pop he currently performs.
> **"**

MARTY FRIEDMAN
Megadeth, Cacophony

Although Marty Friedman has spent only a portion of his long career playing metal, he appears in this book because he spent almost a decade in Megadeth, the band for which he is still best known. He is a man for all seasons, renowned for his expert shredding in any context, whether rock, metal, or the Japanese pop he currently performs. Friedman is a player for whom genre is, rightly, unimportant.

This broad acceptance of all – or almost all – musical environments has been part of Friedman's outlook since the early days of his career. Born in 1962, by his late teens he was working on a melodic shred style of the neo-classical type used by Randy Rhoads, Eddie Van Halen, and other contemporaries on the guitar scene. He was playing in the bands Deuce and Hawaii.

Friedman's first real prominence came in the late 80s with Cacophony, a band that also featured fellow shred master Jason Becker. The title of the second album, 1987's *Speed Metal Symphony*, revealed everything about the intentions of the musicians, the direction in which they were marketed, and the velocity of their solos – but not the nature of the songs themselves, which were a form of melodic power metal rather than speed metal. (Depending on your point of view, speed metal is either a slightly more technical version of thrash metal or simply a synonym for thrash.)

Despite its rather ludicrous nature, the album's exceptionally complex counterpointed leads from Becker and Friedman made them big names in the shredder community. At this stage, Friedman was known for playing Carvin guitars and the occasional B.C. Rich model, such as an Ironbird.

Although Becker was destined to remain a relatively little-known figure outside the guitar world, Friedman gained enormous exposure when he joined Megadeth. When Cacophony split, he was told by up-and-coming guitarist Jeff Loomis – soon to find fame himself with Nevermore – that Megadeth were looking for a new guitarist. Friedman passed the audition (footage of which is available as an Easter egg on the *Arsenal Of Megadeth* DVD and also on YouTube). He rapidly integrated with Megadeth frontman Dave Mustaine's phenomenally intricate guitar style and, more importantly, proved to be a personality match for the notoriously volatile bandleader.

Friedman would turn out to be the longest-running second guitarist in Megadeth. The Mustaine–Friedman version of the band – bolstered by bassist Dave Ellefson and drummer Nick Menza – is regarded by most fans as the classic line-up. Friedman joined Mustaine in playing Jackson guitars, primarily his Kelly KE1 signature model.

Friedman debuted on Megadeth's best-regarded album so far, *Rust In Peace* (1990). Although the band had already released three albums, *Rust* represented the pinnacle of their songwriting and performing skills, and several of the songs became permanent features of the band's live set. 'Holy Wars … The Punishment Due', 'Take No Prisoners', and 'Hangar 18' in particular were examples of complex, semi-progressive thrash with a modern production sheen and impossibly technical solos from both Mustaine and Friedman.

This didn't last, unfortunately. Like Metallica and Anthrax – their peers in the Big Four Of Thrash along with Slayer – Megadeth chose to abandon pure thrash metal in the 90s, a move that paid enormous dividends for Metallica with their self-titled album of 1991. Unlike Metallica, however, Megadeth's initial forays into non-extreme metal were largely disappointing.

Mustaine and his band were expected to equal or even surpass the dazzling, expressive songs of *Rust* but had opted for a more commercial sound to attract a wider audience. This led to ever-decreasing returns on *Youthanasia* (1994), *Cryptic Writings* (1997), and *Risk* (1999), a sequence of releases that divided Megadeth's career, like Metallica and Anthrax, into 80s good; 90s bad. Some of this was attributed by Mustaine to Friedman's desire to move toward alternative-rock; Friedman himself said that he had grown tired of metal, lending some substance to Mustaine's claim.

Whatever the truth, Friedman's tenure with Megadeth was clearly no longer working by the end of the decade, and he opted out, leaving Mustaine to try to find a metal footing for his band. Friedman began a solo career that has led to eight albums so far, and also he guested on albums by a disparate range of artists including Fozzy, Firewind, and Tourniquet.

He also played with a trance artist, Takeomi Matsuura, on one of many Japanese projects, and moved to the country in the early 2000s, developing a parallel career as

> **"by his late teens he was working on a melodic shred style of the neo-classical type used by Randy Rhoads, Eddie Van Halen, and other contemporaries on the guitar scene."**

26/100

a TV personality thanks to his fluent Japanese and the country's love of Western heavy rock. To the surprise of those who recall his early days as a sweaty thrasher, he plays with nationally-known pop artists, writes columns in the Japanese press, and presents several TV shows, including *Rock Fujiyama* and *Jukebox English*. He also performs voiceovers for the popular American cartoon *Metalocalypse*.

Friedman now plays Ibanez guitars. He is one of the very few musicians in this book to emerge from the heavy metal scene to become a known figure in the wider world.

> **▶▶◀ Genius moment**
> Just pick up a copy of the 1987 Cacophony album Speed Metal Symphony and you'll get the message.

Friedman on greats

"There are so many great players, but by far the best heavy metal guitarist is James Hetfield. He's been coming up with riffs that have made millions of people headbang furiously for decades. His sense of playing great metal is without peer. I love the way he plays so solidly, confidently, and tightly, and solos tastefully when necessary. He's the perfect heavy metal guitarist. His singing at the same time as playing is also amazing. Dave Mustaine is also really good at that. In terms of technicality, no one comes near Ron Jarzombek, period."

GLEN TIPTON
Judas Priest

None other than Kerry King of Slayer told me in 2003, "A sleeper candidate for the position of most accomplished guitarist in the world could well be Glen Tipton." Who are we to ignore his words?

Tipton is the oldest guitarist in this book by a matter of months – just pipping Tony Iommi. He was born in 1947 and plays guitar, guitar synth, and keyboards in the venerable Judas Priest. Like so many musicians born in the 40s and early 50s, he was well placed to experience the explosion of rock music that led from rockabilly and skiffle in the 50s, through beat and psych in the 60s, to prog, hard rock, and the nascent heavy metal that erupted in the early 70s.

Perhaps uniquely among the players in this book, Tipton did not begin learning to play guitar until he was 21, when the rock music revolution was well underway. Jamming first in The Flying Hat Band and then Judas Priest, an established act that needed a second guitarist for the recording of their debut album, Tipton evolved a bluesy, mostly legato style with a clear homage in its early stages to 70s guitarists such as Gary Moore.

Priest's debut album, 1974's *Rocka Rolla*, may not have been much of a commercial success but it did have Tipton's influence all over it – from the songs

> *He is one of the very few musicians in this book to emerge from the heavy metal scene to become a known figure in the wider world.*

25/100

themselves, some of which he rewrote on joining the band, to the solos, although the poor sound of the album was said to be the fault of producer Rodger Bain rather than the band.

A period of enormous success followed, with *Sad Wings Of Destiny* (1976), *Sin After Sin* the following year, and two albums in 1978 – *Stained Class* and *Killing Machine*. All are enduring examples of the band's craft. The songs were pure metal in its earliest, most naïve form. As singer Rob Halford always claimed, Priest were perhaps the very first heavy metal band – even Black Sabbath, their antecedents by four years or more, thought of themselves as a heavy rock act at times. Check the first Priest live album, *Unleashed In The East* (1979), for raw evidence of Tipton's musicianship – but be aware that rumours of studio overdubs on that record still abound today.

Priest's commercial peak came in 1980 with their best-known album, *British Steel*. Tipton was by now the prime mover of the band, along with fellow guitarist K.K. Downing, and had evolved a duelling-guitar style with Downing that was emulated by many bands, in particular Iron Maiden, the leaders of the New Wave Of British Heavy Metal (NWOBHM).

The singles 'Breaking The Law' and 'Living After Midnight' were among the best known of their songs, although (or perhaps because) neither qualify as heavy metal or even as particularly heavy rock. Instead, they show that the Priest songwriting team knew when to place memorable hooks over shredding for shredding's sake. Tipton achieved this with a humbucker-equipped Strat and a Gibson Les Paul, as well the occasional SG.

As the band progressed through the 80s, Tipton took a hint from the rest of the metal scene and began to develop a more technical guitar style. This was reflected in his choice of guitar, a signature Hamer, which he used for many years. By the middle of the decade he was using tapping and sweep picking in some of his solos, perhaps influenced by the new wave of guitar heroes who were making themselves heard in the USA. Although the albums released at this time were regarded as something of a letdown after the behemoth that was *British Steel* – with 1986's *Turbo*, all synths and glam-metal overtones, a particular embarrassment – the band were now becoming something of a cult act thanks to films such as *Heavy Metal Parking Lot*, shot at a Priest show. Struggling to sound contemporary, Priest were beginning to sound like yesterday's men, and they faced a court case in 1990 after the suicide of an American fan.

However, Judas Priest's fortunes hit a temporary second peak with the *Painkiller* album, released in 1990. Boosted by a new drummer, Scott Travis, and upgraded to a more modern sound and tempo, the band received an enormous lift from the subsequent tours with Pantera, Sepultura, and Megadeth in support. The new audience attracted by these younger acts appreciated Priest's updated guitar style, with both men now sweeping, tapping, and hitting pinch harmonics for all they were worth.

This didn't last, and Priest's golden era came to an end when Halford left in 1993 for a new band, Fight (which played semi-extreme metal and required more aggressive vocals than the melodic crooning of before). The rest of the decade was

> **"Tipton is the oldest guitarist in this book by a matter of months – just pipping Tony Iommi."**

25/100

GLEN TIPTON

tough for Tipton and Downing, whose songs with Halford's replacement Tim 'Ripper' Owens weren't taken as seriously as they should have been. And in any case, the 90s were a fallow period for classic heavy metal.

Thanks to the *Metalogy* box set, Halford's return, and the rise of a new, classic-rock-loving audience in the new century, Priest have achieved something of a return to the public eye in recent years. At the time of writing, the band are touring their latest album, *Nostradamus* (2008), on which Tipton is on startling form. Always a Marshall amp man, Tipton has refined his previous balls-out sound into an epic, more atmospheric tone that perfectly suits the album's semi-operatic material.

> **"**
>
> *Always a Marshall amp man, Tipton has refined his previous balls-out sound into an epic, more atmospheric tone.*
>
> **"**

▶▶ Genius moment

The title track of Nostradamus (2008) is immense – all mid-tempo downpicking and ravishing melodic solos. Whether you're new to the band or a Priest veteran, there's plenty of axe-related fun to be had here.

Tipton on songwriting

"It was difficult for us to write *Angel Of Retribution* [2005] at first, because we thought, after 14 years apart, what do people expect from Priest? So in the end we just wrote what comes naturally to us. It's not a modern album, because that's not what we think people expect from us, so we've written a classic Priest album. There's no detuned guitars, and no death metal vocals. It's not too far advanced from what Priest fans think is acceptable. It's got some light and shade and it's got some very powerful stuff. There are some incredible tracks on there, although as always we've broken rules – there are some tracks on there which will make people think, 'Is that heavy metal?'"

SAMOTH (Tomas Haugen)
Emperor, Zyklon

Black metal is comparatively under-represented in this book – not because guitarists from that genre of music are less talented than their counterparts in the heavy, thrash, death, or doom metal scenes, but because the music they play, according to its parameters, does not require particularly technical or expressive playing.

One of the dark pleasures of black metal is its ice-cold atmospherics, coupled with a destructive misanthropy in the lyrics that makes complex guitar playing almost redundant. But there are exceptions, the most prominent of which was the now-defunct Norwegian quartet Emperor – effectively a duo of Tomas 'Samoth' Haugen and Vegard 'Ihsahn' Tveitan.

The scope of Emperor's vision was breathtaking. The first wave of black metal in the 80s focused mainly on Bathory, Venom, and Mercyful Fate, establishing the idea of Satanic lyrics barked or screamed over a simple, muddy thrash metal background. When the genre's second wave arose in 1990 or thereabouts, it didn't take long for the new bands to elevate their music to a far more sophisticated level. Samoth and Ihsahn spent a couple of years early in the decade singing about Satan and his minions and playing pretty fundamental riffs, like everyone else on their scene. But soon they emerged with a wholly new and unsettling sound that rested firmly on their awe-inspiring musical skills.

Samoth (a simple inversion of his given name) is an expert player of guitar, bass, and drums. He formed Emperor in 1991, inspired by Mayhem guitarist Øystein 'Euronymous' Aarseth to follow a black metal path – as distinct from the death metal approach in vogue at the time. Initially he played drums but switched to guitar when bassist Mortiis (and later Tchort) and drummer Faust joined the band. A self-titled EP appeared on the British label Candlelight, but any further progress was halted when Samoth and Tchort were prosecuted and given jail sentences for church-burning, a popular pastime among the members of the black metal Inner Circle, as they were labelled by a frothing media.

The first real Emperor album was recorded and released after an older and wiser Samoth had served his time and the Inner Circle had collapsed on the death of Euronymous. *In The Nightside Eclipse* appeared in 1994 and completely redrew the boundaries of black metal, introducing complex arrangements and swathing them in a vast, symphonic production that left listeners spellbound. Samoth's lead guitars and machine-like riffing were just a fraction of the huge, expansive sound, achieved by recording the album at Bergen's famous Grieg Hall, the Grieghallen. The album's fantastical cover art and intimidating song titles – 'I Am The Black Wizards' is an enduring classic to this day – made the package all the more impressive.

Anthems To The Welkin At Dusk (1997) took this approach further, firmly establishing Emperor, and was a precursor of the symphonic black metal scene. The album featured more razor-sharp riffs from Samoth beneath the layers of keyboard and pummelling percussion, as well as ambient and orchestral sections that lent the recordings great depth. As the years passed, however, a slight difference could be heard between the playing preferences of Ihsahn and Samoth. Ihsahn was more responsible for the symphonic art of Emperor, while Samoth was leaning more towards a lean, angular form of death metal.

IX Equilibrium (1999) was the last true collaboration between the two men, and although it was a fine recording, it did not seem to contain any progressions. Nor did the final Emperor album, *Prometheus: The Discipline Of Fire And Demise*, released in 2001. *Prometheus* was composed and mostly played by Ihsahn, with Samoth already forming his next band during its production.

Emperor announced their split shortly afterwards, with Ihsahn going on to a solo career that has yielded two successful albums to date. Samoth formed the death metal band Zyklon (not to be confused with an earlier project, Zyklon-B). He dispensed entirely with Emperor's electronic and acoustic orchestration, instead employing a ferocious, stripped-down sound that sounded completely modern.

The 2001 debut album *World Ov Worms* was terrifying, with its shattered-steel riff textures, blistering solos, and guttural vocals from frontman Secthdaemon. Two more albums so far – *Aeon* (2003) and *Disintegrate* (2006) – have reinforced Zyklon's position as a death metal band to reckon with. The fact that Samoth's fellow guitarist

> **"**
> One of the dark pleasures of black metal is its ice-cold atmospherics, coupled with a destructive misanthropy in the lyrics that makes complex guitar playing almost redundant.
> **"**

24/100

Destructhor was recently loaned to the pioneering death act Morbid Angel says much about the phenomenal musicianship of the entire band.

Emperor fans were rewarded in 2005 and '06 when the band reformed for a series of festival dates, although when they split again Ihsahn and Samoth assured us that it would be for the very last time. In between these commitments, Samoth contributed guest guitar to Scum, a supergroup also featuring Chasey Chaos of Amen and Happy Tom from Turbonegro. He also runs a record label, Nocturnal Art.

> ▶▶ **Genius moment**
>
> Samoth's guitar parts have been so complex and detailed since the early 90s that it's difficult to select just one riff or solo. But let's go with the title track of 2006's Disintegrate, Zyklon's most recent album at the time of writing (although a fourth album is due for release). If it's fearsomely tight tremolo picking you want – and why wouldn't you? – here's the place to listen.

"

As I grew interested in thrash, death, and black metal, there was nobody playing guitar in that style where I lived, so I decided to take it up myself.

"

Samoth on heroes

"As I grew interested in thrash, death, and black metal, there was nobody playing guitar in that style where I lived, so I decided to take it up myself. I was never really focused on lead guitar. It was always much more about riffing.

"Metallica were definitely a great influence, but it was just as much about James Hetfield's rhythms as Kirk Hammett's leads. Sepultura with Andreas Kisser and Max Cavalera were also a great inspiration – lots of great riffs and cool leads as well. Slayer's Kerry King and Jeff Hanneman are of course the ultimate riff duo, and a great inspiration to this day. I would also list Celtic Frost's Tom Warrior as an influence: we're obviously not talking master guitar shredding here, but lots of dark catchy groove and dirty licks.

"As far as more modern technical shredders do, I'd say Jeff Loomis of Nevermore is pretty fucking awesome. I've always liked that band, and his leads float very well with the Nevermore tunes. And there are of course great death metal guitarists like Trey Azagthoth, Chuck Schuldiner, and Erik Rutan, who I like just as much for the power of their riffs as their skills in shredding."

PHIL DEMMEL
Machine Head

Few of the musicians in this book have had to wait as long for the limelight as Machine Head's lead guitarist Phil Demmel. In his late 30s when his band received real acclaim, he truly served his time on the metal circuit before finally taking his place among the axe pantheon.

Demmel was born in 1967, and as a San Francisco resident was ideally situated to take advantage of the Bay Area thrash metal wave that dominated the club scene there throughout the mid 80s. His first proper band was Vio-lence, a well-known act

on the local thrash circuit that also featured in its ranks Robb Flynn, who quit early on to form a new band, Machine Head.

While Flynn struggled to get his new band some exposure, Demmel endeavoured to make Vio-lence work, but it was not to be. San Francisco simply had too many original metal bands at the time, and the music industry was spending all its time searching for the next Metallica or Testament – and Vio-lence could never hope to equal those.

Giving up on Vio-lence, Demmel formed Torque, a band that played a hybrid of half-thrash, half-classic-heavy-metal. Also, he recorded a solo studio album. Torque was followed by Technocracy (rudely nicknamed Techno Crazy by detractors). But this band too did not go far, and Demmel was obliged to quit the industry for a while to work in his family's business. With a failing marriage and his hopes for a future as a professional musician fading, it must have been a bleak period.

A call in 2001 from his old sparring partner Robb Flynn saved the day. Machine Head, who were into a successful career with the Roadrunner label, had run into some difficulties. Their latest single, 'Crashing Around You', had been issued just after the 9/11 attacks on the USA, and the accompanying video had been banned from MTV because it contained shots of falling buildings. The Roadrunner label cut its losses by reducing the band's financial support, and they left the label.

Guitarist Ahrue Luster also chose this moment to leave the band, and Flynn asked Demmel if he would step in and fill the gap. He agreed.

This was a wise move, even though Machine Head's commercial success was on the wane. Demmel completed some outstanding tour dates with the band, and two years later he was asked to join as a full-time member. His recruitment coincided with a renewal of fortunes for Machine Head, who returned to a more classic metal style with their next album, *Through The Ashes Of Empires*. It was released in 2003 in Europe through Roadrunner, and the band returned to that label's US arm after protracted negotiations.

Demmel can be heard at his best on 'Imperium', released as the lead single from *Ashes Of Empires* and a perfect example of the modern metal sound. With a grinding first half and a back end that sounds remarkably like Haunted-style Swedish thrash metal, the song re-established the band's metallic credentials after Flynn had spent too long flirting with a rap-metal sound. The album was such a success that the new Flynn–Demmel line-up headlined at 2005's Wacken festival to 40,000 headbangers – quite an achievement for a band that had effectively been on the rocks four years earlier.

However, all this turned out to be merely a precursor to the enormous acclaim for Machine Head's next album, *The Blackening*, released early in 2007. Chock-full of long, multi-sectioned songs given a powerful production by Flynn and emphasising the duo's phenomenal lead and rhythm chops, the album scooped a shelf-load of industry awards. The most extreme track, 'Aesthetics Of Hate', was unforgettable for its fast tempo, stop-start riffs, and the extended guitar duel at its centre (most of which was edited out for the single release).

Demmel had just been awarded his own signature guitar, a Jackson with the title Demmelition King V, on which he delivered razor-sharp sweeps and melodic, bluesy

> Few of the musicians in this book have had to wait as long for the limelight as Machine Head's lead guitarist Phil Demmel. In his late 30s when his band received real acclaim, he truly served his time on the metal circuit before finally taking his place among the axe pantheon.

23/100

JEFF HANNEMAN

lines that soared cleanly and exotically above the fast riffing executed by Flynn, himself no mean shredder.

After spending much of 2007 on tour with metal luminaries such as Lamb Of God and Trivium, Machine Head returned to the studio to work on the follow-up to *The Blackening*. At the time of writing, their stock has never been higher – due in no small part to the guitar playing of Demmel.

▶▶| Genius moment

Try anything by Vio-lence for a taste of nostalgia, avoid Torque and Technocracy, and head straight for 'Imperium' or 'Aesthetics Of Hate' by Machine Head, on both of which Demmel delivers a supertight rhythm part and expert solos.

Demmel on things

"I remember seeing Trivium play for the first time on the Roadrage tour a couple of years ago, when they were still in their teens. Our sound guy said, you gotta see these guys. I remember thinking, holy shit – these guys are tasty! I respect the fuck out of their frontman Matt Heafy – I remember going up to him once, when I was wasted, and saying: 'Man, can you show me some of those things?' Ha ha ha!"

JEFF HANNEMAN
Slayer

The ultimate extreme metal guitar team is Kerry King and Jeff Hanneman of Slayer, who not only interchange riffs and solos of blinding speed and complexity but have evolved a unique, atonal lead style of their own. There have been analyses of their solos over the years, with one newspaper critic hilariously describing the sound as 'free jazz' and many more simply labelling it noise. But the shrieking, dissonant sound of the average Slayer solo can't be described in such easy terms.

The only real way to appreciate the guitar playing of either man – and in this case the slightly less expressive Hanneman – is to understand Slayer's history. The influences they have absorbed over the years absolutely define and explain their sound.

Born in 1964, Hanneman grew up in the California suburb of Oakland at the exact period in musical history when American punk and metal were on the cusp of popularity. Southern California hardcore punk was an addiction for Hanneman in his teenage years. He loved the intense speed and aggression of the songs as well as the rebellious lyrics. But at the same time he was drawn in by the international heavy metal scene. In fact, his love of hard-rock-bordering-on-metal acts such as Kiss and AC/DC predated his ongoing obsession with punk.

When Hanneman met the other members of Slayer in 1981, he was a diehard punk, sporting spiked blonde hair and an array of Minor Threat and Black Flag T-

" Southern California hardcore punk was an addiction for Hanneman in his teenage years. "

LEFT Thrash metal's most brutal band: the mighty Slayer. Guitarist Jeff Hanneman is second from left.

> **"**
>
> As I grew interested in thrash, death, and black metal, there was nobody playing guitar in that style where I lived, so I decided to take it up myself.
>
> **"**

shirts. The other musicians in the band – King plus bassist–vocalist Tom Araya and drummer Dave Lombardo – were strict metalheads, into the new sounds of Iron Maiden and Motörhead as well as vintage hard rock such as Deep Purple and Black Sabbath. But they were instantly converted by the punk scene's raw speed, and quickly applied the style to their own songs – which got faster and faster as a result. As the band got more into punk, Hanneman grew his hair and revisited his old Judas Priest albums, complementing the rest of Slayer as the band became the perfect punk-meets-metal ensemble.

Hanneman played a Gibson Les Paul on the earliest Slayer recordings and briefly dabbled with B.C. Rich guitars, but finally he landed up with ESP, where he has stayed since the early 90s. He now has a signature ESP model, painted with the Heineken logo (his beer of choice) but with 'Heineken' rewritten as 'Hanneman'. He uses Marshall JCM-800 amps that drive Marshall cabs with Celestion speakers. His signal passes to the amps through EMG pickups and a Dunlop Crybaby From Hell wah pedal. Perhaps the most crucial element of Hanneman's style is his picking hand, which is extremely tight. He only relaxes it on rare occasions, such as Slayer's 1996 album *Undisputed Attitude*. This consisted of covers of hardcore punk classics – and did not require any of the usual supertight palm-muting.

Hanneman is just as well known for his songwriting skills as for his dexterity on the guitar. He composed several of Slayer's most enduring songs. Their best-known album, 1986's *Reign In Blood*, features 'Angel Of Death' as its opener. This is a perennially controversial song because of its lyrics, which detail the horrific human experimentation of Auschwitz scientist Josef Mengele. Hanneman grew up in a family of war veterans and had read of Mengele's appalling crimes. He wrote of the "pathetic harmless victims" subjected to "surgery, with no anaesthesia", pumped with fluid, burned, frozen, "sewn together", "abacinated" (having their eyes burned out), injected with substances, and having their eyes dyed different colours.

Musically too, 'Angel Of Death' was utterly uncompromising. Most of the riffs were delivered at about 200bpm, apart from a classic midsection composed of a snaky riff of hammer-ons and pull-offs in a catchy, descending pattern. The song's solo section established a Slayer template, with King and Hanneman alternating leads over a sequence of four bars, with the band tuned down a half-step, as they were for all of *Reign In Blood*. Ending with a frantic kick-drum solo from Lombardo and squealing to a halt, it is one of the most gripping thrash metal songs of all time.

Hanneman was constantly accused of right-wing political views for years after the release of 'Angel Of Death'. His detractors couldn't understand why he would write a song about the detested Josef Mengele if he didn't support his actions – despite Hanneman's endless explanation that the song merely listed, rather than condoned, the Auschwitz atrocities. On the 1990 album *Seasons In The Abyss*, Hanneman wrote 'War Ensemble', another tune about warfare that has been a constant presence in the band's live set, as is 'Mandatory Suicide', a 1988 song about death in the trenches of war.

Slayer's albums have been at their best when King and Hanneman, the band's primary songwriters, are more or less equal contributors, as on *Reign In Blood*. In 1998, the band committed a near-fatal error with the *Diabolus In Musica* album,

RIGHT All hail the new wave of shred – with Children Of Bodom frontman Alexi Laiho in the vanguard.

ALEXI LAIHO

21/100

which flirted dangerously with the sludgy nu-metal style popular at the time – the first and only time that the band have strayed any distance from their thrash metal roots. Most of the album was written by Hanneman, as King had backed away in disgust at the state of the contemporary music scene. It contained Slayer's all-time low, a song called 'Stain Of Mind', based on a two-chord riff that sounded exactly like nu-metal poster-boys Korn. Luckily, such transgressions are now ancient history.

▶▶⊦ Genius moment

Hanneman has written so many genre-defining songs that it's almost impossible to choose one, but the intro of 'War Ensemble', from Seasons In The Abyss (1990), has a twisty little figure that would test anyone's picking hand to its limits. It's a perfect example of how Slayer combine melody and speed to such devastating effect.

ALEXI LAIHO
Children Of Bodom

As appreciation for melodic soloing has grown in recent years, bands such as Finland's Children Of Bodom have risen to fame. Singer and lead guitarist Alexi Laiho, nicknamed Wildchild for his prolific partying, lays down world-class leads over the semi-extreme, semi-mainstream metal played by his band, aided by a gift for composing highly memorable melodies. Together with his knack for a soundbite and his waiflike good looks, Laiho has become something of a figurehead for the modern heavy metal guitar scene. He delivers his solos on a signature ESP sharkfin although he has occasionally used Jackson custom guitars.

The 13-year-old Laiho founded a band with drummer Jaska Raatikainen in 1992, calling it Inearthed. Early songs were along the lines of old-school death metal bands such as Entombed, the Swedish pioneers who were regarded very highly in neighbouring Scandinavian countries at the time. Even in their demo era, the band were still interested in melody as much as aggression, and used keyboards for extra atmospherics. Signing to the local Spinefarm label, the band renamed themselves Children Of Bodom (a reference to three still-unsolved murders committed at Finland's Lake Bodom in 1960). They embarked on a record–tour–record routine that has sustained them to this day – although it took at least five years to build any kind of international profile.

It's interesting to follow Laiho's progression as a guitarist. Children Of Bodom's debut album from 1997, *Something Wild*, features a lot of fast, intricate shredding in the neo-classical idiom – which he later confessed was an attempt to play in the style of his idol Yngwie Malmsteen. He toned down the classical stuff on the band's later albums, working toward his own musical identity, although elements of homage to his other heroes such as Zakk Wylde remain in his playing today.

European metal fans took readily to Laiho's fast alternate picking and mastery of

"

Laiho, nicknamed Wildchild for his prolific partying, lays down world-class leads over the semi-extreme, semi-mainstream metal played by his band, aided by a gift for composing highly memorable melodies.

"

sweeps and pinch harmonics, which complemented the speedy, melodic riffing of the Bodom songs. In fact, the genre-spanning nature of the band's songs meant that they were accepted by audiences on a variety of bills, with tuneful power metal acts like Sinergy or extreme metal acts such as Hypocrisy and Agathodaimon. Sinergy was fronted by Laiho's some-time spouse Kimberley Goss, to whom he was married from 2002 to 2004. Both Laiho and his fellow Bodom guitarist Roope Latvala joined Sinergy for a period in 1999.

A step up for Children Of Bodom came with the 1999 album *Hatebreeder*, with a single and video clip accompanying the release. The band then played in Japan with In Flames – another act combining extreme metal with melodic soloing and hooky choruses – and recorded the *Tokyo Wildhearts* live album there. Another level of metal acceptability came when they chose producer Peter Tägtgren for their 2001 album *Follow The Reaper*. At the time, Tägtgren was the European extreme metal producer of choice.

However, for subsequent albums it became apparent that Bodom could step out of the metal box and become something closer to a household name. This happened in 2005 with *Are You Dead Yet?*, a simpler, more trad-metal album than previous works, but still retaining some of the melodic death metal elements of old.

As time passed, the industry began to take note of Laiho's prowess on the guitar, with *Metal Hammer* magazine awarding him Best Guitarist award at the 2006 Golden Gods ceremony. More exposure came when Bodom toured with Slayer on the first Unholy Alliance tour the following year, with Laiho forming an unlikely bond with fellow social drinker Kerry King. Laiho sustained a shoulder injury when he fell over at a bowling alley (really), and this put his guitar-playing out of action for a few months that year, leading to the cancellation of some live shows. But the band have continued their rise to glory, releasing *Blooddrunk*, playing alongside Megadeth, and appearing regularly in the rock press.

Laiho is a fan of fast cars (he owns various American hot-rods), faster guitars, and beer. He has become one of the newest poster children for heavy metal in recent years. Whether or not you like his music, you can't deny that he's earned his success. Even Kirk Hammett of Metallica, when asked by *Rolling Stone* to name the best guitarist in the world, said: "It's the one and only Joe Satriani or that fucking amazing wild child Alexi! Oh, what power he has!"

> **There's still stuff that I want to learn – like chicken-picking with my fingers, I suck at that big time. I won't necessarily need it, it's just for the sake of learning new things.**

▶▶▌ Genius moment
Pick up Hate Crew Deathroll (2003) and go straight to 'Angels Don't Kill', played in drop-C tuning and a perfect example of Laiho's precise picking.

Laiho on rhythm

"One of my favourite guitarists is Zakk Wylde, not only with Black Label Society but on the Ozzy Osbourne albums he did, too. The rhythm guitars were fuckin' crazy – a lot of guitarists only listen to leads when they want to hear guitar played well, but I think people should pay equal attention to the rhythm parts. I made that mistake when I was 16. There's still stuff that I want to learn – like chicken-picking with my

21/100

fingers, I suck at that big time. I won't necessarily need it, it's just for the sake of learning new things. It's more about what I *don't* use. For example, I don't use the harmonic minor; I'm not into it. I like the blues shapes – the pentatonic. I add the flat five and the major six and whatever the fuck to that. Just basic major and minor scales, and the diminished thing where you do an arpeggio. When you don't overdo it, it can sound pretty cool."

HERMAN LI
Dragonforce

Power metal peaked in the early 90s, as fans of Helloween and Gamma Ray will recall, before levelling out for the rest of the decade. Relatively few innovations appeared on that scene for many years, until the sudden, shocking arrival of British band Dragonforce in the early years of the new century. Accurately styling themselves 'extreme power metal' thanks to their music's combination of thrash metal speed and upbeat melodies, the band included two incredibly talented guitarists, Herman Li and Sam Totman. Li is also the band's producer and backing vocalist, and is among the most accomplished musicians anywhere in metal.

Born in Hong Kong but raised in New Zealand and the UK, Li evolved a very fast, melodic lead style with all the tricks we've come to associate with the modern shredder – string-skipping, hybrid picking, sweep-picking, tapping, and the obvious fast alternate picking and legato picking. He delivers these alongside Totman in songs that are usually paced around 200bpm, with the occasional slower section. Keyboard-heavy and symphonic, Dragonforce's music sounds uplifting even when the band write songs with minor-chord choruses (like their best-known song so far, 'Through The Fire And Flames'), leading to much criticism from conservative metal fans who think their material is too lightweight or 'un-metal'.

Li is an interesting character as well as an expert guitarist. His interview soundbites make him far more memorable than the regular monosyllabic shredder. Li is renowned for off-stage partying and his love of video games. He incorporates brief snippets of sounds from old-school games such as Pac-Man into his playing. He trains daily with his road crew in the art of Brazilian ju-jitsu.

When he's not doing any of that, he plays an Ibanez signature model called the E-Gen, featuring scalloped 21st to 24th frets and an Edge Zero whammy bar that he uses to its maximum. For those interested in Li's technique, Dragonforce helpfully included in the 'Through The Fire And Flames' video a close-up shot of Li's hands during the long solo section where he alternates leads with Totman. Remarkably, when the song starts and he and Totman deliver a harmony line, both men can be seen employing a reversed fretting-hand position, reaching over the top of the neck rather than the more conventional style. Many of Dragonforce's guitar lines use an octaver for a high-pitched, slightly unhinged sound, often the first thing the listener notices. More than a few metal fans, upon hearing the band for the first time, assumed that the music they were listening to had been sped up, artificially or otherwise, thanks to this effect.

"

Li evolved a very fast, melodic lead style with all the tricks we've come to associate with the modern shredder.

"

Li's dexterity and the constant flow of melodic ideas which inform his playing have earned him much acclaim. In 2005 he was awarded *Metal Hammer* magazine's Dimebag Darrell Young Guitarist Award, presented by Zakk Wylde. Guitar magazines worldwide have recognised him (individually and with Totman) with several more awards. He wrote a regular column in the UK's *Total Guitar* magazine, which described some of the techniques he employed in Dragonforce songs. Clinics and appearances at several events devoted to high-speed guitar, such as the first Shred School event in Los Angeles in 2007, have set Li on a path that one day will probably elevate him to the level of a Joe Satriani or a Steve Vai.

Dragonforce have enjoyed a long and unorthodox history. They formed in 1996 after the demise of Li and Totman's earlier band, Demoniac, a black metal outfit based in New Zealand. It's hard to imagine the resolutely optimistic guitar duo performing the grimmest music known to mankind. Totman told me recently: "We used to do interviews and say that the albums had been written in the midst of torment and depression, whereas actually we were riding around the studio on skateboards." Little wonder that the band didn't make an international impression.

The first Dragonforce songs, released on MP3.com, were immediately popular thanks to their unusual sound when compared to the rest of the power metal movement. The success of 'Valley Of The Damned', which attracted over half a million downloads, led to a deal with Sanctuary, who released two albums before the band were scooped up by Roadrunner, where they remain today. Their albums – *Inhuman Rampage* (2006) and *Ultra Beatdown* (2008), a deliberately slower collection with more light and shade than previous records – have done well, thanks largely to the band's incessant touring and the instrumental flamboyance of Li.

If power metal is too cheesy for you and extreme metal is too heavy, try Dragonforce – it could be the perfect combination you've been looking for. Thousands of metallers have already signed up, and if the relentlessly cheerful nature of the music is too much for you, you can at least admire the phenomenal guitar playing.

"

We never think of ourselves as great guitarists, but one thing I can say without sounding big-headed is that we are influential in the world of guitars – as in making people pick up the guitar.

"

▶▶❙ Genius moment

Li's playing on Ultra Beatdown (2008) reaches a peak of activity on 'Heroes Of Our Time'. It is, frankly, ludicrous.

Li on modesty

"We shouldn't be in this book, ha ha! We never think of ourselves as great guitarists, but one thing I can say without sounding big-headed is that we are influential in the world of guitars – as in making people pick up the guitar. Marty Friedman is one of my favourite players. He has this unique sound, and great note choice. Anyone can play really fast with good technique, but at the end of the day it doesn't mean you're gonna sound like yourself. You have to have your own sound so that people will hear it and say, 'I know he's with *that* band.' It's more important to play one style which is your own than to play 20 other styles which belong to other people."

20/100

MICK THOMSON

19/100

MICK THOMSON
Slipknot

The hulking man-mountain Mick Thomson is as intimidating as the riffs he plays in the nine-man nu-metal band Slipknot – at least superficially. He is not known for his pleasant character or willingness to tolerate the many music-business fools that plague any band above a certain level of success. He is known for his aversion to company of any kind when he returns from Slipknot's extensive tours. "When I get home I hole up for weeks on end," he told me in 2004. "I'm the kind of guy who gets angry about pretty much everything."

As you might expect, Thomson honed his considerable chops in a grisly death metal band called Body Pit before joining Slipknot's early line-up in 1996. He claims his approach is based on three things – fast tremolo picking; precise, Metallica-style downstrokes; and the pinch harmonic and heavy approach of Morbid Angel axeman Trey Azagthoth.

Hold on, though. Thomson's guitar style isn't based solely on heaviness and speed – as revealed by the mixture of influences he drew on in his youth. Although he was a huge fan of technical death metal bands such as Death and Pestilence, he was also a devotee of the classic rock shredders, from Yngwie Malmsteen ("He could pick up a fuckin' bayonet and make it sound good") to Michael Romeo. There's subtlety behind that blackened death-mask.

Thomson was a longtime B.C. Rich player in the 90s but switched to Ibanez in the early 2000s. His signature Warlock bore the word HATE on the fretboard, while the new Ibanez MTM-1 has SEVEN engraved there instead, a replica of the tattoo on his forearm. It's the number he chose when he joined the band, because in its early days the members went by numbers and nicknames rather than their given names. He plays a seven-string from time to time and has said that he keeps a collection of 98 guitars at his home.

Brutal and melodic guitar styles have made their way into Slipknot's songs, with the Iowa band's first two albums focused heavily on punishing rhythm playing. Lead guitars were deemed passé at the height of the nu-metal boom. Listen to '[Sic]' from Slipknot's 1999 self-titled debut album for a perfect example of a clean, purely downstroked riff with exquisite palm muting. By 2001's *Iowa*, Slipknot had found a darker, more sinister sound, partly thanks to the drop-C tuning of many of the songs: listen to 'Everything Ends' for a layered, wailing approach that is worlds away from the clean aggression of the debut album.

Volume 3 (The Subliminal Verses) in 2004 was a step further. As the nu-metal wave receded and record buyers found a renewed appreciation for classic rock and metal, the 'no guitar solos' restriction was quietly dropped. Thomson and Slipknot's other guitarist Jim Root were finally allowed to exercise their blinding lead skills, and this they did in abundance. 'Pulse Of The Maggots' included a memorable solo section written as a tribute to Thomson's idols Slayer, with alternating shred-outs from both guitarists.

Thomson remains among the most gifted guitarists of the post-nu-metal scene and among the very few whose careers survived the downfall of that movement.

> **"** When I get home I hole up for weeks on end, I'm the kind of guy who gets angry about pretty much everything. **"**

19/100

LEFT **Slipknot's Mick Thomson: anything you can do, he can do faster, and he might just dismember you while he's at it...**

> if you're stuck in a bus with eight other fuckers, you have to be able to release it quick. If you bottle it up, things get pretty bad. Certainly this helps keep me from doing real bad shit.

The band described their fourth album, 2008's *All Hope Is Gone*, as another step forward – and with each album delivering markedly different vibes from its predecessor, their claim seems plausible. However, whether Slipknot will continue to deliver albums for many more years is not known. The volatility of each musician – and apparently they are all as troubled as Thomson by the world around them – makes a long-term career unlikely.

▶▶ **Genius moment**

Check 'Duality' from the 2004 album Vol. III: The Subliminal Verses for an example of the perfect pinch harmonic, enunciated with millimetre-perfect precision in the song's main riff. Don't attempt to replicate it, unless your thumb and pick are perfectly in synch and the gain on your distortion is at or near maximum. Elsewhere, Thomson's perfect tremolo picking (accompanied by the first blastbeats recorded by a nu-metal band) can be heard on 'Eeyore', the hidden track from Slipknot's self-titled 1999 debut album.

Thomson on the job

"I've been doing this so long, it's a fuckin' way of life. The shows are very physical. It's like going to the gym. You end up pretty depleted by the end of the show, so when I'm at home I usually just play video games and sleep. When I go home, I'm like: don't talk to me, don't knock on my fuckin' door. I cut myself off from the world. But if I have to drive to the mall, just parking the car makes me want to cut people into little fuckin' pieces and play with their organs. All that is fuel for angry music, especially if you're the kind of person I am, where pretty much everything pisses me off. So it's not hard to find fuckin' inspiration, ha ha! Also, if you're stuck in a bus with eight other fuckers, you have to be able to release it quick. If you bottle it up, things get pretty bad. Certainly this helps keep me from doing real bad shit."

KERRY KING
Slayer

Kerry King and his fellow Slayer guitarist Jeff Hanneman redefined thrash metal guitar playing in the 80s. They kept the flag flying in the 90s and are still keeping the style pushed-out and angular to this day. If you've never heard Slayer, you've missed out on a huge chunk of musical history as well as some of the most addictively energising sounds of all time. Here's how it happened – and why it matters.

King – like Hanneman born in 1964 – was brought up on classic hard rock and heavy metal in the 70s. He experienced something of an epiphany in 1981 when he heard the first thrash metal band, Venom. The speed and violence of their songs permanently altered the way he approached the guitar, and their cod-Satanic lyrics made him realise how much fun he could have writing outrageous songs that made people above a certain age feel uncomfortable.

RIGHT The classic shot from the back of Slayer's 1986 LP, Reign In Blood. The then-hirsute Kerry King is pictured at far left.

KERRY KING

18 / 100

My goal before a gig is to play the fastest riffs in the set, so I'll make a point of getting 'Angel Of Death' down.

As you will recall from Hanneman's entry a little earlier in this book, the members of Slayer had their horizons abruptly broadened when Hanneman introduced them to hardcore punk, which was raging in California at the time. The speed of punk particularly influenced drummer Dave Lombardo, who played each new Slayer song incrementally faster every time the band rehearsed it. This placed Slayer in a unique position when they began recording demos and playing gigs on their home turf in Orange County: punk and metal crowds flocked to them because of their fusion of the best of both scenes.

King had developed a phenomenally tight picking hand at an early stage, following the lead of fellow LA band Metallica and their pioneering frontman James Hetfield (although he'll never admit it). He soon evolved a lead style that was indebted to Iron Maiden and Mercyful Fate, with legato hammer-ons and dramatic, melodic lines.

For Slayer's first album, *Show No Mercy* (1983), his approach revealed the band's influences for all to see. However, by the following year – and the awe-inspiring *Hell Awaits* album – this changed as the King–Hanneman team pursued an atonal, squealing style that disgusted critics and enthralled fans in equal measure. They have refined and re-refined this throughout Slayer's career, with King acknowledged nowadays as a guitarist with that rare asset – a unique lead style. It's not known if he could play melodic shredding should he choose to, but he never has. Perhaps one day he'll surprise us.

As well as the dissonant shriek of his solos, King's greatest guitar strength is his superbly muscular rhythm style. The riffs are played to microsecond accuracy despite their great speed – Slayer's songs peak at about 240bpm, making them among the consistently fastest guitarists in this book, alongside Dragonforce – and require powerful palm muting and tremolo picking of fiendish precision.

Every Slayer album has one or more warp-speed songs, and fans looking for particularly high-velocity entertainment should immediately seek out 'Chemical Warfare' (*Haunting The Chapel* EP, 1984), the title track and 'Praise Of Death' (*Hell Awaits* album, 1985), all of *Reign In Blood* (1986), 'Silent Scream', the first half of 'Ghosts Of War', and the second half of 'Live Undead' (*South Of Heaven*, 1988), 'War Ensemble', 'Hallowed Point', and 'Born Of Fire' (*Seasons In The Abyss*, 1990), 'Dittohead' and 'Mind Control' (*Divine Intervention*, 1994), most of *Undisputed Attitude* (1996 – but be warned that this is an album of punk covers, and the guitarists' picking-hand precision is reduced accordingly), 'Bitter Peace', 'Scrum', and 'Point' (*Diabolus In Musica*, 1998), 'Payback' (*God Hates Us All*, 2001), and 'Flesh Storm', 'Consfearacy', and the midsection of 'Supremist' (*Christ Illusion*, 2006). All these songs are usually delivered at a higher speed (and a corresponding reduction in tightness) when played live. Now go and burn yourself the ultimate Slayer compilation.

But King is not merely about speed for its own sake. His slower songs are massively, crushingly heavy thanks to a skilled engineering and mastering team on most (unfortunately, not all) Slayer albums, and a willingness to experiment with tunings. 'Spill The Blood', the closing track on Slayer's fourth album, *South Of Heaven*, was their first to feature a clean guitar, used in the flat-picked intro riff.

This approach was echoed in the title track of *Seasons In The Abyss* (a hit in 1991), '213' from *Divine Intervention*, and 'The Final Six' from *Christ Illusion*. It is a highly effective and sinister device. Meanwhile, 'Gemini' – an original song on the otherwise all-covers *Undisputed Attitude* – featured King's first use of a seven-string guitar, used in a slow, doomy fashion with plenty of slides toward the lowest register.

▶▶︎ Genius moment

There's a moment in 'Fictional Reality' from the much-maligned *Divine Intervention* (1994) in which King executes a tapped pattern on his low E-string, all within the lowest seven frets. Although the album's strange production doesn't make it easy to hear, listen carefully and you'll hear something that I don't think has been attempted in metal before.

We don't have space here to cover the other iconic aspects of Kerry King – his body art, his many feuds with other musicians (in particular Dave Mustaine of Megadeth and Robb Flynn of Machine Head), his antagonistic stance toward organised religion (although he is not a Satanist, as many have assumed), his live and studio guest appearances with Megadeth, Pantera, the Beastie Boys, Sum 41, Marilyn Manson, and many others, or his friendship with the late 'Dimebag' Darrell Abbott.

But we can at least mention his choice of weapon. He's been a career-long endorser of B.C. Rich, starting out on a red Mockingbird, decorated with spatters of black paint by Slayer roadie (and later drummer extraordinaire) Gene Hoglan. He has several custom versions in different finishes of his signature guitar, the KKV. He also has his own Marshall head, the JCM-800 2203KK, which features a built-in noise gate to assist with the palm muting.

A heavy metal legend if ever there was one, Kerry King should be at the top of anyone's list of guitarists to investigate. He has estimated that Slayer have approximately five years left in them before they quit. Frontman Tom Araya is 47 as this book goes to press – a ripe old age for anyone playing thrash metal night after night. So if you haven't seen King's unique band in action, don't leave it too long.

> "
> A heavy metal legend if ever there was one, Kerry King should be at the top of anyone's list of guitarists to investigate.
> "

King on warming-up

"To me, it's like if you're working out and you go from lifting 20 pounds to 50 pounds. You don't lift 20 pounds and then say, hey, I'm going for 50. When I warm up before a show, I start out by playing 'Propaganda' by Sepultura, because it's got some pedalling, but it's not fast pedalling. I don't warm up with, say, [Slayer's song] 'Angel Of Death', because if you cramp up it blows your gig. I'll warm up with something slow and then build up to where I need to be in an hour. My goal before a gig is to play the fastest riffs in the set, so I'll make a point of getting 'Angel Of Death' down. A lot of times I'll play 'Born Of Fire' because that has a lot of speed and intermittent picking in it."

18/100

17/100

IHSAHN (Vegard Sverre Tveitan)
Emperor

Vegard 'Ihsahn' Tveitan is best known for his work in the Norwegian black metal band Emperor, whose history was recounted in detail in the entry for Tomas 'Samoth' Haugen a little earlier in this book. Ihsahn is a composer of extreme vision, invoking fantastical and mythological imagery in his expansive, complex music. As well as playing guitar to a phenomenally high standard, he also plays bass and keyboards and provides both melodic and brutal vocals.

Tveitan was born in the small town of Notodden and is still resident there. He formed a band with Haugen in 1991 called Thou Shalt Suffer, partially funded by a government grant for musicians. At first, the two multi-instrumentalists pursued the death metal style that was in vogue at the time, but they soon realised its limitations and switched to black metal and a new name, Emperor. Tveitan renamed himself Ihsahn, for which no explanation has ever been supplied, although he insists that it isn't a reversal of 'Nazi' as has been claimed. Haugen became Samoth: simply his given name, Tomas, backwards.

The band's new sound was much wider in frequency and its range of content than before, and far more malevolent, with huge swathes of orchestral keyboard providing a rich, ambitious feel. The band would become the third biggest-selling black metal act ever, after Cradle Of Filth and Dimmu Borgir, notching up over half a million sales during the next few years, before calling it a day in 2001.

The band were consistently dogged by controversy – thanks to the jailing of their first drummer Bård 'Faust' Eithun for the murder of a gay man in Lillehammer in 1992, Samoth's prison time for church-burning the following year, and their consistent adherence to Satanic principles – but as the years passed much of this seemed to diminish, leaving them merely as respected musicians.

The reasons for Emperor's (entirely amicable) split help to understand Ihsahn's musical approach. Samoth had tired of the symphonic black metal style that Emperor had established and that had been emulated by many other bands of their genre, while Ihsahn wanted to improve and expand upon that sound, bringing in other influences such as progressive rock.

Samoth duly formed the futuristic death metal band Zyklon, while Ihsahn played with his wife Ihriel's band Peccatum, set up a record label, Mnemosyne Productions, and prepared his first solo album. While fans waited, news came that his home town had presented him with the Notodden Kommunes Kulturpris, an award in recognition of his contribution to local culture.

Ihsahn's solo album, *The Adversary*, was announced in late 2005. The run-up to its release coincided with a brief (and popular) Emperor re-formation for festival shows the following summer. When the album was released that April, it was a revelation – an intricate, detailed record of great scope that required several spins to understand. Guitar was just a small part of the sound, although Ihsahn played with extreme precision and great expression. He brought several brands of metal to the table, including melodic thrash, blackened death metal, and more of

"
Tveitan renamed himself Ihsahn, for which no explanation has ever been supplied, although he insists that it isn't a reversal of 'Nazi' as has been claimed.
"

LEFT Black metal's most accomplished guitarist may well be Ihsahn, who fronted Emperor for a decade before going solo.

17/100

the shimmering, orchestral black metal of Emperor. Guitar solos were not the focus of the sound on most of the songs, with harmonised lines appearing much more frequently, but as always Ihsahn's rhythm guitar was perfectly enunciated, whether with precise downstrokes or reverb-heavy arpeggiated chords. He played all the instruments on the album apart from drums, supplied by session player extraordinaire Asgeir Mickelson, and a vocal guest spot on the song 'Homecoming', which came from Ulver frontman Kristoffer 'Garm' Rygg.

A video shot for the song 'Invocation' shows Ihsahn delivering a series of riffs and, halfway through, a cleanly-picked chordal section. He has used Ibanez guitars since the mid 90s and was recently reported to be using their new eight-string model, the RG-2228 so beloved of Divine Heresy and Meshuggah.

In 2008, Ihsahn released *angL*, his second solo album. The vast soundscapes of *The Adversary* were still there, but on repeated plays it became apparent that he had used more areas of light and shade, with equally dynamic execution of heavy and lighter guitar parts. Metal was still the bedrock of the music, but the songs had more of an eccentric, oblique direction that placed the album firmly in the prog-metal camp. Ihsahn has already devoted one record to the devil and another to an angel, and so fans wait expectantly for the next album from this artist whose great instrumental expertise is still secondary to his unique vision.

> **"**
> Ihsahn has already devoted one record to the devil and another to an angel, and so fans wait expectantly for the next album from this artist whose great instrumental expertise is still secondary to his unique vision.
> **"**

▶▶ Genius moment

Visit Ihsahn's second solo album angL (2008) for evidence of his continuing moves away from metal and into more opaque, experimental areas of music. 'Unhealer', which features guest vocals from Opeth's Mikael Åkerfeldt, contains blistering rhythm parts and atmospheric effects.

Ihsahn on a favourite

"Although there are many to choose from, I think I must go by personal preference and say Andy La Rocque of King Diamond. I've always found his playing to be very inspired and convincing. His choice of notes and passionate execution, especially on solos, has really appealed to me and my philosophy of 'play it like you mean it and believe it'."

TOM MORELLO
Rage Against The Machine, Audioslave

Quite a few readers will be surprised at the inclusion in this book of Tom Morello, whose best-known work was with the rap-metal act Rage Against The Machine in the early to mid 90s. After all, to some Rage was a metal band, but not to others – and I can see a clear argument in favour of both sides. But the riffs that Morello laid down in that band were metal, beyond all reasonable doubt. If you're still upset about this, feel free to email me a rude message.

Morello was born in New York City in 1964 and raised in Chicago. He inherited a highly political family. His Kenyan father had been a Mau Mau guerrilla while his Italian-American mother was a teacher and anti-censorship campaigner. Morello was an active musician and actor in his youth, singing in a Led Zeppelin covers act at age 13 and learning the guitar. By 1984 he had struck up a friendship with future Tool guitarist Adam Jones, who played bass in his band The Electric Sheep, a mainstream heavy metal outfit with politically-themed lyrics.

Punk was also a huge influence on Morello, resonating with his musical tastes and his anti-establishment stance. But it's amusing to note that his first real exposure came with a Van Halen-style pop-metal band called Lock Up. This shortlived act, formed after he moved to Los Angeles following graduation from Harvard, released an album on Geffen with the laughable title *Something Bitchin' This Way Comes*. Despite the lightweight riffs (readily available for viewing on YouTube), Morello – who had already honed an experimental guitar style thanks to a daily routine of eight hours' practice as a student – was already dropping in unusual sound effects from his guitar through an array of pedals.

A chance meeting with vocalist Zack de la Rocha at a club show in LA prompted Morello to put together a band with Brad Wilk on drums (who had previously auditioned for Lock Up) and de la Rocha's friend Tim Commerford, a bass virtuoso. Rage Against The Machine was the new band, formed just in time to take advantage of alternative rock and metal's Year Zero, 1991.

The year 1991 saw the release of three era-redefining albums: Metallica's *'Black Album'*, Nirvana's *Nevermind*, and The Red Hot Chili Peppers' *Blood Sugar Sex Magik*. It marked the start of a half-decade period in which old-style heavy metal was swept away by waves of grunge and alt.rock, leaving all the biggest and most tenacious bands without an audience.

Fortunately, Rage Against The Machine's self-titled debut album of 1993 immediately tagged the band as innovators. While de la Rocha's barked rapping and grunts revealed his hip-hop background, the furious, rock-solid backing of the rest of the band on songs like 'Killing In The Name' (RATM's first single and still their best-known song), 'Bombtrack', and 'Know Your Enemy' were as metallic as you could get in the early 90s and still be regarded as part of the mainstream. And Rage were mainstream all right: signed to Epic and headlining Lollopalooza, despite their underground origins. Elsewhere, the riffs had more in common with funk than metal, although the two fused naturally to form the beginnings of the nu-metal scene – which, like many new musical movements, started promisingly before losing its way shortly after.

In Rage, Morello used a series of Fender Strats and Teles through many pedals, including a Dunlop Crybaby and a Digitech WH-1 Whammy, the mainstays of his processed, divebombing lead sound. He employed a harmoniser on some of his jazzier solos, boosted by a DOD volume pedal. He has used flangers, tremolo pedals, and phasers during his career, although at this early stage his main sound was a meatier, compressed overdrive, executed with needle-sharp palm-muting and a noise gate for an added staccato texture.

All this amazing dexterity led Morello over the next few years to be asked to guest on albums by artists as diverse as Anti-Flag, The Crystal Method, and The

> **Morello formed an impromptu glam-metal trio with Faith No More's Billy Gould and Tool's Maynard James Keenan, called Shandi's Addiction, for a 1994 Kiss tribute album, Kiss My Ass.**

16/100

Prodigy, as well as playing on the soundtracks of *Talledega Nights* and *Dodgeball*. He even formed an impromptu glam-metal trio with Faith No More's Billy Gould and Tool's Maynard James Keenan, called Shandi's Addiction, for a 1994 Kiss tribute album, *Kiss My Ass*.

Despite all the technology, the real core of Morello's playing lies in his inventiveness. He might pluck the strings with objects other than a plectrum, including an allen key, or scrape his guitar's cable over the pickups for a rubbing, scratching sound. He makes extraterrestrial noises that don't usually enter the guitar's vocabulary. More than a few listeners assumed that music software was being used, leading to a rather lofty disclaimer in the *Rage Against The Machine* album's liner notes to the effect that no sequencers or samplers had been employed.

Rage were the quintessential touring band for some years in the 90s, perhaps due to the anthemic nature of their songs – the "Fuck you, I won't do what you tell me!" refrain of 'Killing In The Name' is one of the most gripping live moments ever. Because of this, their three other studio albums were less successful than their debut, with hardly a hit by the time they came to record their last, the covers album *Renegades* released in 2000.

De la Rocha left and the other three recruited Soundgarden singer Chris Cornell for a new group, Audioslave. They scored a major hit in 2002 with the single 'Cochise', a Zeppelin-esque song featuring Morello tapping a pencil on the strings, and a triple-platinum self-titled debut album. Morello used a Gibson Les Paul among other instruments in the new band.

Audioslave split in 2006 after two more records, before the entirely unexpected reunion of Rage Against The Machine, who have played several festival dates since then. The biggest of these so far has been the Lollopalooza festival in August 2008, where the played alongside Radiohead and Nine Inch Nails. Morello also plays acoustic folk under the name The Nightwatchman, where he exercises his more mellow instincts in line with the various political organisations to which he is affiliated – most prominent among them is Axis Of Justice, co-founded with System Of A Down frontman Serj Tankian.

It's a sign of Morello's popularity among guitar fans that he is now represented as an end-of-level boss in the popular Playstation/Wii game *Guitar Hero*, and has been asked to jam with musicians of the stature of Bruce Springsteen. He is one of a kind.

> **"**
> Morello also plays acoustic folk under the name The Nightwatchman, where he exercises his more mellow instincts in line with the various political organisations to which he is affiliated.
> **"**

▶▶ Genius moment

Of the hundreds of riffs that Tom Morello has donated to the guitar community – many of which you'll hear emanating from rehearsal rooms on any given night – let's pick the last riff from 'Bullet In The Head'. Any budding guitar hero should throw away his or her Guitar Hero console and play this until reaching perfection.

16/100

KIRK HAMMETT
Metallica

Metallica, the biggest-selling heavy metal band that has ever existed, made their fortune on the back of three prize assets. First, they have written some of the most essential metal songs ever composed, which will live on for decades, perhaps centuries, and will mark them permanently as the Led Zeppelin of their generation. Second, they have toured, and toured, and toured until they dropped, and then got up and toured some more. There can be few inhabited countries left that have not hosted a Metallica show at some point. Finally, three of the four members possess almost inhuman musical skills: the fourth – the drummer – is merely competent rather than a virtuoso, but he has written many of their most enduring songs and so has never been unduly troubled by this fact.

Kirk Hammett, who was born in 1962 in San Francisco, the future home of thrash metal, has been a highly regarded master of many guitar styles for 25 years. He began learning the instrument in 1977, just as classic rock peaked in the USA and the first wave of heavy metal was declining in the UK and Europe. Overseas bands such as UFO, the Scorpions, and Iron Maiden informed his playing for the next few years, and he was heavily influenced by the clean, melodic leads of those acts. His elder brother, a guitarist, bass player, and fan of heavy rock, introduced him to Jimi Hendrix, Black Sabbath, Led Zeppelin, and many more of the world's finest guitarists. Hammett grew up fuelled with enthusiasm for his instrument.

He graduated rapidly from his first guitar – a model from the Montgomery Ward mail-order catalogue – to a 1978 Fender Stratocaster and then a '74 Gibson Flying V, which he still uses today after replacing the stock pickups with EMGs in 1989. Hammett evolved a fast, accurate picking technique and a melodic shred approach, later described as "very European" in the American musical climate of the day.

By 1980, Hammett and his school-friends – including Les Claypool, later to become the frontman of Primus – were playing in metal bands influenced by the current NWOBHM. He co-founded San Francisco band Exodus and played on their 1982 demo, helping to push them towards early dominance of the Bay Area metal scene.

Also in 1982, the Los Angeles thrash quartet Metallica made the move up to SF, because of the city's more receptive metal scene but also the reluctance of their new, San Fran-based bassist Cliff Burton to relocate. Once settled into the city, Metallica utterly dominated the local metal scene, transforming it with their fast, relatively brutal music and inspiring a crop of acts – among them Exodus – to speed up themselves. Hammett was rapidly developing a powerful guitar style, coached by shredder extraordinaire Joe Satriani, whose own career was yet to take off.

Hammett didn't have much time to progress with Exodus. He was asked to join Metallica in the spring of 1983, when they fired guitarist Dave Mustaine for his drinking habits. Hammett flew in to New York, where the band were in the process of recording their debut album, as Mustaine boarded a Greyhound bus back to California. At the time, neither man knew how crucial these events would turn out to be in the history of heavy metal.

I wanna be the best I possibly can be, and I want it to be perfect – and that's just unrealistic, but I can't get that out of my head.

15/100

Mustaine went on to found the very successful thrash act Megadeth, while Metallica needed a reliable guitarist who would support the songwriting of singer James Hetfield and drummer Lars Ulrich without challenging them for the leadership of the band. Hammett, a rather introspective character, filled this position perfectly, and his solos on *Kill 'Em All* complemented the band's music in similar fashion. His leads were based on Mustaine's solos on the previous demos but expanded and polished, adding a touch of class to Metallica's primitive thrash metal.

Hammett's musical evolution was astounding through *Ride The Lightning* (1984), *Master Of Puppets* ('86), and *...And Justice For All* ('88) – which, as it turned out, marked Metallica's golden era. Just as each album was a step ahead of its predecessor in songwriting complexity and ambition, so were Hammett's solos.

He delivered them through a variety of guitars and frequently – too frequently for some listeners – through a Dunlop Crybaby wah pedal. Although he often deployed the '74 Flying V for lead (and rhythm, on stage only), Hammett settled on ESP guitars early in his career, with the KH-2 superstrat (and versions with different designs and finishes) becoming his main touring guitar for almost two decades. His alternate picking and legato playing, played in a range of styles from bluesy and emotional (the introduction of 'Fade To Black' and the first solo in 'Creeping Death') to all-out warp-speed with some dissonance and divebombs ('Disposable Heroes' and, perhaps his finest moment, '...And Justice For All') made him a hugely respected soloist by the end of the decade.

By 1990, Metallica had tired of complex songwriting, which had reached a prog-metal level on the *Justice* album. The writing sessions for their next album focused on stripped-down, simpler arrangements. They reaped enormous rewards on *Metallica*, the so-called *'Black Album'*, released the following August. Hammett duly toned down his soloing, focusing on melody and emotion over speed and aggression. Possibly to his chagrin, one of the most famous Metallica solos ever recorded appeared on that album, at the end of the ballad 'Nothing Else Matters'. It was played by Hetfield.

In critical terms, it was downhill from then for Metallica. Reviewers largely despised the series of albums they released after 1996: the alternative-metal *Load*, the lamer sequel *Reload*, a covers album *Garage Inc.*, and a live orchestral collaboration with the San Francisco Symphony, *S&M*. In the band's defence, these albums all shifted many millions of copies and they grossed ever larger sums from touring, irrespective of the complaints of the critics.

Hammett expanded his lead guitar into new territories. Fans may not always have relished these moves, but they spoke volumes about his interests as a guitarist. His first slide solo, for example, came on *Load*'s opening track, 'Ain't My Bitch', and elsewhere he introduced a range of effects, such as a voice-tube, into his rhythm parts (which he and Hetfield began to share after 1996).

Despite Hammett's induction into the *Guitar World* Hall Of Fame in 2002 (he was the first player to be so honoured), he reached a career low-point with the following year's *St. Anger* album, which featured no solos. The band could be seen in the accompanying *Some Kind Of Monster* documentary arguing over whether to feature solos or not, eventually trampling over Hammett's eminently reasonable protests. He said that avoiding leads for the sake of fashion inevitably made a band seem outdated

> **"**
> I'm never very confident. A lot of that has to do with the fact that sometimes soloing comes really easy for me, and I question it. I'm like, 'That was too easy! That must mean that maybe it's not good.
> **"**

15/100

KIRK HAMMETT

when those fashions inevitably changed. The album itself was terrible, whether or not it had leads, and has gone down as a black spot on Metallica's already inconsistent CV.

However, their 2008 album, *Death Magnetic*, featured plenty of expressive soloing, even if still no match for their 80s work.

Equipped with signature amp heads from Randall and an arsenal of guitars that now include Strats and Les Pauls, Hammett is the consummate metal guitarist – even if his band has not always been the perfect vehicle for him. He has earned his place in metal history several times over.

> "
>
> **He has earned his place in metal history several times over.**
>
> "

▶▶▍ Genius moment

Where to start? The superb tapping on 'Creeping Death'? The faithful, split-second-accurate re-creation of the solo on Diamond Head's 'Am I Evil?'? The layers of melody on 'Sanitarium (Welcome Home)'? The clever exploitation of the chromatic backing riff in 'Don't Tread On Me'? In fact, any and every Metallica album released up to and including 1991 is worth investigating.

Hammett on perfection

"I'm never very confident. A lot of that has to do with the fact that sometimes soloing comes really easy for me, and I question it. I'm like, 'That was too easy! That must mean that maybe it's not good.' Also, I wanna be the best I possibly can be, and I want it to be perfect – and that's just unrealistic, but I can't get that out of my head."

RALPH SANTOLLA
Deicide, Obituary, Iced Earth

The Italian-American guitarist Ralph Santolla can play any style of music, but his trademark is fast, melodic soloing with classic-rock influences, and he's played a crucial role in many different bands. So versatile is Ralph that he is perhaps the only musician in this book to have found success with a hair-metal act as well as a death metal band.

Santolla first found major acclaim in 1993 when he took up the position of touring guitarist in Death. This revealed much about his talent before he played a single note – famously, Death mainman Chuck Schuldiner only recruited the metal scene's very best musicians into his band. Although Santolla didn't actually record with Death, who were between albums at the time, he is immortalised in the video for 'The Philosopher', which is readily available on DVD and online. When you watch, note his superstrat painted with the Italian flag – and how he's trying not to laugh in the final shot.

That classic prog-metal composition came at a turning-point for the veteran Florida extremists, when they metamorphosed from being merely another metal act (albeit one of serious talent) to a musical phenomenon with few boundaries. In this,

Santolla emulated his illustrious predecessor James Murphy, whose stylish lead playing on Death's *Spiritual Healing* album (1990) had given them a lift to a new level of technicality.

After Death, Santolla played with Iced Earth, a band whose music –fast, traditional heavy metal with occasional thrash metal influences – has received huge attention for the epic songs of its primary composer Jon Schaffer, which deal in intricate detail with history and warfare. Santolla's playing was perfect for the band: his fast, spiralling leads added majesty to the already landscape-wide songs. That approach reached a peak on 2004's *The Glorious Burden*, which contained within it the 32-minute song 'Gettysburg (1863)'.

In addition to his Iced Earth performances, Santolla saw prestigious stints with Eyewitness, Millennium, and the Sebastian Bach band – yes, the Skid Row singer who had inspired a million teenage boys to apply hairspray and eyeliner in the 80s. He is also much acclaimed in the metal community for his exemplary work with two more Florida death metal bands, Deicide and Obituary.

When Santolla joined Deicide in 2005, it was a logical move for both band and musician. Santolla had for some years been teaching one of the band's recently-departed guitarists, Eric Hoffman, and knew the rest of the band well. Deicide at the time were effectively singer–bassist Glen Benton and drummer Steve Asheim, as Eric and his brother Brian had both decamped. The band were supremely talented at what they did but were on something of a commercial downturn when Santolla joined. The Hoffman brothers' lead style, a less gripping form of the classic atonal, Slayer-style squeal, had become slightly outdated, and fans welcomed Santolla's classy, warm melodicism.

▶▌ Genius moment

Go to YouTube and watch Deicide's phenomenal 'Homage To Satan' immediately, if you haven't already. Not only is it a fast, powerful death metal song with some of singer Glen Benton's most uncompromising vocals to date, it also features a long, melodic solo section delivered by Santolla – a complete shock for fans who had been expecting more of the standard Eric Hoffman squeal.

The first Deicide album on which Santolla played, *The Stench Of Redemption* (2006), was widely regarded as a welcome step back toward the band's creative peak in the early 90s, with the consensus that Benton and Asheim had been newly inspired by the recruitment of Santolla and also Jack Owen, who had recently left the death metal scene-leaders Cannibal Corpse.

The new line-up's second record, *Till Death Do Us Part* (2008), was more of the same, to the relief of the band's fans. The vast barrage of riffage and solos that Santolla delivered on Dean and Jackson guitars through Randall amps was, if anything, more intense than that of *Redemption*. (Santolla's Catholic beliefs were thought by many fans to be a cause of conflict between him and the resolutely Satanist Benton, but this was not the case, as both men explained on many occasions.)

> **So versatile is Ralph that he is perhaps the only musician in this book to have found success with a hair-metal act as well as a death metal band.**

14/100

ALEX SKOLNICK

Obituary recruited Santolla after he relinquished his post in Deicide between the two albums. They needed a second guitarist to fill in for Allen West, who was serving a prison sentence at the time. To the confusion of some observers, Santolla has retained a place in both bands. At the time of writing, he is planning to tour with both Deicide and Obituary, organising his time so that the two schedules do not overlap. Florida death metal fans are thus in for a double treat.

Santolla on the best

"I can't narrow this down to just one guy. I'll say Alexi and Roope from Children Of Bodom have to be considered, because technically they're incredible – and they don't just bullshit to play fast, they make incredible music with great feeling. They're a huge inspiration to me. On the Deicide album *The Stench Of Redemption*, which seems to have gotten a lot of attention for my guitar playing, I never would have played that stuff or approached it that way if it hadn't been for touring with those two guys. Watching them play every night took me back to some stuff that I used to play a long time ago – all the sweeping and the fast alternate picking that I used to do but had let fall by the wayside.

"Michael Romeo from Symphony X is a fuckin' fantastic guitar player and a great musician – plus he smokes cigarettes and drinks Jack Daniels, so he's definitely up there. Also I would say Michael Amott, because he brings the stuff that I like – Michael Schenker, Gary Moore – to extreme metal in a way that no one else did before. And he writes incredible stuff too."

"

The Italian-American guitarist Ralph Santolla can play any style of music, but his trademark is fast, melodic soloing with classic-rock influences, and he's played a crucial role in many different bands.

"

ALEX SKOLNICK
Testament

Melodic thrash metal took some time to arrive in the 80s, evolving out fast, raw early incarnation of the genre that dominated until the bands got past the lust for pure speed and aggression. The idea of speedy riffs combined with melodic elements took over when the guitarists in bands like Annihilator and Testament, who had learned their chops from old-school trad-metal, brought harmonious playing techniques to extreme metal.

Although Testament founder Eric Peterson is an excellent guitarist, his fellow axeman Alex Skolnick is nothing less than a world-class virtuoso. His skills had their downside, however, as he outgrew the thrash scene relatively quickly.

Skolnick was born and raised in Berkeley and became an important force on the Bay Area thrash metal scene from its earliest days. By 1983, he had studied under San Fran's resident guitar guru Joe Satriani and was ready to apply his skills in a band. He chose to sign up with Legacy, a band formed by Peterson and struggling to achieve a stable line-up. Personnel came and went, but Skolnick and Peterson formed an instant bond and quickly wrote an album's worth of songs.

Little progress was made until 1986, when the band – now called Testament to avoid legal trouble with an existing Legacy – signed with the Megaforce label, the New York company that had discovered and launched the careers of their Bay Area

LEFT The super-dexterous Alex Skolnick of Testament, whose love of jazz equals his passion for metal.

13/100

> **Melodic thrash metal took some time to arrive in the 80s, evolving out fast, raw early incarnation of the genre that dominated until the bands got past the lust for pure speed and aggression.**

contemporaries Metallica. The relationship between band and label was founded in depressing circumstances: at their audition, band and label owners Jon and Marsha Zazula were reeling from the news of Metallica bassist Cliff Burton's premature death in a coach crash in Sweden the previous day.

Testament made rapid progress thanks to the dazzling guitar playing and songwriting on their 1987 debut album, confusingly titled *The Legacy*. Like Metallica, Testament made an instant impact with their anthemic, smoothly-produced songs, which offered speed and power aplenty while allowing Skolnick's solos full rein. In fact, the Metallica comparisons always dogged Testament, who later showed some annoyance that they weren't included in a Big Five of thrash metal, having rivalled Anthrax and Slayer in album sales for several years.

Testament hit a blistering creative peak with 1989's *Practice What You Preach*, which brought them millions of fans. By this stage, Skolnick's devastating legato runs were an integral part of the Testament sound, delivered on a variety of Ibanez superstrats. But the only way was down after the band failed to match the momentum of Metallica and Megadeth in the 90s.

Following a sequence of poorly-performing records, Skolnick jumped ship. He'd tired of the thrash metal approach and disagreed with Peterson over the direction that the group should take in the wake of the new grunge movement. As the death throes of metal resounded all about them, Skolnick proposed that Testament take a softer, more commercial route into rock (which, as we know in retrospect, would have been their death-knell). Peterson wanted to extend the extremity and go toward death metal, the approach the band ultimately adopted in the mid 90s and that has ensured them a career to this day.

In 1992, Skolnick found himself without a band for the first time in almost a decade. His first move, unsurprisingly, was to join Florida power metallers Savatage, who played fast, smooth music with elegant soloing and hooky choruses – rather like his vision of where Testament should have gone. After playing on the band's 1994 album *A Handful Of Rain* and their subsequent live record, *Japan Live '94*, he returned to California and played with Exhibit-A, and then Skol-Patrol, who were known for their funked-up take on TV cop show themes – and virtually ignored by the metal community as a result.

This hardly troubled Skolnick, who was on a trajectory away from heavy metal and toward the skilled guitarist's habitual target, jazz-rock. In The Alex Skolnick Trio he delivered supremely technical fusion licks alongside bassist Nathan Peck (replaced in 2003 by John Davis) and drummer Matt Zebroski.

Skolnick initially seemed to take a light-hearted view of his trio, focusing on bebop covers of established rock and metal tunes by Black Sabbath, Deep Purple, Kiss, Iron Maiden, and even Testament (whose 'Practice What You Preach' was given the Latin treatment and retitled 'Practica Lo Que Predicas'). However, after the 2002 covers album *Goodbye To Romance: Standards For A New Generation*, he composed original material for the follow-up releases, *Transformation* (2004) and *Last Day In Paradise* ('07). By then, he had returned to Testament after a 15-year hiatus, playing on their new album and proving clearly that while jazz might be his current passion, it isn't his only speciality.

13/100

> **▶▶▌ Genius moment**
>
> Check out the incredible soloing all over Testament's 2008 comeback album The Formation Of Damnation. The songs aren't a match for their 80s material, but Skolnick's solos are as accomplished as anything he's ever done.

Skolnick on the guru

"My favourite metal guitarist is Randy Rhoads. He brought a previously unheard-of level of musicianship and outside influences to metal, wasn't overly concerned with how 'metal' his image was, and planned to continue studying and growing for the rest of his life – which was tragically cut short. He was and is a role model for my own career."

PAT O'BRIEN
Cannibal Corpse

One of many interesting things about Pat O'Brien, apart from his fearsome picking skills, his machine-like ability to choke off millisecond-perfect pinch harmonics, and his fluid, expressive leads, is the small but crucial fact that he has played in a melodic metal band, Nevermore, and a monstrously abrasive one, Cannibal Corpse – and been eerily at home in both.

O'Brien first joined Nevermore in 1994, when the Seattle quartet first came to international prominence. The band's powerhouse, the virtuoso guitarist Jeff Loomis, had given them a boost when he'd joined earlier that year, and the musical bond between Loomis and O'Brien quickly solidified across two prestigious tours, the first with Blind Guardian in Europe and the second supporting the mighty Death across America.

A debut album showcasing Nevermore's particular brand of progressive metal immediately won fans of dexterous guitar playing, and O'Brien was able to add his own contributions when the next record, *The Politics Of Ecstasy*, was released in 1996. He immediately attracted attention for the epic, intricate guitar parts in the songs, based on the Timothy Leary book of the same name and exploring the processes of the mind in the lyrics.

Meanwhile, Cannibal Corpse, the Florida-based death metal band, had recently lost guitarist Rob Barrett to Malevolent Creation, and O'Brien was asked to join them. He parted from Nevermore amicably and stepped up to the phenomenally gory, uncompromising music of Cannibal Corpse – music that has since made them the biggest-selling death metal band in the world. O'Brien formed a guitar team with Jack Owen that was unfeasibly fast and complex, not to mention bone-crushingly heavy.

O'Brien was using his longtime favourite guitars, by B.C Rich, as well as the occasional Jackson, and remained with Rich until relatively recently, when he signed up with the Polish manufacturer Ran, a brand also used by Annihilator's Jeff Waters. O'Brien's signature guitar is a beautiful green-camouflage V with a symmetrical

" One of many interesting things about Pat O'Brien, apart from his fearsome picking skills, his machine-like ability to choke off millisecond-perfect pinch harmonics. **"**

12/100

FREDRIK THORDENDAL
Come back! Meshuggah are lovely chaps really. The intimidatingly talented guitarist Fredrik
Thordendal is at far right.

pointed headstock, not dissimilar to the B.C. Rich Vs that he used for many years.

O'Brien has become an integral part of Cannibal Corpse, forming an expert guitar team at first alongside Owen, who departed to join Deicide in 2005, and then Rob Barrett, who returned from Malevolent Creation upon Owen's departure. The guitarists' unison riffing is massively impressive, with bassist Alex Webster's unusual songwriting (based on dissonant scales and unusual triads) forming the basis of Cannibal Corpse's style. Webster, O'Brien, and the other songwriters in the band have a subtle but crucial groove in their riffs: without this catchy, slightly funky element, the brutality of the music would be overpowering. The ability to deliver a hooky device such as a pinch harmonic in each bar – even at 200bpm – is key to the band's live performances, and fortunately both guitarists have this skill in abundance.

Death metal is often dismissed by the uninformed (or just stupid) as a wall of noise that requires little musical skill, an unfortunate consequence of the foggy studio production of the early death acts, which did little for the riffs or the subtleties of the vocals and arrangements. This all changed when producer Scott Burns took up residence at the renowned Tampa studio Morrisound in the early 90s, bringing a clarity to the music that emphasised its extremity. Cannibal Corpse were among the first acts to benefit from Burns's adroit console-tweaking skills, and together they established a benchmark in extreme metal production that remains unsurpassed today. Without Burns, gifted guitarists such as Pat O'Brien would never be fully heard.

> **"**
>
> **Death metal is often dismissed by the uninformed (or just stupid) as a wall of noise that requires little musical skill.**
>
> **"**

▶▶| Genius moment

It's obviously 'Frantic Disembowelment', from The Wretched Spawn (2004). A version of this song without vocals was on YouTube at the time of writing, providing education for anyone who doubts the musical skills of the members of Cannibal Corpse. It is a showcase for every rhythm guitar trick that exists in heavy metal. There are no leads, but this is an irrelevance: the riffs that O'Brien executes in unison with bassist extraordinaire Webster are as complex and fast as a dozen guitar solos. The song begins with a speed-picked figure that extends across the full range of notes, before it is replaced by a series of intricate power chords that would be manageable if they weren't executed at such a punishing tempo. The final riff includes a quick upstroke and a flurry of hammer-ons before the song slams to a halt.

O'Brien on the master

"It's Tony Iommi – he invented heavy metal with songs like 'Sign Of The Southern Cross', 'Children Of The Grave', 'Disturbing The Priest', 'Black Sabbath', 'Sabbath Bloody Sabbath', 'The Eternal Idol', 'Hand Of Doom'... basically, everything! As for Cannibal Corpse, we use Boss Metal Zone distortion pedals, which seem to be the most consistent for what we do – and I've bought tons of different distortion pedals. I'm always trying to outdo them, but they win every time. The distortion's backed off a little bit, just to add to the gain on the amp and give it a little extra edge. We also use Mesa/Boogie Rectifiers and the guitars have EMG 81 pickups, which I can't beat."

12/100

FREDRIK THORDENDAL
Meshuggah

As you will recall from Mårten Hagström's entry, Swedish quintet Meshuggah are among the most technical and experimental bands on the planet. While Hagström holds down the rhythm guitar sections with almost inhuman precision, Fredrik Thordendal plays lead and rhythm, and brings a whole range of sounds and techniques to the band in the process.

Thordendal also played bass on a 1995 tour, after the band's bassist, Peter Nordin, was obliged to withdraw from live shows due to inner-ear problems. To the surprise of many observers, Thordendal played many of his normal guitar parts – including solos – on the bass, as well as conventional bass parts. On another occasion, Thordendal – a carpenter by trade – severed the tip of the middle finger on his left hand in an industrial accident, Tony Iommi style, and was obliged to refrain from playing the guitar for some months after the fingertip was replaced. This, then, is a band who have been through more than their fair share of hardship.

Meshuggah don't make things easier for themselves, writing phenomenally complex music that is far too detailed to be understood in a single hearing. Thordendal's guitar parts sometimes adhere to the overall time signature of a given song, but are just as likely to follow a time of their own, part of the polyrhythmic approach, anchored by drummer Thomas Haake, that has become a Meshuggah trademark. Haake himself often adds to the complexity by playing simultaneous patterns with hands and feet in different signatures, making for an overall sound that can seem dissonant on first listen. Also, the time of various parts can change at a moment's notice, often according to a rotating pattern, and when this is added to the many styles that Thordendal applies to his solos – jazz, blues, metal, funk, or a combination of these best labelled as 'progressive' – it is understandable that Meshuggah's music has gained a cult following rather than mainstream appeal.

On their early albums, Meshuggah had not yet reached their current level of musical intricacy. The obvious influences on their 1991 debut album, *Contradictions Collapse*, were the classic thrash acts of the 80s. Thordendal admires players with great downstroke precision, such as Anthrax's Scott Ian, and this was evident in songs that were fast and technical, but not yet astoundingly technical. However, he added jazz-fusion licks to 1995's *Destroy Erase Improve*, while the other musicians were also developing a more complex style, and critics decided that the album marked Meshuggah's first foray into what they labelled math-metal, prog-metal, or even post-metal. *Chaosphere* (1998) was even faster and more extreme, with the band's death-metal foundation even more apparent than before.

In guitar terms, 2002 was Meshuggah's Year Zero. As you'll recall from Hagström's entry, Meshuggah began experimenting with eight-string guitars for that year's *Nothing* album, commissioning custom models from Nevborn for recording sessions. The idea was to detune the eighth string, an F-sharp, by a half-step (semitone), but when the Nevborn guitars were found to need extra

> **"** Thordendal – a carpenter by trade – severed the tip of the middle finger on his left hand in an industrial accident, Tony Iommi style, and was obliged to refrain from playing the guitar for some months after the fingertip was replaced. **"**

11/100

work, Hagström and Thordendal used downtuned seven-string instruments instead. After the album's release, the guitarists switched to the completed Nevborns and then to newer versions by Ibanez, re-recording the guitar parts on *Nothing* in 2006 and reissuing it the same year.

Here's the interesting bit for guitar fans. Because the eight-strings are tuned so low, it's not possible to play power chords at the lower end of the range (let alone barre chords) because the low sound simply gets lost in the mix. Even the most competent engineer and sophisticated studio can't make sounds that are almost inaudibly low come through clearly, so Thordendal stays away from those chords in his playing. Instead, he plays single-note riffs and unusual chords that cover the instrument's full range, which can be reproduced with clarity without interfering with the bass guitar's frequency range. This led to a more ambient approach on the 2005 album *Catch Thirtythree*, with a single 47-minute composition divided into 13 subsections, the sheer scope of which allows for more experimentation from the musicians.

After a decade of expanding the math-metal approach, Thordendal and band returned to a more straightforward approach on their 2008 album *ObZen* (a portmanteau of 'obscene' and 'Zen'). This surprised observers yet again, because the band were now using simpler, stripped-down arrangements. Haake played much of the record in regular 4/4 time, and Thordendal focused as much on clarity of expression and atmospherics as experimental playing.

By this point in his career, Thordendal has become renowned as a virtuso on the heavy metal scene. He released a successful solo album, *Sol Niger Within*, in 1997 that was full of his instantly recognisable jazz-influenced chromatic runs and licks. Thordendal often uses a clean, untreated sound – not what you'd expect when you see the intimidating size of his Ibanez eight-string – but he is not averse to using a distortion tone with moderate gain. The sound of his guitars is heavily shaped by their custom Lundgren pickups, his MIDI breath controller, and a series of pedals including a Digitech delay and a Rocktron Juice Extractor. All this complex noise comes through a TC Electronics preamp and a Marshall or Mesa/Boogie head.

For anyone who is still sceptical, Meshuggah matter because they've broadened the parameters of metal. Guitarists such as Fredrik Thordendal play in their difficult, sometimes indigestible way for a reason – because it adds colour to the wider palette of the music. In this case, it happens to be within the framework of heavy metal, and it requires the vast skills of Thordendal and his band to take shape. Let us be grateful that we're living in these exciting times for the electric guitar, as we move on to the hallowed Top Ten.

> **"**
> Guitarists such as Fredrik Thordendal play in their difficult, sometimes indigestible way for a reason – because it adds colour to the wider palette of the music.
> **"**

▶▶❙ Genius moment
Check out Thordendal's insane guest lead on the song 'Psychic Pain' by Darkane on their Insanity album. Executed with the full roster of shred techniques, his solo also retains a genuine melodic hummability.

11/100

CHUCK SCHULDINER
Death, Control Denied

Death metal was an American invention, unlike its British-born antecedent, thrash metal. The origins of the genre's name are disputed, with rival claims for its invention coming from the late Tomas 'Quorthon' Forsberg of Bathory as well as the staff of the German Noise label, who issued the *Death Metal* compilation LP in 1984. Most experts say that Jeff Becerra of the San Francisco band Possessed created the 'death metal' tag, and he made it the title of one of the songs on his band's debut album, *Seven Churches*, released in early 1985.

Possessed may have been the first death metal band out of the blocks, but it was a close thing. As they rose to prominence, a younger, more isolated act, Mantas, were doing something rather similar at demo level. This Florida band had been formed by the 16-year-old Charles 'Chuck' Schuldiner in 1983 and recorded a demo that year, *Death By Metal*.

Raw, fast, and utterly unsophisticated, Schuldiner's songwriting bore little hint of the complexity to come. He had started to learn the guitar at the age of nine, after losing his older brother in a car accident. His parents bought him the instrument in an attempt to help him through his grief. After some initial reluctance, he took avidly to the instrument, practising for entire weekends at a time.

Schuldiner formed Mantas with his schoolmates Barney 'Kam' Lee (vocals, drums) and second guitarist Rick Rozz. He continued to record more demos after *Death By Metal*, including *Reign Of Terror* and an in-concert recording (*Live At Ruby's Pub*) – both of which appeared the following year, after a name-change to Death. By this point, the band, still without a bass player, were making a name for themselves on the Florida live scene, bolstered by 1985's *Infernal Death*, *Rigor Mortis*, *Back From The Dead*, and *Infernal Live* tapes.

In 1986, Schuldiner parted with Lee and Rozz, having negotiated a deal with the Combat label for a full album. Crucially, he had met another like-minded musician, Chris Reifert, a drummer, vocalist, and guitarist whose taste for horror-movie-style slasher lyrics matched his own. The pair recorded a demo, *Mutilation*, in spring 1986 – after Schuldiner had endured a brief and unsatisfactory stint in the Canadian thrash metal act Slaughter – before embarking on songwriting sessions for the first Death LP, *Scream Bloody Gore*, released in 1987.

Scream Bloody Gore was a turning-point in extreme metal. Influential though the Possessed album *Seven Churches* had been two years previously, more than a few metalheads regarded it as merely thrash metal with harsh vocals. *Scream* extended and elevated the concept a little further, with Schuldiner's throaty roar and the dark, doomy production taking another step towards extremity. The solos were understated and delivered uncertainly, with Schuldiner clearly searching for a musical identity. He played all the guitar and bass tracks in fast unison, uninterested at this stage in attempting anything other than a fast, bloodsoaked rampage.

In 1988, Death recorded *Leprosy*, a smarter, cleaner, and more thoughtful album, with the leads a more prominent feature of the overall sound. Reifert had departed to

> " Schuldiner had started to learn the guitar at the age of nine, after losing his older brother in a car accident. His parents bought him the instrument in an attempt to help him through his grief. "

10/100

CHUCK SCHULDINER

found the even more extreme death–gore metal band Autopsy, leaving Schuldiner to recruit his old Mantas sparring partner Rick Rozz along with bassist Terry Butler and drummer Bill Andrews.

By 1990, Schuldiner had reached the ripe old age of 23, and with that maturity came a newfound desire to expand his musical and lyrical creativity. Replacing Rozz with the renowned session guitarist James Murphy, he composed the groundbreaking *Spiritual Healing*, another extreme metal milestone.

At this point, an entire death metal scene had arisen in Florida, with Morbid Angel and Deicide exceeding the speed and violence of Death's output with their use of blastbeats, a fast drumming technique with the snare drum playing 16th-notes. This device, borrowed from the hardcore punk scene and the new grindcore movement pioneered in the UK by Napalm Death and Carcass, lent the music much more intensity. Schuldiner must have noticed that these rival bands on the Florida scene were using the technique, but to his enormous credit he persevered with his own vision.

Spiritual Healing had an iconic jacket designed by Megadeth sleeve artist Ed Repka, whose art had also adorned the earlier Death albums. The album was the first step toward a progressive death metal style' The complex writing is exemplified by the riff immediately before the long, melodic solo in 'Defensive Personalities'.

Next, Schuldiner stepped out of the safety zone and really stretched his abilities to the fullest, recording the *Human* album with a band of extraordinarily gifted musicians, including bassist Steve DiGiorgio, Paul Masvidal on guitar, and Sean Reinert on drums. Questioning social ills such as suicide as well as the mysteries of the cosmos, Schuldiner wrote songs that were a universe away from the gore themes of *Scream* and the quasi-political commentary of *Spiritual Healing*, overlaying the fiercely complex music with opaque lyrics.

Human was one of the first albums to combine extreme metal with progressive elements, an approach that Schuldiner continued and expanded on the remaining Death albums, *Individual Thought Patterns* (1993), *Symbolic* (1995), and *The Sound Of Perseverance* in 1998.

What they have in common is a constantly restless songwriting style in which riffs are interchanged and juxtaposed in a complex, asymmetrical sequence.

Schuldiner's melodic, fast alternate picking was a constant feature of his solos, delivered on his instantly recognisable B.C. Rich Stealth, as were his frequent returns to tremolo-picked death metal passages from the old days. His strength lay in the many types of guitar-playing he had mastered, and they manifested themselves in a high-profile supergroup called Voodoocult, in 1994, in which he temporarily played alongside ex-Slayer drummer Dave Lombardo and Kreator guitarist Mille Petrozza.

Such were Schuldiner's skills that – like Alex Skolnick of Testament before him – he then set off in a direction that took him away from extreme metal, as Death went on hiatus in 1998. His new band, Control Denied, played a combination of straight heavy metal with progressive elements, a mixture that attracted much praise for the band's sole album, *The Fragile Art Of Existence* (1999). Aided by DiGiorgio again, as well as drummer Richard Christy (another Death alumnus), singer Tim Aymar, and

> **"**
>
> Schuldiner remains one of the metal genre's greatest innovators. As a guitarist, as a songwriter, and as that innovator, he was one of a select elite whose vision has shaped the music we listen to today.
>
> **"**

LEFT The most visionary man in this book? Chuck Schuldiner of Death (second left).

10/100

guitarist Shannon Hamm, Schuldiner seemed to be well on track to building a successful second band.

However, Schuldiner was diagnosed with cancer of the brain stem in May 1999, making the title of the current release by Control Denied somewhat prescient. As is so often the case, radiotherapy reduced the tumour and surgery removed the remaining material but the cancer returned, two years later. Although Schuldiner had continued to write and record with Control Denied in the interim, problems meeting his medical bills and the gradual erosion of his health meant that much of his time was spent away from the studio, and the new music remained unfinished.

Many of his fellow musicians – Foo Fighters, Kid Rock, Korn, and The Red Hot Chili Peppers, among others – donated time and money towards a fundraising campaign, but Schuldiner died on December 13 2001 after a severe bout of pneumonia. His death at the age of just 34 was a tremendous blow to Death's fans, who might reasonably have expected another three decades of virtuoso music from him. What made the tragedy even worse was that over his short musical career – a mere 14 years – Schuldiner had followed a steep curve of evolution, both as a musician and songwriter. If he had moved from raw death metal to prog-metal to melodic heavy metal in that short time, what might he have accomplished if he'd been granted a full lifespan? We will never know, and, for many thousands of his fans, that fact still hurts bitterly.

In the years that have passed since then it has been a source of comfort for many Death and Control Denied fans that Schuldiner has not been falsely deified in the way of so many fallen icons. He is known today, just as he was known in his lifetime, as a driven character who could be difficult to work with, as his standards were so high. Schuldiner demanded, and received, the best possible performances from his fellow musicians, as he used only the most talented and committed people on his records. This led to a degree of quality control that meant there is very little inessential material on any post-1990 Death album – and not much before that point, either.

Schuldiner's legacy has not been without its controversies. His mother, Jane Schuldiner, who administers his estate and music, has been involved in a legal struggle for some time over the remaining Control Denied recordings, some of which were issued by a European label in 2004 as part of the *Zero Tolerance* compilation. The feeling among fans seems to be that the recordings deserve to be finished and issued in a manner appropriate to Schuldiner's last recorded work, although the compilation itself sold well.

Death's entire catalogue was reissued by Century Media at the turn of the century, and the 1995 album *Symbolic* received a luxury reissue by Roadrunner in 2008. Hopefully more of these albums – each of them proof of Schuldiner's phenomenal musical skills and presence – will be reissued soon. B.C. Rich recently announced that a version of the Stealth guitar that he used on so many great songs will go into production shortly. Fans reacted to the news with a mixture of delight and cynicism, probably due to the revenues and publicity that Dean gained from their Razorback model, released after the untimely death of 'Dimebag' Darrell Abbott.

> **Schuldiner demanded, and received, the best possible performances from his fellow musicians, as he used only the most talented and committed people on his records.**

RIGHT Swedish prog-metal mavericks Opeth are led by the astounding Mikael Åkerfeldt.

MIKAEL ÅKERFELDT

Schuldiner remains one of the metal genre's greatest innovators. As a guitarist, as a songwriter, and as that innovator, he was one of a select elite whose vision has shaped the music we listen to today. He is much missed.

> ▶▶▎ **Genius moment**
>
> 'The Philosopher' from the 1993 album Individual Thought Patterns features a tapped intro and perfectly precise alternate picking throughout, as well as a picking-hand precision that has rarely been equalled. But any and all of Death's albums display Schuldiner's maverick genius.

MIKAEL ÅKERFELDT
Opeth, Bloodbath

"Some people tell me that I'm a guitar hero," Opeth frontman Mikael Åkerfeldt told me in 2007, "but I can't see where that comes from, because there are so many other guys who are so much better than me. The guys who go widdly-widdly? I can't play that fast. I've always relied on emotional playing: I'm more into single notes than a million notes. In fact, I've never been a lead guitarist, I was sort of pushed into the position of lead guitar in the band. I always valued writing songs more – even though my childhood dream was to be fuckin' Yngwie Malmsteen! I've never been able to play like that, but I certainly appreciate people who like my playing."

Welcome to the world of Mikael Åkerfeldt, whose music comes so far ahead of his guitar skills that his highly evolved playing seems almost an irrelevance to him. Yes, he doesn't often play the fast, melodic solos that are ubiquitous in heavy metal and its subgenres. But he is a pioneer in almost all other areas of the instrument, especially when he's combining acoustic and folk passages with the grisliest of Swedish death metal.

Opeth are now the consummate progressive-metal band, opening up musical boundaries one by one as their albums have appeared over the years and fortuitously coinciding with the rise of a new breed of heavy metal fan. This new headbanger, mentally as well as physically mature, is prepared to invest some time and intellect into new music, seeking out profundity and digesting the most complex and arcane of musical statements – just as the first wave of prog-rock fans did in the early 70s.

Born in Stockholm in 1974, Åkerfeldt first formed a band when he was 14. He called it Eruption. After recording naïve songs such as 'We Hate Hip-Hop' in a raw, unsophisticated death metal style – and realising that Eruption was probably never going to add up to much – he applied for the bassist's position in Opeth, a band founded by vocalist David Isberg.

As the story famously goes, Isberg told the rest of the band that Åkerfeldt was going to join, whereupon they all left, leaving Åkerfeldt and Isberg as the sole members. New musicians were recruited, notably guitarist Peter Lindgren, but Isberg

" Some people tell me that I'm a guitar hero, but I can't see where that comes from, because there are so many other guys who are so much better than me. **"**

himself left two years later, leading Åkerfeldt to take over the vocals. His singing alternated between death grunts and a clean, melodic style.

From the very beginning, Åkerfeldt wrote songs influenced by two distinct influences: 70s prog-rock bands, such as Comus; and classic traditional and extreme metal acts like Black Sabbath, Slayer, and Morbid Angel. Folk, classical, and jazz sounds also appear in Opeth's work, with complex arrangements and exquisitely-crafted atmospherics characterising the music.

Åkerfeldt tends to leave most of the guitar solos to his colleague: Lindgren until 2006, and now ex-Arch Enemy shredder Fredrik Åkesson. Åkerfeldt does still play many of the harmony lines, however. In fact, unison and harmony leads were a major element of the early Opeth albums, although Åkerfeldt moved away from them in the mid 90s, stating that they had become too common in the wake of Carcass and other melodic death metal bands.

Opeth released their debut album, *Orchid*, in 1995, and it was immediately marked out as slightly different from its death-metal contemporaries thanks to its cover art (a pink flower), its lengthy songs, and their resolutely nonconformist arrangements. The idea of using two vocal styles was new at the time, too, adding to the album's innovations.

On *Orchid*'s 'Requiem', Åkerfeldt plays the first of many acoustic sections. The acoustic guitar has gradually risen in importance in Opeth since then, to the point where it is almost as prominent as the electric. The band expanded this multi-faceted approach on the following year's *Morningrise*, which included more of the lighter, non-metal passages for which Opeth were becoming known.

Your Arms, My Hearse (1998) was another commercial step up for Opeth, who changed their approach slightly to include more heavy sections and relatively short songs, in a nod toward their roots. But the band did not find real recognition until *Still Life* (1999), regarded as one of Åkerfeldt's best albums to date. It is a concept album that follows the progress of a woman, Melinda, who is murdered by her lover at its end. The record allowed Åkerfeldt plenty of opportunities to explore the outer territories of the guitar, with even a jazz solo on the acoustic track 'Benighted'.

Blackwater Park (2001) was named after a German prog-rock band, and it marked Opeth's deserved commercial breakthrough. Some of this can be attributed to the fantastic production provided by Porcupine Tree maestro Steven Wilson. Åkerfeldt and Wilson admired each other's work, and the match of songwriter and producer turned out to be an inspired one, as both men seemed to know intuitively what the other wanted and how to achieve it.

After *Blackwater Park*, Opeth's fortunes took an upward swing – as Åkerfeldt later admitted, he had been surviving on a tiny income from the occasional royalty cheque and a job in a guitar shop. However, his employment had come to an abrupt end when a guitar was stolen from the store by a thief while Åkerfeldt was busy talking to the robber's accomplice, so the success of the album was timely.

Opeth recorded two albums in 2002, with one of them delayed a year before release. *Deliverance* ('02) and *Damnation* ('03) were intended to display the two sides of the band: the former devoted to super-heavy death metal with a small number of

" As the story famously goes, Isberg told the rest of the band that Åkerfeldt was going to join, whereupon they all left, leaving Åkerfeldt and Isberg as the sole members. **"**

mellower moments; the latter a more introspective album of lightweight songs. Although neither record surpassed *Blackwater Park* commercially or creatively, the sheer scope afforded by two albums' worth of material made for few limits on Åkerfeldt and Lindgren's guitar playing.

A move to the powerful Roadrunner label was followed by 2005's *Ghost Reveries*, a magnificent example of the now-established prog-metal genre. Åkerfeldt wrote songs that included Mellotron and other rich instrumentation but didn't neglect the riffage or the solos, and for these the band returned to their aggressive origins. Their new popularity was consolidated with *Watershed* in 2008, so named because Åkerfeldt regarded it as a turning-point for the band – perhaps due to the motivating boost given to the band by Lindgren's replacement, Fredrik Åkesson, whose superb solos added enormous melodicism to the songs. Åkesson even gave Åkerfeldt some tuition for his picking technique, Åkerfeldt revealed later.

Opeth were now a world-class band, but they have never lost touch with their roots in Swedish death metal. In fact, Åkerfeldt also performs vocals in the brutal death metal supergroup Bloodbath, a project co-founded by members of the doomdeath band Katatonia and the producer Dan Swanö. A long way away from even Opeth's harshest songs, Bloodbath play fast, groove-laden riffs straight from the school of Chuck Schuldiner, overlaid with Åkerfeldt's most guttural vocals. The *Breeding Death* EP of 2000 was a revelation for fans of the old style of death metal, which had been largely superseded by the new melodic version, and was followed by an album, *Resurrection Through Carnage*, in 2003.

Although Åkerfeldt doesn't play guitar in Bloodbath, his presence as the resident star brings huge publicity. Nonetheless, he quit for four years to focus on Opeth, and his replacement during that time was Peter Tagtgren of Hypocrisy. Åkerfeldt returned for another EP, a live DVD, and a studio record in 2008, demonstrating once more that his dual approach – performing both melodic and brutal music – is alive and well.

Åkerfeldt has amassed a quantity of guitars over the years, but is usually seen playing one of a series of Paul Reed Smith Custom 24 models in a variety of finishes. He also uses Gibson Flying Vs and Les Pauls, Fender Stratocasters, and a B.C. Rich on occasion. For his acoustic songs, he usually employs a Martin or Takamine instrument, admitting (with some embarrassment) that he even attempted to play a lute during one Opeth session. His amps are made by Laney.

As a guest artist, Åkerfeldt has performed with dozens of bands, notably Dan Swanö's Edge Of Sanity, his Bloodbath team-mates Katatonia, Porcupine Tree, Soilwork, and others.

> **"**
>
> From the very beginning, Åkerfeldt wrote songs influenced by two distinct influences: 70s prog-rock bands, such as Comus; and classic traditional and extreme metal acts like Black Sabbath, Slayer, and Morbid Angel.
>
> **"**

▶▶ **Genius moment**

'Atonement' from Ghost Reveries (2005) features a plethora of guitar tones from Åkerfeldt – including, remarkably, a sitar (or an exact digital impersonation of one). It marks one possible way into the world of Opeth for those yet to take the step. Alternatively, the Watershed song 'Heir Apparent' (2008) features a monstrous death-metal riff section that sits perfectly between mellower sections.

Asked if Opeth are a prog band rather than a metal band these days, Åkerfeldt mused: "We certainly have those roots, but there's much more to the palette than that, so you can't really say we're a death metal band. Prog-metal? Not completely true either, because there's a negative vibe to that term. I like to think that we're somewhat progressive and that we have our own sound. I generally just say that we're a metal band – or if I'm talking to an old guy, I say we're a rock'n'roll band just like The Beatles."

Åkerfeldt on gods

"Black Sabbath is obligatory for any metal fan. They were the first metal band I ever heard. I was scared of them. There's something about their music that makes me feel the same to this day. One thing that I really like about Tony Iommi is his jazz style: when I was growing up I was very much into the heavy songs, of course, but a bit later on what impressed me most were solos like the one he did on 'Planet Caravan'. It's outstanding, and very jazzy. He also did that at the end of 'Symptom Of The Universe'. Not many metal guitarists give him credit these days for his taste – he is a very tasteful player, in that the notes he chose to play were always the right ones. I like everything Iommi has been involved with – including the Tony Martin and Glenn Hughes records.

"All the guys I grew up with – everybody from Yngwie, to Uli Roth, to Michael Schenker – could be the best metal guitarist of all time, but I'm gonna go with a versatile player who is good at rhythm and lead: Eddie Van Halen. It's impossible to play like him. Obviously the songs and the riffs that he's written, as well as the millions of solos, are amazing. I've been listening to him all my life and I don't know if he's a great jazz player or acoustic player, but I love the fact that – as with Dimebag – when the solo starts, the rhythm stops. Being the sole guitar player in that band is just amazing. But I could have said Tony Iommi, or Matthias Jabs, who I think is highly underrated."

> "
> The guys who go widdly-widdly? I can't play that fast. I've always relied on emotional playing: I'm more into single notes than a million notes.
> "

JAMES HETFIELD
Metallica

In the 70s, Keith Richards of The Rolling Stones was occasionally called the world's best rhythm guitarist. While this is hard to demonstrate, given the impossible mastery that the title implies, it's easier to nominate Keef's counterpart in the heavy metal world. The most accomplished rhythm player anywhere in metal or its subgenres is Metallica frontman James Hetfield.

Metallica, the biggest-selling metal band ever, have attained such a peak of iconhood that it's easy to forget their blistering instrumental skills. Multimillionaires whose every action attracts headlines, they're the ultimate idols of heavy music – rendering their musical activities almost secondary. Look behind the San Francisco mansions and the endless controversies – Napster, *Playboy*, *St Anger* ... any metaller who's been paying attention will know the drill – and it's obvious that

8/100

8/100

the quartet have earned every cent because of their early dedication to mastering their instruments.

Much of Metallica's chequered history is covered here in the entry for their lead guitarist, Kirk Hammett, so we won't revisit much of it – although a certain period in their history, during which Hetfield stunned his contemporaries and the metal-consuming public with a certain aspect of his playing, is worth placing under the microscope. Pay attention now.

It's a miracle that Hetfield attained any guitar skills at all, given his turbulent childhood – but not a miracle generated by Christian Science, under whose religious yoke he laboured from his earliest years. Like so many metallers in this book, he was born in the early 60s, meaning that he reached his teens at a peak time for international heavy music. Although he shared his birth year of 1963 with Hammett, who grew up in San Francisco – an eight-hour drive from Hetfield's home town of Downey, Los Angeles – he shared little else with the culturally privileged Hammett, being obliged to adhere to his parents' strict religious beliefs.

The famous story that is always quoted at this point is of a Christian Scientist girl in Hetfield's class at school, who proudly showed him her deformed arm that had healed badly after a break. It was left untreated because God could apparently be trusted to heal injuries through his divine benevolence. It's little wonder that Hetfield retreated to the dark shadows of heavy metal as soon as he possibly could, motivated still further to abandon his family's faith by the death of his mother when he was 16.

Having studied the piano and drums in his pre-teen years, Hetfield took up the guitar at 14, inspired by Aerosmith, Black Sabbath, and Thin Lizzy. A sequence of bands followed – Obsession, Phantom Lord, and Leather Charm – while he worked on his guitar technique. This period of Hetfield's life – 1978 to 1980, between the ages of 15 and 18 – is often ignored in official and unofficial biographies, because what we're rushing toward is the period in 1981 when he first met the Danish drummer Lars Ulrich, dismissed him for his rudimentary skills, met him again when Ulrich's drumming had improved, and formed a band called Metallica.

But it was in those early years that Hetfield spent day after week after month devoted to his guitars, hacking out riff after riff in an attempt to match his idols – which by 1979 and '80 included New Wave Of British Heavy Metal newcomers Diamond Head and Iron Maiden, as well the slightly more established Motörhead.

Here's the thing. Riffs were, then as now, the core of any heavy metal and hard rock song. Back in those far-off days, the art of the precise downstroke was still in its infancy, with players usually allowing a chord to ring a little before the next stroke. The staccato, palm-muted sound that we have been associating with metal for 25 years now was not common back then. It was Hetfield who played the largest part in promoting that style, not necessarily because he was the only guitarist playing that way, but because his band experienced rapid success with songs based on that tight downstroke style.

Hetfield's picking-hand technique evolved over rehearsal sessions with his school buddies long before he met Ulrich and formed Metallica. Once he was in the band, his super-tight downstrokes became the key feature of a series of demo tapes that

The most accomplished rhythm player anywhere in metal or its subgenres is Metallica frontman James Hetfield.

were circulated on the tape-trading underground of the day. Many musicians who went on to be household names of their own were astounded by Hetfield's machine-like picking on cassettes such as the legendary *No Life 'Til Leather* of 1982.

Hetfield scraped away at the strings like some kind of single-minded robot, cupping his hand around the bridge for a perfectly taut sound that made heavy metal sound not brash nor rude nor sexy but more like the future. The apocalypse had arrived, and it came in the shape of the right hand of a spotty teenager from the wrong side of the LA tracks.

Metallica's career history has been recounted too many times to bear repeating, but if you need more detail, you're politely referred to the author's bestselling 2004 biog *Justice For All: The Truth About Metallica*. What concerns us more here are the key points in the band's career where Hetfield has proved his prowess on the guitar, over and over again.

After *No Life 'Til Leather*, Metallica signed to the New York label Megaforce and recorded their first album, *Kill 'Em All* (1983), which made an instant impact. Metal fans loved *KEA* for its technicality; punks loved it for its speed (it was the first American thrash metal album); and, most importantly in this case, guitarists worshipped the record for its tight, scratchy riffing, executed with all the unplayed strings damped to silence. Of course, today the band themselves would (quite rightly) never hail this album as a masterpiece of guitar playing, pointing at the uninterested producers, the cheap studio equipment, and their own youth and naivety as major stumbling-blocks.

When we examine the next album, 1984's *Ride The Lightning*, you have to agree with them. *Ride* makes *Kill* sound as if it had been recorded by monkeys. The silky-smooth production, by Flemming Rasmussen at his Copenhagen studio Sweet Silence, was a gigantic leap forward not only for Metallica but for the new extreme metal genre, which required a sympathetic sound in order not to sound cacophonous. The opening song, 'Fight Fire With Fire', remains the fastest that Metallica have ever recorded in terms of beats per minute, and yet you can hear every stroke of Hetfield's warp-speed tremolo picking. This is due in part to Rasmussen's sensitive engineering in the studio but also to Hetfield's insanely precise picking – and he was still only 21 years old.

Hetfield's finest hour came with *Master Of Puppets*, released in 1986 and easily Metallica's best work. Often regarded as the best thrash metal album ever made, or second only to Slayer's *Reign In Blood* (released the same year), *Puppets* was melodic, crushingly heavy, and intricately arranged, ticking all the right boxes for the metal audience then as now and enduring to this day.

Once again, Hetfield's rhythm picking was split-second precise – but in case you're thinking that the old dog was playing the same old trick yet again, take a closer listen: the songs were a little slower in places, making picking precision even more important, not less. And where the songs were faster, Hetfield was syncopating his riffs, adding accents of great subtlety to the tremolo picking. Guitarists should try playing the fast "Soldier boy / Made of clay..." riff in 'Disposable Heroes', or better still try to transcribe it for tab or notation, and you'll see what I mean. Actually, don't try.

" Hetfield scraped away at the strings like some kind of single-minded robot, cupping his hand around the bridge for a perfectly taut sound that made heavy metal sound not brash nor rude nor sexy but more like the future. **"**

8/100

JAMES HETFIELD

By now, Hetfield had perfected a studio technique where he would lay down identical rhythm tracks – one on each side – and then add a third layer, which he laughingly called the thickener. It required near-infinite patience and a sense of timing that was second to none to get the rhythm parts "tighter than a gnat's ass", as he put it. This approach was crucial for the 1998 album ...*And Justice For All*, Metallica's most progressive record to date.

Justice featured long, complex songs dominated almost completely by the rhythm-guitar parts. The drums occupied a relatively high frequency range, with the kick drum given a top edge that was unusual for the day, and the bass guitar – infamously – was mixed almost completely out.

"It's not really about ability: it's writing a good riff and knowing what tempo it needs to be, where it lives in the song."

From this point on, Hetfield's rhythm guitar has dominated Metallica's sound. Some critics have attributed this to the death of their bassist Cliff Burton in 1986, after the release of *Puppets*. They claim that Burton, a virtuoso bassist, would never have allowed the rhythm guitar to fill the sound so completely. Whatever the truth, Hetfield and his vast riffs – executed with inhuman accuracy – became the talk of metal guitar players, then and always. He rarely strayed into lead guitar territory, apart from a quick ten-second burst on 'Battery' (the opener of *Master Of Puppets*), a world-class solo on the soupy ballad 'Nothing Else Matters' from the planet-shafting '*Black Album*' of 1991, and a few harmony lines when playing live.

So much for the good half of Metallica's career. As most of you will know already, the band delivered a series of albums from 1996 that ranged from average to utterly terrible, exploring alternative rock and disposing of thrash metal. Compared to the heart-in-mouth glories of the 80s albums, these records represented a long and painful decline. As I write this, Metallica are about to deliver their best work since the '*Black Album*', a reasonably exciting record called *Death Magnetic* that the band are hoping will undo some of the damage incurred. A tour will follow – always the best way to experience this frustratingly inconsistent band.

▶▶❙ Genius moment

Anything and everything Hetfield played on Metallica's first three albums make a frankly intimidating demonstration of how to pick like a machine. By the time of ...And Justice For All in 1988, the music was getting a little samey at times. Hetfield based the riff to 'Eye Of The Beholder' on the same E/G/F-sharp sequence he'd used on 'Disposable Heroes' from Master Of Puppets, released two years before, so some of the Justice tracks can be skipped. The 1991 'Black Album' was a masterpiece of the riff master's art, so you can't really miss out on that. After that came, er ... there was ... did I say that the first three Metallica albums were the best? Maybe just stick with them.

You'll no doubt see Hetfield playing a variety of ESP guitars on stage, the company with whom he has remained since the 80s. You won't see his famous ESP Explorer with 'EET FUK!' written on it, because it now resides in America's Rock & Roll Hall Of Fame & Museum. You might see a similar model with 'More Beer!' on it (or perhaps not, since he went through rehab for alcoholism in 2002), a Flying V with red or green flames on it, or the Truckster, an ESP Les Paul-shaped axe with fake wear painted on.

8/100

The huge noises that Hetfield makes with these instruments may be coming out of Krank Krankenstein and Revolution 1 heads into Mesa/Boogie or Marshall cabinets, or he may be using a Mesa/Boogie rig composed of preamp, power amp, and cabs. Whatever the setup, if Metallica play plenty of pre-'96 songs, you're guaranteed a good time. Just keep watching his picking hand.

Hetfield on fun

"I'm pretty comfortable with my down-picking. I don't see how it could get much faster. It's not a race. It's not really about ability: it's writing a good riff and knowing what tempo it needs to be, where it lives in the song. Certain riffs, you speed up two beats and it doesn't sit right: it's all about what the riff feels and at what tempo you play it. Obviously playing all the fast rhythm stuff is pretty fun, because you can put so much emotion into that, but one of the most fun parts for me is clean stuff, when you can really get creative with sounds and different amps and effects and things like that. I really enjoy doing dual-harmony solos too."

TREY AZAGTHOTH (George Emmanuel III)
Morbid Angel

Florida's death metal scene back in the late 80s was a raw, uncultured beast, a seemingly random flurry of blastbeats, Satanic or slasher-themed lyrics (or both), custard-gargling vocals, and a murky production. None of us really knew if we were listening to black metal or death metal, and most people weren't too sure what thrash metal was, either. The extreme metal genre was experiencing severe growing pains – and very few fans could have predicted what came next.

What happened was that a small group of death-metal bands climbed out of the primeval Florida ooze, kicked away the desperate, grasping hands of the lesser musicians clinging to their heels, and gave some serious thought to their music.

Five major acts emerged in the early 90s, each with a unique vision that led to an individual identity. These were: Death (see Chuck Schuldiner's entry), with their progressive approach; Obituary, whose sound rested on the sick, über-intestinal vocals of John Tardy; Deicide, whose total blasphemy made them controversial (see entries for current guitarists Jack Owen and Ralph Santolla); Cannibal Corpse, originally from New York state, whose groove-laden riffs and horrific lyrics have made them the biggest-selling death metal band ever (see Pat O'Brien and Rob Barrett); and Morbid Angel, a quartet whose epic vision makes them one of the most enthralling bands of all, metal or otherwise.

The line-up of Tampa-based Morbid Angel has changed frequently over the years, but the band is effectively driven by two individuals – singer–bassist David Vincent and guitarist Trey Azagthoth. Born George Emmanuel III, Azagthoth adopted his stage name (or 'spirit name' as he calls it) early on in his career, presumably influenced by his love of the occult writing of HP Lovecraft – Azathoth, without the g, is the name of the 'blind idiot god' in Lovecraft's mythos.

> **"**
> Azathoth, without the g, is the name of the 'blind idiot god' in Lovecraft's mythos.
> **"**

7/100

TREY AZAGTHOTH

Azagthoth's absolutely world-class guitar-playing formed the backbone of Morbid Angel's first four albums, each of which has long been recognised as a genre classic. The riffs, which exude a weird, slightly twisted ambience thanks to Azagthoth's fondness for string-bends and sudden tempo changes as well as an array of effects, complemented by atmospherics and synths, give Morbid Angel's songs a unique identity that millions of metalheads find compulsively addictive.

Azagthoth was born in 1965, making him one of the most senior death metal artists, and he began learning to play guitar in 1981. Forming Morbid Angel three years later and refusing to heed the criticism of those who pointed out the existence of the thrash bands Dark Angel and Death Angel, he evolved a guitar technique heavily influenced by Eddie Van Halen, whom he cites as an influence in the sleevenotes of many albums.

Expanding on Van Halen's famous fretboard-tapping technique, Azagthoth often creates an artificial bridge with his fretting-hand forefinger to shorten the neck scale while he taps, aided by massive distortion. He uses the whammy bar for wide-interval divebombs and a Morley wah for added expression.

As a lead guitarist, Azagthoth is almost unparalleled in the death metal scene, but it's his rhythm playing that makes Morbid Angel what they are. Playing the complex, ever-shifting dynamics of the songs is one thing, but composing them in the first place is another feat entirely, especially as they run the gamut of styles from fast tremolo-picking (as in 'Maze Of Torment') to slow, dark downstrokes with super-precise pinch harmonics ('Fall From Grace'). Some songs – 'Nothing But Fear' is a prime example – incorporate sludgy, cacophonous chords that stumble into each other in deliberate chaos before seguing into a heartstoppingly fast riff of immense speed and clinical dexterity.

Azagthoth has infused Morbid Angel with his unorthodox worldview since the band's inception. Claiming a series of unusual influences on his songwriting – Mozart is one example – he wrote lyrics on the band's first couple of albums that were more or less Satanic, tying in with the death metal ethos of the day. This didn't last long, however, and his songs are informed by his interests in the *Simon Necronomicon* (itself a mixture of various mythologies), ancient Sumerian texts, and modern mystics such as Deepak Chopra. Add to this an obsession with modern video games such as *Quake* and the spiritual implications of quantum theory (at its deepest, a revised view of the nature of reality), and it's apparent that his take on life is unusual, to say the least.

Somehow, all this philosophy seems to come out in Azagthoth's guitar playing, with weird, atonal scales and extreme dynamics underlining the band's opaque, sometimes indecipherable songs. He refers to his state of mind while playing solos as a place called the Temple Of Ostx, for example – just one example of his relentlessly individual thinking.

Morbid Angel had yet to evolve their complex belief systems and musical talents when they debuted on record. They had made a series of demos, and been bootlegged (one of which, *Abominations Of Desolation*, came out officially several years later). But serious public attention didn't come their way until their 1989 debut album *Altars Of Madness*, released by the Earache label, based in Nottingham (in central England, a far cry from the swamps of Florida).

> **"**
> he evolved a guitar technique heavily influenced by Eddie Van Halen, whom he cites as an influence in the sleevenotes of many albums.
> **"**

7 / 100

> **As a lead guitarist, Azagthoth is almost unparalleled in the death metal scene, but it's his rhythm playing that makes Morbid Angel what they are.**

Altars was an immediate underground success, with its occult aura allied to furious riffs and Vincent's harsh but decipherable vocals, making it a dark pleasure for thousands of headbangers – a number that would expand to millions over the following decade. Songs such as 'Chapel Of Ghouls' and 'Evil Spells' were impossible to pin down, with their complex arrangements and riffs that changed tempo and key at a moment's notice.

'Immortal Rites' on the album has an impossible-to-copy slow-to-fast break punctuated by four riff-stabs that form the high point of any Morbid Angel show. But for sheer picking speed and whammy-bar abuse, head straight for 'Maze Of Torment'. The album also broke new ground by featuring blastbeats from drummer Pete 'Commando' Sandoval, a device pinched from grindcore that added enormous weight to the sound.

The only downside of the *Altars* album was its relatively lightweight production. You had to boost the bass and the volume in order to do the music justice. This changed on 1991's unearthly *Blessed Are The Sick*, which possessed a deep, clear sound that emphasised the meaty nature of the riffage. Vincent's voice had dropped deeper, too, thanks to a couple of years of touring, and the band were playing with more expression and economy.

Everything about Morbid Angel was more serious by this point, from the cover art (Delville's 19th-century gothic painting *Les Tresors De Satan*) through the liner-note dedications to the lyrics. Azagthoth, who had previously played many of his riffs on a B.C. Rich Ironbird, was also now using Mockingbird models and the occasional Jackson Warrior, a set-up he retained until 2008, when he began using a new Dean Flying V-shape guitar known as the X-Core.

Morbid Angel made history in 1992 by becoming the first death metal band to sign to a major record label. Hooking up with Giant, a subsidiary of Sony, they incurred some displeasure among their fans, many of whom responded with predictable calls of sell-out. However, Azagthoth was expanding his music at the same time, believing that those who do not evolve, die. He picked up a seven-string guitar for the first time. Tuning his instrument down a whole-step, he introduced new depth to Morbid Angel's songs on the next album, *Covenant* (1993), which featured stomach-shaking tunes such as 'Blood On My Hands' and the slow, stately 'God Of Emptiness', which Vincent later identified as the song of which he was most proud.

The next Giant-released album was 1995's *Domination* (and you will have noticed that Morbid Angel release albums in alphabetical order). But this was a step too far for the band. It featured industrial sounds and an overall tone that Azagthoth later claimed was too commercial – although this was hardly true by most people's standards. It was Vincent's last record for 13 years, as he quit the band a year or so later.

It's true that 'Dominate' was a little lightweight compared to the occult anthems of old, and 'Where The Slime Lives' had a repulsive vocal effect that alienated some listeners, despite its excellent riffs and pinch harmonics. However, the sheer speed and vitriol of 'Dawn Of The Angry' and 'Hatework' (notable for the shredding of second guitarist Erik Rutan) showed that the band had retained at least some of their power, despite ambient keyboard pieces such as 'Dreaming', contributed by Azagthoth.

Giant Records liquidated after *Domination* and Morbid Angel re-signed to Earache

7/100

after a long tour and a live album, *Entangled In Chaos* (1996). However, it was clear that that the band had passed an important point with Vincent's departure, although the split had been amicable. Death metal itself was now a different creature to the streamlined version of the *Blessed Are The Sick* and *Covenant* years, and Azagthoth was obliged to rethink his strategy. Recruiting a new bassist–vocalist, Steve Tucker, and performing all the guitar parts on the next album himself, Azagthoth focused on a faster, harsher, and generally more extreme sound that paralleled the rise of American grindcore in the latter years of the 90s.

When *Formulas Fatal To The Flesh* was released in 1998, fans didn't really know what to think. Tucker's vocals were as powerful as Vincent's, but they were pitched rather lower in an overall mix that seemed slightly compressed when compared to the ambitious, widescreen feel of *Domination*. The tempos were faster, with more reliance on Sandoval's blastbeats, but in some ways it felt as if Azagthoth had mislaid some of the malevolent atmosphere that marked Morbid Angel out from the rest of the death metal and grindcore pack. Anybody could play fast, brutal songs, critics remarked, but what Azagthoth had forgotten was that the eerie elegance of his early albums had made his band unique.

Still, guitar fans were thrilled when an EP called *Love Of Lava* accompanied the reissue of *Formulas* in 1999. This release – self-indulgent hubris though it undoubtedly was – contained nothing more nor less than Azagthoth's isolated guitar solos from the album. A masterclass in shredding, the EP allowed Azagthoth's followers the chance to dissect his leads without the huge sounds of the band blotting them out. At the time of writing, the audio tracks are still available to download from www.morbidangel.com, a decade after the CD's release.

The thrills of *Love Of Lava* aside, fans of Morbid Angel were in for a fallow period for the next few years. As extreme music expanded and diversified, there were other avenues of excitement for headbangers to follow – and Azagthoth's music just wasn't up to scratch. Sure, *Gateways To Annihilation* (2001) and *Heretic* (2003) were polished, energetic albums, but like *Formulas* they lacked a certain something.

It appeared that the something was David Vincent, who rejoined the band in 2005 for touring and, three years later, a new album, which was still in preparation as this book went to press. The reunited band, now with new second guitarist Thor 'Destructhor' Myhren of Zyklon, played a new song, 'Nevermore', live in 2008, and it promised much for the new record, with plenty of fast tremolo picking and a breathtaking energy level.

> **▶▶ꟾ Genius moment**
> There are innumerable riffs and solos on the first four Morbid Angel albums that make the listener think, 'Why haven't I heard that before?' Forced to pick one, many of those who appreciate the Azagthoth approach would point to the phenomenally complex and fast riff that comes before the line "From churning words of mindlessness..." on 'Immortal Rites' from Altars Of Madness (1989) – see Youtube for live footage. He said it all with that first song on his first album. Genius, without question.

"

self-indulgent hubris though it undoubtedly was — contained nothing more nor less than Azagthoth's isolated guitar solos from the album.

"

7/100

Morbid Angel are back, it seems, with all the vast power and authority that made them so compelling in their earliest days. The art of playing death metal guitar remains in safe hands with Trey Azagthoth at its helm.

TONY IOMMI
Black Sabbath

This entry is about Tony Iommi, but it's also about the invention of heavy metal, and therefore it's also about some people's erroneous concept of what heavy metal is. Iommi is that important.

As you may recall from the introduction of this book, it's possible – essential, in fact – to draw a line between heavy metal and heavy/hard rock. Both are equally entertaining and valid forms of music, but in this marketing-driven age it's important to know what you're being sold. Categories are junk, invented by music journalists in order to keep their record collections in order, and only geeks enjoy genre-spotting.

But if you don't know your Black Sabbath from your Black Widow, someone somewhere will take advantage and the facts will be twisted. Or to put it more bluntly, someone will tell you that The Kinks were the first heavy metal band, a stunning fallacy that endures to this day. The next thing you know, Dave Davies is named as one of the Top Ten metal guitarists ever. This has to stop.

I'll stop preaching now and simply inform you that heavy metal – which is made up of chunky, overdriven riffs, depressive, angry and/or ominous vocals, and lyrics about death and debauchery, all of which are best enjoyed at heightened volume – was invented by Tony Iommi of Black Sabbath. Everything else that came before him – Jimi Hendrix, Deep Purple, Led Zeppelin, The Beatles' 'Revolution', Link Wray, Vanilla Fudge, Blue Cheer, and, yes, The Kinks, every single one of which has been named as the starting point of metal over the years – was rock of the heavy variety.

Tony Iommi tuned his guitar down, creating a doomy sound; his singer Ozzy Osbourne sang about death, paranoia, the occult, and Satan, often a quarter-step flat; and the band stood around in industrial wasteland a lot. That made them heavy metal. Deep Purple's Ian Gillan had a great, operatic voice and sang about Little Richard and fast cars, making his band heavy rock. Led Zeppelin played folk-rock. Hendrix played amped-up blues. The Kinks were mods with a broken guitar amp. 'Revolution' was a protest song. You get the picture. As for the story of how Iommi invented the beast that we now know and love as heavy metal, read on.

Frank Anthony Iommi, for it is he, was born in 1948 in a miserable post-war English suburb of Birmingham called Aston. Like so many other kids raised in that shellshocked era, he worked in a variety of factories after he'd left school as early as possible, only relieving the tedium by playing guitar in various bands in the evenings. One day, he inadvertently chopped two of his fingertips off.

Here's the story in his own words, as he told me in 2005. "I was a teenager working in a factory on a pressing machine: it pressed sheet metal. I got my middle fingers on my right hand caught in it and, without thinking, I pulled them out

> **"**
> This entry is about Tony Iommi, but it's also about the invention of heavy metal, and therefore it's also about some people's erroneous concept of what heavy metal is. Iommi is that important.
> **"**

RIGHT Tony Iommi of Black Sabbath. Need we say more? The man is a god.

TONY IOMMI

> **I was a teenager working in a factory on a pressing machine: it pressed sheet metal. I got my middle fingers on my right hand caught in it and, without thinking, I pulled them out quickly. The weight on them was so great that parts of those fingers stayed behind.**

quickly. The weight on them was so great that parts of those fingers stayed behind – down to the first joint on the middle finger and most of the way down to the joint on the ring finger. The nails were broken off and then surgically re-implanted."

Iommi continued: "To this day it hasn't really healed. There's only a couple of layers of skin over the ends of the bone, and if I bend those fingers, they still hurt. Believe me, I've looked into every conceivable way of getting them repaired surgically, but I'm afraid that if I do that I'll lose the technique which I had to develop to get round it. They want to pull the skin forward from the rest of the finger to make a bigger covering at the fingertip, but I really don't want to do that.

"Some of the other suggestions they've made are basically not much different to what I do already, which is wearing fibreglass clips on the ends of those fingers. The surface of the clips has to be a perfect balance of gripping the string and not gripping it too much. It's really hard to get it right. I made the first ones myself years ago, but nowadays I get a hospital to do it for me."

Ouch. Still, Iommi's pain was our gain. He was obliged to tune the strings of his guitar down two whole-steps in order to reduce their tension and thus the strain on his knackered digits. As you'll know if you've ever tuned down, the lower notes give a distorted guitar riff much more weight. So it was that Iommi invented heavy metal downtuning.

He worked his way through more bands: Mythology, The Polka Tulk Blues Company, and Jethro Tull, a brief but rewarding experience that taught Iommi how real bands worked. He wound up in Earth, which soon changed its name to Black Sabbath, after a popular horror film of the day.

The early 70s were Tony Iommi's golden years. He invented riff after riff and presented them to his supremely talented rhythm section to jam over – Terry 'Geezer' Butler on bass and Bill Ward on drums. Iommi took full advantage of the public's newfound appetite for heavy music and pushed the metal envelope further and further. Doom-laden songs from the band's first three albums – including 'Paranoid', 'War Pigs', 'Iron Man', and the unholy-trinity song, 'Black Sabbath' on *Black Sabbath* by Black Sabbath – have been classic metal tunes for almost 40 years. Although Iommi's solos were initially warm, blues-based, and full of mid-tones, he later played faster, cleaner lines as the concept of heavy metal matured and the guitar solo became paramount in the listener's expectations.

Unlike his nearest contemporaries in this book – K.K. Downing and Glen Tipton of Judas Priest, also from Birmingham – Iommi has never mastered modern tricks such as sweep picking, preferring to combine fast legato playing with slow, expressive melodies rather than compete in the alternate-picking championships. This is why he isn't at the Number One spot in this book, even though you'll notice that many of the guitarists I interviewed have nominated him as their top metal axeman of all time.

Not that Iommi appears to give a stuff about the competition. I asked if he felt outclassed by the many fast-shredding guitarists – not one but two generations younger than him – who have come to prominence over the last few years. He shrugged. "I'd love to be able to play all these different techniques," said Iommi, "but I just don't feel as though I'm capable of them at the moment. My thing is to just go in and play whatever feels right at the time."

6/100

He added that four decades of metal haven't been kind to him physically. "I've got a problem with my thumb – the cartilage has gone, so it's just bone on bone. The doctors have suggested an operation to fuse the two joints together and make it stiff, which I'm really worried about. Apart from that, there's not a lot they can do – I have to take painkillers. I did have shots in my hand a few times, but you can only do those for so long.

"Also, I broke a tendon in the same arm when I was lifting weights, and it's still broken – and I broke three tendons in that arm a few years ago, just from wear and tear. I had them repaired, which took a while to heal, but on this last tour – at the last New York show – I was doing some exercise, and bang! One of them went in my bicep. I haven't got time to get it repaired. It's really annoying, because these things all happen to the same [right] arm – first I cut the fingertips off, and then I had carpal tunnel problems, and now all the tendons are going. I'm falling to bits, basically."

So many riffs over so many years: this is what happens when you play guitar in a band that hasn't stopped moving since the psychedelic era. Sabbath's discography reads like a list of must-have albums – *Sabbath Bloody Sabbath*, *Sabotage*, and, after the departure of Ozzy, *Heaven And Hell*, *Born Again*, and *The Mob Rules* – but it hasn't all been easy going.

Black Sabbath suffered in the late 80s and early 90s from the double-headed chimera of unfashionability and personnel problems. They went through too many singers for fans to take them seriously – Ronnie James Dio, Ian Gillan, David Donato, Glenn Hughes, Ray Gillen, and Tony Martin among them – and made ill-advised collaborations with artists such as Ice-T along the way.

But Iommi always persevered, never letting the band die and never failing to come up with riffs. In 1996, his patience was repaid with the first of many slots on his ex-singer Ozzy Osbourne's travelling festival, the Ozzfest, which led to a rise in Sabbath's stock, a new best-of album, and a solo album, *Iommi*, recorded with a host of high-profile guests. Two more solo albums, *The DEP Sessions* (2004) and the following year's *Fused* (both recorded with Glenn Hughes), kept Iommi at large. And the reticence of Ozzy when it came to new Sabbath activity was no hindrance in 2007, when Iommi reformed most of the Ronnie James Dio-led version of the band and toured extensively under the name Heaven And Hell.

Iommi is nothing if not consistent, and his weapon of choice over the years has tended to be one of his many Gibson SGs. He has played a signature SG for many years now, using Iommi-branded amps by GH and a simple effects set-up that includes a Tycobrahe wah, a Korg delay, and some basic chorus, octaver, and compression gear – a signal path that anyone with a couple of grand can replicate. But will that make you sound like Tony Iommi? No, not even if you're the best guitarist on the planet – because no one plays like him. To play like Tony Iommi, you'd need to have invented heavy metal.

> "first I cut the fingertips off, and then I had carpal tunnel problems, and now all the tendons are going. I'm falling to bits, basically. "

▶▶▏ Genius moment

Everything from 1970 to 1975. Yes, everything. Even after that, Iommi's guitar playing remained world-class, until he was outpaced by the rise of the technical shredder in the mid 80s.

6/100

5/100

'DIMEBAG' DARRELL ABBOTT

Iommi on retirement

"I don't think about retiring. I've been asked about it since I was 25 years old, and the answer is: I'll keep doing it until I can't do it any more. Or until people don't want to hear it. If you really love it, you've got to stick with it. We've all heard people tell us, 'You're playing the wrong stuff,' and 'Don't play that, play this,' but if you can just do what you believe in, eventually it'll come through."

'DIMEBAG' DARRELL ABBOTT
Pantera, Damageplan

Darrell Lance Abbott was one of the most influential metal guitarists of the 90s. His flamboyant personality and guitar style were essential elements of his band, Pantera. Dimebag's tragic death in 2004 at the hands of a mentally disturbed gig-goer, and the immense impact that this has had on the heavy metal community, is still obscuring his talents as a musician. However, in years to come it is certain that guitar fans will recall his dedication and innovation as a guitarist as much as his status as a fallen hero. His nickname of Dimebag or Dime has become so well-known that referring to him as Darrell or even Abbott feels somehow contrived – a true sign of iconhood – and so we'll use his nickname here.

Part of the attraction that Pantera fans felt for Dimebag came from his Southern roots, expressed in a good ol' boy style that was as infectious as it was genuine. Born in Dallas, Texas, and raised there by his father, country musician Jerry Abbott, Dimebag and his older brother Vinnie Paul grew up surrounded by different styles of music, from country to rock to metal and beyond. He was inspired to pick up the guitar after Vinnie Paul took up the drums, and Dime spent his earliest years as a musician attempting to emulate the riffs of his hero, Ace Frehley of Kiss.

Dime was self-taught, as he told me a few months before his premature death. "I don't know all the fuckin' scales. I know a handful, maybe. You know what? If I knew all the scales, I'd know what something was gonna sound like before I played it. And then there'd never be that experience of stepping out there and saying, 'Lemme see if I can make this solo fly! Can I get that last lick in there?' And if you can turn a sour note into a good one just by bending it a half step, you can almost make it sound like it was meant to be.

"For me, the best scale in the world is the chromatic scale. I use every fuckin' note, whether the chord is major or minor or whatever. If I picked up the guitar every fuckin' day and went through the ritual, I wouldn't play the kind of riffs I play. The fuckin' greatest riffs I've ever written – 'Cowboys From Hell, 'Walk', all that shit – came after I picked up a guitar for the very first time, after a day or two when I haven't played it. It's like when you haven't had a piece of ass for a long time."

Once the Abbott brothers had gained enough chops to play a set of songs, they recruited a bassist, Rex Brown, and a singer, Terry Glaze. This was the early 80s, and painful as it is to recall it today, the fashionable music of the day was hair-rock of the Poison, Warrant, and Bon Jovi mould. Teasing their hair up into bouffant manes,

> **Darrell Lance Abbott was one of the most influential metal guitarists of the 90s.**

LEFT Dimebag doing what he did best – shredding at enormous volume.

5/100

> **"**
>
> I don't know all the fuckin' scales. I know a handful, maybe. You know what? If I knew all the scales, I'd know what something was gonna sound like before I played it.
>
> **"**

applying make-up, and squeezing into leather and spandex, the band strutted their stuff in local Texas clubs for years before they made any serious progress. They'd named themselves Pantera, after the Spanish for panther, and they stood out from the pack because of their impressive musical skills, gained form night after night of playing songs by Judas Priest, Van Halen, and Iron Maiden – an invaluable training-ground for any metal band.

Releasing no fewer than four albums on their own Metal Magic label – each of which bore embarrassingly naïve artwork – the band struggled onward, only taking a step up at the end of the decade when they replaced Glaze with a new singer, Philip Anselmo. Demoing new and much harder tunes with Anselmo and dropping their ridiculous glam image almost overnight, Pantera signed a deal with Atco and released the *Cowboys From Hell* album in 1990.

The response was immediate. Stripped of all the extraneous embellishments, the new Pantera sound was a crushing mixture of Dimebag's frequency-obliterating guitar riffs, Anselmo's new, hardcore vocals, and a drum and guitar interplay derived from the thrash metal scene. Although Brown's bass was virtually eradicated from the album as a result of the all-encompassing guitar tracks, the huge sound became a Pantera trademark – to which they stuck on 1992's career-best album, *Vulgar Display Of Power*.

Vulgar Display featured all-time classics such as 'Walk' and 'Fucking Hostile' – the latter an example of pure thrash metal – and the record elevated Pantera to the level of third biggest-selling metal band of the decade, after Metallica and Iron Maiden. The first half of the 90s was Pantera's commercial peak, consolidated by the 1994 album *Far Beyond Driven*, which topped the *Billboard* album charts.

The live arena was where Pantera shone most brightly. Their shows struck a perfect balance of drunken debauchery (Anselmo often smoked a joint between songs; Dime chugged endless beers) and the razor-sharp precision that the songs required. By the 1997 live album *101% Proof*, however, the band had peaked and, unfortunately, the only way from there was down. Anselmo developed a heroin addiction in order to cope with crippling back pain, and overdosed on one occasion. His live performances became erratic, as he turned to alcohol and then prescription painkillers; in interviews he seemed permanently intoxicated, slurring his words. Tensions grew between the singer and Dimebag, and by the band's less-than-stunning swansong, *Reinventing The Steel* (2000), the writing was on the wall.

The end of Pantera came in the wake of 9/11, when the band were stuck in Ireland, mid-tour. Unable to fly home and forced to endure each other's company, arguments raged and Anselmo simply walked away to work on his various side projects. The Abbott brothers waited for his return in vain, but in 2003 called an end to Pantera and founded a new act, Damageplan.

Expectations were high for Damageplan, in which Dimebag and Paul played alongside ex-Halford singer Patrick Lachman and bassist Shawn Matthews (later replaced by Robert 'Bobzilla' Kakeha). However, their sole album, *New Found Power* (2004), was adequate rather than essential: the songs, based on the groove-metal riffage that had made Pantera's first three albums so memorable, now seemed a little out of date. The presence on 'Reborn' of Zakk Wylde, Dimebag's obvious sibling in style and attitude, lifted the album slightly, but in total it was hardly the

5/100

RIGHT **When Dimebag played, we listened. The metal world is a darker place without him.**

'DIMEBAG' DARRELL ABBOTT

5/100

explosive launch that Damageplan so badly required. Added to this was a war of words between the Abbotts and Anselmo.

Their ex-singer was playing in Superjoint Ritual, preparing for back surgery, and struggling with the anger he felt about the loss of Pantera. This culminated in the Christmas 2004 edition of *Metal Hammer* magazine, in which Anselmo told me: "Dimebag deserves to be beaten severely."

Neither this barbed comment nor the lacklustre nature of Damageplan's album would have mattered much, had it not been for the death of Dimebag on December 8 that year. At a Damageplan gig in Columbus, Ohio, a Pantera fan named Nathan Gale climbed onto the stage and shot Dimebag dead at point-blank range. He also killed two fans and one of the band's employees. Gale, an ex-Marine who had been diagnosed with mental problems, attempted to escape with a hostage before being shot and killed himself by an off-duty policeman who happened to be in the area.

The impact of Dimebag's death resonated far and wide, even making national TV news shows. Heavy metal was supposedly a niche area of music, but the loss of one of heavy metal's finest was felt by millions of people. The killing was described as "metal's 9/11" in more than one publication, and writers fell over themselves to heap praise on the likeable nature and unearthly guitar skills of a musician whose most recent album they had largely ignored. Most of them lacked the vocabulary to do justice to Dime's abilities, and the fact that most years since then have been marked by a release of some kind – a Pantera best-of here, a DVD there – indicates the commercial opportunity provided by the tragedy.

So what kind of guitarist was Dimebag? First, like all the truly great players of the era, he was a master of both rhythm and lead guitar, pushing out the boundaries in both fields. His heroes – Tony Iommi, Eddie Van Halen, Ace Frehley – were masters of melody in their solos and economy in their riffing, skills that he brought to Pantera and Damageplan.

One of Pantera's trademark devices was the tremolo-picked riff-and-kick-drum interchange, honed over hours and days of rehearsal: Vinnie Paul locked in with Dimebag with a synchronised attack that many astounded observers could only attribute to some kind of fraternal telepathy. This sound was much copied in the late-90s metal scene, although the device itself was derived (at least in part) from the speed-picking of the thrash metal giants of the previous decade.

Dave Mustaine of Megadeth famously ignited an on-off feud with Dimebag. Asked if he thought his songwriting style had been influential on the new wave of metal bands, Mustaine told MTV: "I'm not gonna name anybody cos I'm not gonna promote them. OK, we'll say 'panther' in Spanish and Portuguese. You're welcome, guys. We might as well be cooking their dinner for them, or pushing their little wheelbarrow to the bank for them."

Dimebag exhibited a firm grasp on a full range of guitar styles. A posthumously-released collaboration with country artist David Allen Coe displayed his chops when it came to blues and country, while earlier Pantera songs such as 'Cemetery Gates' showed that he could play cleanly and emotively when needed.

Traditionally, Dimebag's guitar decay in Pantera was controlled tightly by a noise gate, leading to a staccato sound that can be approximated with precise palm-muting

> **like all the truly great players of the era, he was a master of both rhythm and lead guitar, pushing out the boundaries in both fields.**

5/100

if you don't have the necessary pedal or amp feature. In Damageplan, however, Dime used a sludgier, less precise approach. His leads in both bands featured the full range of shred techniques, although he was occasionally criticised for his constant use of legato hammer-ons and pull-offs over alternate picking. However, when he chose to do so, his picking was second to none; he also used sweeps and tapping when they suited the song, rather than simply to show off his abilities. Another Dimebag trick was the artificial harmonic, heavily distorted and extended into a long, deep divebomb with the whammy bar. Most of all, Dimebag's solos were never boring: his ideas were apparently limitless.

Dime looked back on his early days with commendable honesty. He told me: "It wasn't till *Cowboys From Hell* that I found my sound and my style. Nowadays, I'm playing a bit darker and looser with Damageplan than I did with Pantera. A bit less of the noise gate. There's a lot more sludge than there was with Pantera."

Perhaps the finest advice ever given to young metal guitarists came when he concluded the interview. "You grow up, you learn how to do shit, and you come into your own. We used to play three one-hour sets a night in clubs, seven nights a week, and I went through every fuckin' Van Halen, Iron Maiden, Led Zeppelin, and Judas Priest song ever written. You learn a lot from that shit. Make sure you go to the old school – Rhoads, Iommi, Eddie Van Halen – for the lead chops. And do what's right for *you*." RIP, that man.

> **"**
> We used to play three one-hour sets a night in clubs, seven nights a week, and I went through every fuckin' Van Halen, Iron Maiden, Led Zeppelin, and Judas Priest song ever written.
> **"**

▶▶◀ Genius moment

'Walk' remains one of Pantera's best-known songs, because of the effective simplicity of its riff, executed largely in E5. The idea of a virtually one-note riff might seem laughable – but you try playing it in perfect time and see how you get on. The downstrokes are executed with great accuracy and punctuate the drum pattern, so you ought to try playing 'Walk' with a metronome – after all, it famously took Dimebag and Vinnie Paul many hours to reach perfect unison.

Dimebag on Zakk

"Not kissing his ass or anything – because we *are* fuckin' blood brothers – but I honestly think he's the very best guitar player of today. When it comes to picking, when it comes to fuckin' shredding, he's got everything that a great guitar player needs. He's got more chops than anybody. The dude can sit there and play for like 40-million hours and not stop, y'know?"

ZAKK WYLDE (Jeffrey Wiedlandt)
Ozzy Osbourne, Black Label Society

Zakk Wylde and Dimebag often mutually nominated each other as the world's best guitarist, and their remarkable mastery of all elements of the instrument has always made them neck and neck in lists such as this one. In fact, had Dime not been

4/100

ZAKK WYLDE

murdered in 2004, fans might well have had the luxury of seeing the two men play together in a G3-style guitar band. When I spoke to Slayer's Kerry King not long after Dimebag's death, he confirmed that such an event had been planned, and that he would have been the third player.

Wylde, whose slightly more accomplished alternate picking and willingness to experiment with non-metal techniques such as chicken-picking places him just ahead of Dimebag on this list, is a charismatic character over and above his guitar playing, just as Dime was. A hulking, muscular figure with a huge beard and a fondness for endless bottles of Sierra Nevada beer, Wylde is the heavy-metal archetype. He told one interviewer that he liked to keep his life "real simple", basing it on playing the guitar, lifting weights, and spending quality time with his wife and children. This unreconstructed persona is at least partly a stage front, as he has revealed himself to be a sensitive, even aesthetically aware fellow behind the bluster.

Born in New Jersey in 1967, Zakk Wylde – or Jeff Wiedlandt as he was known before stardom approached – began learning the guitar in 1982, spending up to 12 hours a day on the instrument. He also played the piano and sang. Of his relationship with the guitar and how it started, he recalled: "The first riff I learned was either 'Iron Man' by Black Sabbath or 'Smoke On The Water' by Deep Purple. I was eight years old and I had this shitty acoustic with the action a mile high. Later on, when I moved to electric guitar, I got a Gibson L-6S, like the one Carlos Santana played. A copy, not the real thing – my parents didn't have that kind of fuckin' money.

"And I've played Gibsons ever since," Wylde continued. "People bitch about them not staying in tune – you're in New York when you hit the whammy bar and you're in Cleveland when you come back up, know what I'm saying? But that's the charm of it. I like the shitty whammy and no locking nut, the whole fuckin' thing."

While playing with Jersey bands Stonehenge and Zyris, Wiedlandt developed a neoclassical shredding style inspired by one of his idols, Ozzy Osbourne's guitarist Randy Rhoads. In a clear case of a story that you couldn't make up if you tried, in 1987 his girlfriend Barbaranne heard that Ozzy – who had come to the end of a professional relationship with Jake E. Lee, Rhoads's replacement – was looking for a new guitarist. Concluding that he had nothing to lose, Wiedlandt sent an audition tape to Ozzy's management office and (rightly) thought no more of it, as Ozzy dismissed his playing as just another Rhoads clone.

However, shortly afterwards Ozzy was informed by his then-drummer Randy Castillo of a hot new guitarist in New Jersey. Word of mouth recommendation is always the fastest and most effective, and a couple of days later Wiedlandt (for it was he) received a phone call from Ozzy's wife and manager Sharon Osbourne, inviting him to fly to Los Angeles and audition. The meeting went perfectly and he was hired, renaming himself with the nom de shred of Zakk Wylde and finding himself with the job of his dreams.

Fortunately, Wylde was more than up to the task of becoming the latest in a long line of accomplished guitarists who had played with Ozzy – a line that extended back as far as the venerable Tony Iommi, of course. Rhoads had famously introduced neoclassical shredding into Ozzy's music, and Wylde had already mastered that

> "Not kissing his ass or anything – because we are fuckin' blood brothers – but I honestly think he's the very best guitar player of today."

4/100

LEFT Zakk Wylde (Jeffrey to his mother) applying pick to Les Paul. Dimebag called him 'the very best guitar player of today'.

technique, adding a penchant for pinch harmonics and whammy-bar abuse. Although Ozzy's career was hardly in the ascendant at the time – thrash metal and glam-metal were on the rise, and his music fitted into neither category – he was still a big enough name to guarantee instant stardom for Wylde. He suddenly became the toast of the guitar magazines, especially when the 1988 album *No Rest For The Wicked* attracted much praise for its rampant guitar content.

> **Pentatonic scales are the shitty fuckin' scales that are frowned upon and left for people like Angus Young and whatever.**

Of his guitar influences, Wylde once told me: "When I was growing up, it was Al DiMeola, John McLaughlin, and Frank Marino. The first time I heard that Mahogany Rush live album, I was like, how the fuck can anyone play pentatonic scales like this? Pentatonic scales are the shitty fuckin' scales that are frowned upon and left for people like Angus Young and whatever. I thought, you gotta be fuckin' kidding me! These are at hyper speed. It's like the first time I heard Charlie Parker playing the sax, I said, that's a *saxophone*? I was like, holy fuckin' Christ! Then I was into Angus Young and Paul Kossoff. I loved Kossoff's fast vibrato. You hear it: you know it's him. Then obviously Eddie Van Halen and Randy Rhoads. Also Dimebag Darrell is the fuckin' guy. He took guitar playing to another level. And of course Jimmy Page, Robin Trower, and Jimi Hendrix."

It's amusing to compare pictures of Wylde from the late 80s, then in his early twenties, with his current caveman-of-metal image. Back then he was a slim, almost introverted youth, sporting high-waisted trousers and with the required bouffant hairdo. However, then as now, he made a point of playing beautiful high-spec Gibson Les Paul guitars, usually sporting the bullseye logo that has been associated with him for decades.

His career with Ozzy has always paralleled the singer's own fortunes. While mainstream metal suffered in the early 90s and Ozzy's albums fared poorly, the latter half of the decade marked a commercial rebirth for him – and thus for Wylde, his ever-reliable sideman. In 1996, Sharon Osbourne conceived and launched the Ozzfest, the first annual event devoted to Ozzy and a series of supporting metal bands. An immediate success that brought about the reformation of Black Sabbath's classic line-up, the Ozzfest has been an annual fixture for over ten years now, passing through the nu-metal movement and emerging on the other side to embrace neo-thrash and melodic death metal. It has its flaws – certain bands who have played on the bill have complained about their treatment at the hands of the organisers – but the festival re-established Ozzy (as did the MTV series dedicated to his family) and elevated Wylde to the limelight.

Unusually for a stadium-level hired gun, Wylde also runs a successful band of his own, Black Label Society. Based on a biker ethos and sharing some of its ideas with those of the Hell's Angels – dividing its fanbase into local chapters, and so on – Black Label Society play a hard rock–heavy metal crossover, with Wylde as the frontman. His incredibly fast alternate picking is the focus of the sound, as well as the expert stoner–doom riffage, making for an overall brand of music that owes as much to Soundgarden as it does to Sabbath.

While there are those who question whether Black Label Society would have enjoyed its currently high profile had it not been for Wylde's day job in Ozzy's band, most sane observers would dismiss those criticisms. Wylde is accomplished enough as a songwriter and guitarist to make it work, even without the Osbournes' Midas touch.

4/100

ZAKK WYLDE

Wylde has said of his guitar style: "On every one of my records I try to put something like Eddie Van Halen did. On their first record he did 'Eruption', and people said, what's he gonna do on the next record? So he does 'Spanish Fly'. Then he does 'Cradle Will Rock'. So by the fourth record, you figure, well, he can't beat that. So he fuckin' does 'Mean Streets'! And you go, is that even a *guitar*? What the fuck is he doing?"

In recent years, Wylde has become a media-friendly figure in his own right, giving interviews stuffed with soundbites. He once memorably informed me: "I was always a Sabbath freak. The way those guys have lasted is just incredible. They're living proof that quality endures. Back in the 70s, The Bay City Rollers sold more records than Sabbath ever did, but where are they now?

"And I never got the punk thing," Wylde continued. "I mean: I understand it, the whole fuck-you aspect of it, the whole crash-and-burn part. You can't be a punk band and last. You gotta be Sid Vicious all the fuckin' way. It's not built to last, it's supposed to be: fuck you, I'm outta here. It's the same today. Does that mean I have to wear a fuckin' baseball cap like Fred Durst? Limp Bizkit fuckin' suck ass! Where the fuck are they now? Maybe I should get a tit job and show my midriff off and be the next fuckin' Britney Spears, too. That would sell records, right?"

Wylde is now one of the metal scene's most visible guitarists, thanks partly to the attention that focused on him after the death of his friend Dimebag – whose life he celebrated with the slightly mawkish but huge-selling Black Label Society single 'In This River'.

He's also mightily visible thanks to the guitar industry, in which he is widely known. Wylde's signature Les Paul is a popular seller for Gibson, as are his signature EMG pickups and Dunlop strings. Marshall make him two signature amps, a head and cab with 'Black Label'-branded speakers, and a Microstack practice rig. Meanwhile, the Dunlop Zakk Wylde Crybaby wah and the MXR Zakk Wylde overdrive pedal have been much praised for their sounds. Dimebag himself used the Zakk Crybaby from time to time, returning the favour by giving Wylde a custom bullseye-painted version of the Dean Razorback – which Wylde plays during live versions of 'In This River'. As a person and as a guitarist, he is unique.

> "
>
> Pick one and fuckin' stick with it. You'll never see Yngwie fuckin' Malmsteen playing a Les Paul, and that motherfucker can pick up a goddamn fuckin' bayonet and make it fuckin' sound amazing.
>
> "

▶▶ Genius moment

'Dreamer' was a slightly sucky power ballad released by Ozzy Osbourne in 2005, but it's redeemed by a fantastic solo from Wylde. He delivers several emotional, bluesy licks before a final blast of fast alternate picking, which reminds us that even if the music is poor, the solos are still hot.

Wylde on endorsements

"It always make me laugh when I see these guys with 15 fuckin' endorsements who say hey, I'm playing this guitar now, not that guitar. Well, I got news for you. I'm a Les Paul guy and I always will be. I bleed fuckin' Gibsons. Someone says, you know what? Fuck the Les Paul: the G-string always goes out of tune; I'm playing a Strat now. Well I got news for you – they all go outta tune!

4/100

"Pick one and fuckin' stick with it. You'll never see Yngwie fuckin' Malmsteen playing a Les Paul, and that motherfucker can pick up a goddamn fuckin' bayonet and make it fuckin' sound amazing. Know what I'm saying? The guy's sick. If I even saw a picture of him with a Les Paul, it would look so bizarre. If you saw Angus Young playing a Les Paul, you'd say: what the fuck, the fuckin' apocalypse is upon us now!"

JEFF WATERS
Annihilator

At this stage in the book, we're not merely celebrating great guitarists. We're setting down, for historical purposes, the reasons why certain musicians changed the face of popular music. Most metallers have heard of the names in these upper reaches of the list, but Annihilator – the Canadian thrash metal band led by Jeff Waters – have received less than their fair share of adulation over the years. This book sets out to rectify that situation, at least a bit.

All the best bands sit comfortably between musical genres. Metallica are thrash metal and heavy metal. The Haunted are death metal and thrash metal. Pantera were heavy metal, thrash metal, groove metal, and Southern rock. You get the picture. And Annihilator cover most of the heavy-music ground, effortlessly executing melodic thrash, amped-up power metal, and classic heavy metal.

Where Jeff Waters has broken new ground is in his delivery of fast, thrash riffs – but so cleanly and precisely that they're a world away from the sweaty, dissonant roots of thrash. As he has explained on many occasions, when he first heard the fast, raw riffs played by Venom, he wanted to be in a band that did the same thing – but playing those riffs in a cleaner, more technical style.

Waters was in a position to achieve this in Annihilator, which he founded in 1984. After a couple of initial forays with a full studio band, he played all the guitar and bass tracks himself. Like his contemporary James Hetfield, who was playing metal a couple of years ahead of him, Waters made a point of laying down super-tight, super-precise recordings that did not deviate by more than a few milliseconds from riff to riff. This taut, near-flawless approach gives Annihilator's songs a machine-like robustness, over which Waters can display his other great strength – guitar solos.

Waters's leads are among the very best on the planet. When he requires it, they can be incredibly fast, but they're always melodic and expressive, combining superb clarity with immense speed to make him one of the most freakishly talented soloists anywhere in metal. Over the years, he has contributed guitar to albums by Memorain, Soulscar, Dew-Scented, After Forever, and, most memorably, Children Of Bodom, whose own frontman Alexi Laiho is an enormously gifted shredder.

In 1989, Waters received perhaps the ultimate accolade when he was asked to audition for Megadeth by Dave Mustaine, just as 'Deth were about to hit their commercial peak. Although it didn't take long for Waters to decline the offer, with

" Waters's leads are among the very best on the planet. When he requires it, they can be incredibly fast, but they're always melodic and expressive, combining superb clarity with immense speed to make him one of the most freakishly talented soloists anywhere in metal. **"**

thanks, because he was intent on devoting his energies to his own band, fans of both acts have always wondered what the phenomenal talents of those two guitarists would have added up to as a duo. In the end, Mustaine recruited Marty Friedman, a man of similar talent to Waters, and the band went on to hit the very pinnacle of the thrash metal scene. Waters has no regrets, however, pointing out that both men are natural bandleaders and that, therefore, there would have been serious clashes before too long.

Instead, Annihilator embarked on a long and much-respected career that has encompassed 12 studio albums to date, as well as live records and a compilation. An early boost came with the debut album *Alice In Hell* (1989) and the follow-up *Never, Neverland* ('90), which established the clean, melodic thrash–power metal sound that Annihilator delivered so well.

Waters's guitar tones and occasional vocals, supported by a cast of many musicians, made his band a popular live draw, and he has issued albums every couple of years since then, for various labels. Another career-high came with *Criteria For A Black Widow* (2000). Like *Alice In Hell*, it was a concept record, and it required every guitar technique in the book from Waters. Although he was known in his early years for using a Hamer Flying V, Waters has also used Gibsons and Fenders, as well as an ESP Dave Mustaine model. Nowadays he plays a Ran instrument.

The *Metal* album of 2007 was notable for its wide range of song styles and also for a long list of guitarists from the great and the good of the metal scene who provided guest solos. Asked where the inspiration for the guest-list came from, Waters said: "I'd almost finished this record when I met Corey Beaulieu, who was finishing up the last Trivium record in Florida. Out of the blue, I said: do you wanna do a guitar solo on it? He thought I was joking, so I said why would I be joking? And he said, holy fuck – I would love to do it! He freaked out," laughed Waters.

"And then I thought, shit, it worked for Corey – why don't I ask Michael Amott of Arch Enemy? And why don't I call up my buddy Alexi Laiho from Children Of Bodom and see if he'll do it? And then maybe Jesper Strömblad from In Flames? They're all friends of mine. I even thought hey, maybe I can get hold of K.K. Downing or Dave Mustaine. But my girlfriend said stop: just talk to your friends who like your music – otherwise it'll become a gimmick."

> **"**
> known in his early years for using a Hamer Flying V, Waters has also used Gibsons and Fenders, as well as an ESP Dave Mustaine model.
> **"**

▶▶❙ Genius moment

Try 'Back Into The Palace' from 2000's Criteria For A Black Widow. It contains a fast, super-clean intro riff and a melodic, legato solo that beggars belief. Or check out the Roadrunner United anniversary album The All-Star Sessions from 2005, which featured dozens of current and former Roadrunner artists collaborating on an album's worth of new material. Waters appears on 'The Dagger' and 'Independent (Voice Of The Voiceless)', produced by one of four so-called team captains, Robb Flynn of Machine Head. Then spin the accompanying DVD and skip to the point where both men are pictured sitting at the console. Note that Flynn is clearly gobsmacked as Waters runs through solo after hyper-fast solo. Humble as ever, Waters explains that the solo is moving too fast for his mind to be following his fingers. Now that's metal.

LEFT Annihilator main-man Jeff Waters: bringing fearsome speed and melodicism to metal.

3/100

"I said to everybody, just do your thing – I want you to do this your own way. I love what you do, and I don't want you to feel any pressure to do a 'Jeff Waters' kind of solo. Mind you, guys with the talent of Alexi Laiho could do a Jeff Waters-style solo in about two seconds if I told them to."

Today, Waters is comfortable in the knowledge that his talents are respected by his peers. So what's it like to be a guitar hero to so many? "You know," said Waters, "when you listen to these great guitar players and you realise that they were influenced by something you did, it's a great feeling. It's like having a kid. But you don't let it go to your head. You appreciate the moment, and it's done. And then you're just grateful for everything you've got."

Waters on the best

"Just to set this up properly, I need to say this first. Eddie Van Halen, Angus Young, and Randy Rhoads and are my favourite guitar players, in that order.

"Eddie and Randy for their ability to cover all three essences of the greatest players: writing, soloing, and playing rhythm. It's rare to find a player who does all three exceptionally.

"when you listen to these great guitar players and you realise that they were influenced by something you did, it's a great feeling."

"Angus Young rules for his supreme energy and effort live, and for the amazing blues feel and vibrato in his soloing and playing. Early critics – and even the odd few today – couldn't see past the school uniform and stage show: real players, fans, and critics know that Angus 'sounds' easy to play and copy, but few can get his feel down.

"On the more metal front, Metallica's James Hetfield rules for his tight picking, riffing, and songwriting. The evil duo of Kerry King and Jeff Hanneman reign supreme for their music and energy, and for their never-ending brutal picking. Iron Maiden's Adrian Smith and Dave Murray have inspired guitar players from all styles of music to harmonise their lead melodies.

"Dimebag was the next big gun to come out in the 90s. He captured that Metallica–Sabbath vibe while giving us listeners new twists on the old stuff, along with Vinnie's shuffles and grooves. Dime even slid in some Van Halen into his music, acknowledging the king of guitar: Eddie VH. All four bands – Metallica, Slayer, Iron Maiden, and Pantera – have done so much for guitar playing.

"But since I've been asked to name one player, and only in the metal category, I am gonna go with Mr. Glenn Tipton from the mighty Judas Priest. I was fortunate – an understatement! – to have been asked by Priest twice to tour with them: once in 1991 on their *Painkiller* tour of Europe, along with Pantera, and more recently in 2004 on their first dates of their reunion tour.

"Glenn Tipton, along with partners K.K. Downing and Rob Halford, has come up with the most killer metal riffing, with elite, groundbreaking, original songwriting, and with blues-influenced lead guitar shredding. Judas Priest and Tipton's work are arguably worthy of the term metal more than any other, with Tony Iommi and Black Sabbath their only close rivals.

"Some notable all-round guitar gems from early Priest records would be 'Victim Of Changes', 'The Sentinel', 'Hell Bent For Leather', and 'Electric Eye'. A turning-point for Glenn seemed to happen in 1990 with the *Painkiller* record. Drummer Scott Travis told me that as soon as Glenn heard his former Racer X guitar pal Paul Gilbert play, Glenn's own playing and practising went through the roof – as you can hear on the title track's long, shredding masterpiece solo.

"While he's certainly not the cleanest, fastest, or most technical player, this man is a legend to players who got into metal in the late 70s and 80s. Kids of today may be playing his licks without knowing it. Anyone who jams along to Arch Enemy, Annihilator, Children Of Bodom, and many others may be playing a Tipton (or Downing) lick.

"So – to the younger generation of metal guitar players and to fans who may not be totally familiar with Glenn Tipton's playing, go get every Judas Priest CD you can find. If you can learn his licks, understand his songwriting skills, and be influenced by his killer riffing and methods of putting it all together, then you'll be a great player yourself."

JOHN PETRUCCI
Dream Theater

There is an ongoing argument between those who appreciate heavy metal guitar about the exact point where good technique becomes too much technique. Dream Theater's John Petrucci stands at the centre of this argument as perhaps the most technically gifted guitarist in the world – but here he is at Number Two.

Crucially, the entry after this one is devoted to a guitarist who is equally skilled, and not necessarily more skiled – but whose playing has much more of a nebulous quality about it that most of us would call 'feel', and whose band writes better songs.

In fact, songs lie at the core of this discussion. Dream Theater have recorded several successful albums over their two-decade career and have enjoyed sales in the millions of units, but few observers beyond their immediate fans could point to a single song that has become widely known outside prog-metal circles.

The biggest-selling DT song to date is 'Pull Me Under', from their 1992 album *Images And Words* – the single of which is still the band's only Top Ten hit. The band's detractors point out that while the members of Dream Theater probably add up to the biggest pool of musical talent anywhere outside the classical field, they seem incapable of recording simple, memorable songs that people can sing in the shower. The band's supporters dismiss this claim, pointing to well-attended tours and massive CD sales, all bought by people who presumably love those same songs.

There's no real answer. Let us just acknowledge that Petrucci is a target for equal amounts of respect and mockery for his almost extraterrestrial guitar skills … and leave it at that.

Born in 1967, John Petrucci began learning to play guitar as early as 1976, and by the end of the decade he was listening to prog-rock and jazz-fusion's most prominent guitarists. He once jokingly explained that his heroes are "the Steves and the Als" (Steve Howe, Stevie Ray Vaughan, Steve Morse, Steve Vai, Allan Holdsworth, Al Di Meola, and Alex Lifeson).

> " There is an ongoing argument between those who appreciate heavy metal guitar about the exact point where good technique becomes too much technique. "

2/100

JOHN PETRUCCI

Inspired by this world-class group of musicians, Petrucci joined a band with future Dream Theater keyboard player Kevin Moore in 1979, after spending as much time as he could practising his instrument. His real musical education came in the 80s, when he attended Berklee College Of Music in Boston with his bassist friend John Myung. Drummer Mike Portnoy, singer Chris Collins, and Moore formed the early line-up of Majesty, the precursor to Dream Theater. The die was cast.

Remember, this was the mid 80s. The wheel of fashion turns rapidly and cruelly, and the early songs written by the earnestly bemulleted band bore all the hallmarks of that often tragic period for popular music. Petrucci played exactly as you'd expect an 80s Berklee graduate to play: with super-technical sweeps and tapping adorning jazz-rock licks that often sacrificed emotion and finesse for speed.

This didn't last, of course, as Petrucci matured and his influences broadened. Replacing singer Collins with Charlie Dominici and signing to the Mechanic label, the band renamed themselves Dream Theater after a nearby cinema and recorded a debut album, *When Dream And Day Unite* (1989). Something of a false start for the band, the album didn't do well. Petrucci and the rest fell silent for time, dropped by their label and abandoned by Dominici.

Against all the odds, when the band signed to Atco in 1992 and recruited singer James LaBrie from among 200 applicants, they scored a hit. Although the world had been loudly informed of the possibilities of grunge and alternative rock by this point in the early 90s, the *Images And Words* album was a resounding success, yielding that hit, 'Pull Me Under', and establishing Dream Theater in a way that seemed to promise much success. There was a spirit of experimentation about: at the same time, Death's Chuck Schuldiner was recording his own prog-metal music in Florida to much acclaim, and an audience was obviously ready to buy into the new approach.

To expand their horizons a little, Dream Theater recorded their next album, 1994's *Awake*, not in the States but in sleepy Devon in south-west England. The album was heavier and a little more pessimistic than its predecessor, but it achieved a balance between Petrucci's riffs and the keyboard flourishes of Moore (who quit after its release). The major presence in Dream Theater's songwriting by this point was Petrucci, without a doubt. He was also taking over the lyrics and production. The album was one of the band's best, featuring more complex arrangements than ever before without over-taxing a listener's patience.

However, *Falling Into Infinity* (1997) was less successful, a fact attributed by the band in later years to their label's pressure to record a commercial album after the darker tones of *Awake*. The label hired the ballad-songwriter Desmond Child to assist with songwriting, but the execs failed to predict the inevitable consequence of their interference, and the album was less well received than its predecessors.

Perhaps chastened by this, the suits withdrew for the next album, which appeared in 1999 – and reaped due rewards. The title of *Metropolis Part 2 – Scenes From A Memory* alluded to a song, 'Metropolis Part 1 – The Miracle And The Sleeper', from *Images And Words*. The album was hailed as the band's best work yet by the new rock-loving audience that had gathered by the late 90s. It helped that they now had new a keyboard player, Jordan Rudess, whom the band had played with in the side project Liquid Tension Experiment. His musical exchanges with Petrucci

> " Let us just acknowledge that Petrucci is a target for equal amounts of respect and mockery for his almost extraterrestrial guitar skills ... and leave it at that. "

2/100

were now a high point of the band's approach. *Six Degrees Of Inner Turbulence* (2002) marked a trend for recent Dream Theater albums to become steadily heavier and heavier, with thrash metal elements introduced into the sound and a markedly beefier guitar tone from Petrucci. This continued with the following year's *Train Of Thought*, another riff-heavy album, criticised by some older fans for being too concerned with metal and instrumental pyrotechnics.

Train Of Thought was the latest part of the tightrope the band have always walked, balancing between those who require them to play with complexity rather than heaviness and those who want them to play with more heaviness than complexity. Furthermore, LaBrie's occasional rapped vocal led others to label the album as nu-metal – an absolutely ludicrous claim.

If progressive equals complex or intellectual, then the 2005 album *Octavarium* was Dream Theater's progressive zenith. Conceptually dense in music and lyrics, the record featured eight songs, in different minor keys, and included many thematic references to the 'golden ratio' of philosophical science, with the numbers five and eight constantly occurring, explicitly and otherwise. *Systematic Chaos*, two years later, was more digestible but equally heavy in riff weight, establishing Petrucci firmly as a metal (rather than rock) player. By this point, Petrucci had become known for playing a signature Ernie Ball guitar in six or seven-string versions.

As Petrucci's reputation as a guitarist has grown, so has his following among young players inspired by his example. Matt Heafy of Trivium, for example, has memorised Petrucci's *Rock Discipline* book and runs through it before every gig. The book contains exercises for sweep picking and alternate picking, and warm-up devices designed to allow a player to improve while minimising the chances of injury. It is the most comprehensive book of its kind aimed at the serious shredder. But Petrucci's modern status as a shred guru has its critics. He is regarded by some as an academic musician who merely studied his way to the top – a fallacy, as we've seen.

Perhaps Petrucci's ultimate entrance into the world of the guitar elite was his invitation to play as part of Joe Satriani's G3 event, a showcase tour in which three guitarists (usually Satch plus two others) demonstrate their unearthly skills for guitar fans. Previous performers had included Yngwie Malmsteen and Steve Vai, so Petrucci was entering hallowed company. Three tours of duty followed (in 2005, '06, and '07), allowing thousands of guitar fans the opportunity to witness his devastating chops, also featured in a 2005 solo album *Suspended Animation*.

Petrucci remains one of the world's most admired guitar players, although the debate continues on whether his band can write meaningful rather than simply dazzling music. Don't make your mind up either way until you're fully familiar with his skills, however, because by the time you get to that point, it may not matter any more

Elsewhere, search for video footage of Dream Theater performing Metallica's 'Damage, Inc.' at Ronnie Scott's jazz club in London a few years back (it was on YouTube at the time of writing). With Napalm Death singer Barney Greenway on vocals, the band blast through this very fast, aggressive song with breathtaking nonchalance. Petrucci breezes through the rhythm part – which, remember, has intricately-accented features tremolo-picked with microsecond-precise timing by none other than the greatest rhythm player of them all, James Hetfield.

> "Petrucci remains one of the world's most admired guitar players, although the debate continues on whether his band can write meaningful rather than simply dazzling music."

2/100

RIGHT Petrucci looks astonished at what's over the page...

JOHN PETRUCCI

2/100

Petrucci delivers the solo, one of Kirk Hammett's best and fastest, note-for-note as it is on the record, smiling and nodding absent-mindedly to himself, for all the world as if he's jamming on a slow blues. The rest of the band are fiendishly tight, of course, giving Petrucci the reinforced foundation that he requires to make the song work. And work it does.

> ▶▌ **Genius moment**
>
> 'The Dark Eternal Night' from Dream Theater's 2007 album Systematic Chaos features all the techniques required by the modern metal guitarist. It begins with a smooth, downstroked riff with a fat distortion tone, evolving into a faster, thrash-metal figure along the lines of The Haunted or late-80s Metallica. Then it changes down a gear to a staccato figure with pull-offs before embarking on an atmospheric, harmonised chord sequence and returning to the original riff. It is a thing of beauty.

DAVE MUSTAINE
Megadeth

The heavy metal guitarist who combines the greatest technical ability, the greatest clarity of expression, the fastest and most precise alternate picking, the most fluid legato, the most precise rhythm strokes, and the most consistent all-round metalness – even when metal bands were falling like flies all around him and pressure was on from all sides to change his style – is Dave Mustaine of Megadeth.

This doesn't mean that I think Megadeth write the best songs in metal. For the record, I think Megadeth have been on the wane creatively since 1990. Also, this doesn't mean that I think Mustaine is the nicest, most polite, or most charismatic guitarist in metal. I've interviewed him three times, and from that cumulative couple of hours, I have the impression that he is intelligent, educated, cultured, and funny – but no more so than many other people.

This certainly doesn't mean that I think Megadeth are the fastest or the heaviest or the most innovative (or insert your own adjective here) band on the metal scene. I could name 50 other metal bands for you who play harder and faster than Megadeth. In fact, most of them are in this book.

Read my lips. What I'm saying here is that Dave Mustaine is the all-round most talented, pioneering, and consistent guitarist anywhere in metal. No more, but also no less, than that.

Dave Mustaine's career has been written about so many times that the truth is sometimes hard to separate from the rumours. In many ways, he has been so dogged by controversy over the years that the legend has outstripped the man himself. But we'll give it a go.

Mustaine was born in 1961 in Le Mesa, a medium-sized town in San Diego County, California. He grew up in a family that may or may not have been plagued by an alcoholic father, depending on the sources you consult. Just as with James

> **"**
> What I'm saying here is that Dave Mustaine is the all-round most talented, pioneering, and consistent guitarist anywhere in metal.
> **"**

1/100

DAVE MUSTAINE

1/100

Hetfield, conventional biographies tend to leap forward from here to the formation of the first line-up of Metallica – primarily because relatively little is known about what Mustaine did in the first 20 years of his life.

It was certainly during this time that he learned to play guitar, developing a fluid, fast technique and joining a local metal band, Panic. Not much is known about this band (or at least, not much is known to be true beyond all doubt). Some sources claim that some of the band-members died in a road accident at around the time Mustaine auditioned for Metallica.

Of the audition itself, Mustaine later recalled that the members of Metallica – at the time, frontman James Hetfield and drummer Lars Ulrich, plus bassist Ron McGovney – asked him to join the band before he'd played a note. Once the new quartet were rehearsed and playing shows, they were a formidable band: Hetfield, then too shy to speak to the audience, restricted his contributions to sung lyrics and rhythm guitar, while Mustaine, a much more confident character, got the audience fired up between songs.

Relationships backstage, however, occasionally became strained. Mustaine, who dealt drugs for a living, brought one of his security dogs to a rehearsal at McGovney's house. When the dog jumped onto the bassist's car, Hetfield reacted badly, supposedly either hitting or kicking the animal. Mustaine became angry and a verbal spat began, which ended with Mustaine punching Hetfield in the mouth. He was instantly dismissed from the band, but was readmitted the next day after tempers had cooled.

"If I had to do it all again," Mustaine said later, "I wouldn't have brought the dog. I was dealing drugs to keep myself afloat, so I had these dogs to protect my merchandise. I took one of them up to rehearsal one day, and the dog put her paws on the bass player's car. I don't know if it scratched it or left pawprints on it, or put a fuckin' dent in the car – I don't know. Whatever happened, James kicked it, we started arguing, push led to shove, and I hit him. And I regret it."

On another occasion, Mustaine – a cool, sarcastic character when sober but something of a maniac when drunk – poured a can of beer into the pickups of McGovney's bass. A difficult guy to have around, then. But let's not forget that the rest of the band could be pretty unmanageable after a few beers, too, and that Mustaine was only 21 years old.

Once McGovney had been replaced with the extraordinarily gifted bassist Cliff Burton, the band moved forward with enormous speed, despite the personality clashes. Their live demo tape of 1982 reached Jon Zazula, owner of a record store in New York City, and he invited them over to stay at his house while he shopped around for a record deal.

The demo, *Metal Up Your Ass*, contained all of Metallica's original material so far, most of which ended up on their debut album, *Kill 'Em All*, the following year. If you can track down a copy, compare it to the *KEA* versions – it's an excellent way of contrasting the lead guitar styles of Mustaine and his replacement, Kirk Hammett. Notice how Mustaine's version of the solo in the Diamond Head song 'Am I Evil?' is every bit as fluid as Hammett's, while the superfast riffing of 'Hit The Lights' rivals that of Hetfield himself. At the age of only 21, Mustaine had evolved a tight picking hand that perfectly served the complex rhythm parts of the early Metallica songs.

"

Of the audition itself, Mustaine later recalled that the members of Metallica – at the time, frontman James Hetfield and drummer Lars Ulrich, plus bassist Ron McGovney – asked him to join the band before he'd played a note.

"

1/100

In March 1983, the band duly hired a U-Haul truck, loaded in their gear, and made the long trek to the other side of the country. But Mustaine's drinking – and his behaviour while drunk – was beginning to unnerve the other members of Metallica. They contacted Exodus soundman Mark Whitaker and asked if that band's guitarist, Kirk Hammett, would be willing to take Mustaine's place. The other three Metallica musicians were facing up to the task of firing their current guitarist. As Mustaine later recalled, he woke up one April morning to find the others gathered at his bedside. They handed him a Greyhound bus ticket back to Los Angeles, leaving from Rochester, New York, where they took him that same morning. Hammett was flying in the same day.

Mustaine might have been out of the band, but his legacy remained with them over the next couple of years. On Metallica's debut album, *Kill 'Em All*, released that summer, Hammett used Mustaine's solos as a template to work from. According to Mustaine, he co-wrote four songs on that album. Two further co-credits appeared on 1984's *Ride The Lightning*, and Mustaine later alleged that 'Leper Messiah' from 1986's *Master Of Puppets* had been partly his work. None of these claims have been fully resolved in public, even two decades and more later, although Mustaine's credit does appear in the appropriate places next to the lyrics of those songs in the albums' liner notes.

Kirk Hammett's solos benefited from the professional studio environment – a first for Metallica – and therefore they sound more polished than Mustaine's earlier demo versions. But there was a certain raw aggression in Mustaine's solos that was buffed away in the recording process.

Fuelled by anger at his treatment, Mustaine began recruiting members for a new and as-yet unnamed band. He has stated clearly in endless interviews during the quarter-century since that he wanted his new band to be heavier, faster, and more technical than Metallica. After a shortlived project called Fallen Angels, he hooked up with bassist Dave Ellefson and formed Megadeth with the first of a series of second guitarists and drummers. One of the guitarists was Slayer's Kerry King, who played with Megadeth for a few shows while Slayer were between the *Show No Mercy* and *Hell Awaits* albums. But his stay was a brief one, and King returned to Slayer.

This shortlived Megadeth line-up put on a mighty show (as a visit to YouTube should confirm). Mustaine and King were highly accomplished rhythm and lead players, and the pair delivered blistering licks at high speeds. King was playing solos in a melodic sub-Iron-Maiden style at this stage in his career – the famous atonal squeal came later – and his leads complemented Mustaine's style with audible synergy.

Scoring a deal with the Combat label in 1985 – home to many of the great metal acts in this book, including Death, Exodus and Morbid Angel – Megadeth released a debut album, *Killing Is My Business... And Business Is Good*. It featured the original version of 'The Mechanix', which Mustaine had written with Metallica (and which his old band had included on their own debut LP as 'The Four Horsemen').

Stuffed with twisty, uncategorisable riffs executed at enormous speed, *Killing* was a clear statement of intent, even if the production did no favours to the percussion or Mustaine's high, rather weedy voice. If you need a demonstration of Mustaine's prodigious talent, even at this early stage in his career, keep an ear out for 'The Mechanix', the early demo song that Metallica later retitled 'The Four Horsemen'.

> They handed him a Greyhound bus ticket back to Los Angeles, leaving from Rochester, New York, where they took him that same morning.

1/100

> His solos, always exemplary, showcased all of the tricks we've examined in this book — string skipping, economy picking, hybrid picking, tapping, the obvious sweep, legato, and alternate picking.

Megadeth's verison was faster and more technically demanding, with a nifty main riff that is still one of Megadeth's most challenging riffs to play at high speed.

Killing Is My Business was released in summer 1985 – two years behind Metallica, who were already writing their genre-defining third album *Master Of Puppets* – and was part of the second wave of thrash, rather than the first, with Exodus, Anthrax, and Dark Angel all out of the starting blocks and Testament and Death Angel soon to follow.

Despite the occasional co-billing of the two bands – such as the New Year's Eve 1985 show in San Francisco when Megadeth supported Metallica – Mustaine seemed to harbour some residual anger toward Metallica for some years, only relenting in the early 90s. "The feud has been over since 1992," he told me in 1999. But this cessation of hostilities didn't stop Mustaine falling into heroin addiction in the mid 80s and working his way through a variety of band-members, with only the faithful Ellefson staying the course.

Megadeth's classic second album, *Peace Sells... But Who's Buying?* was released in 1986 after a major-label leap to Capitol. Mustaine was playing a signature Jackson guitar, the King V, and attracting acclaim as one of the world's best rhythm and lead players. His solos, always exemplary, showcased all of the tricks we've examined in this book – string skipping, economy picking, hybrid picking, tapping, the obvious sweep, legato, and alternate picking – but always with great taste. For example, Mustaine often avoids using a whammy-bar, stating that if a player has one, the resulting solo is more likely to contain time-wasting show-off elements such as divebombs.

Mustaine claimed in the early 90s to be a "pioneer" on the rhythm guitar scene, an apparently arrogant statement that is in fact fully justifiable. Like James Hetfield, whose picking speed, precision, and aggression are second to none, Mustaine had evolved a supremely flexible right-hand technique by the end of the 80s. Although Megadeth's third album, *So Far, So Good... So What?* (1988), was marred by a featherweight production and a silly cover-version of The Sex Pistols' 'Anarchy In The UK', it paved the way for their career-best album, *Rust In Peace*, which was released in 1990.

While we're on the subject of that lame version of 'Anarchy', Mustaine told me: "Part of the reason why I'm not really fond of *So Far, So Good... So What?* is because of the mastering. I was trying to get clean at the time – I'd decided that I didn't want any more drugs in my life – and the guitarist we were using, Jeff Young, messed around with the sound on the album. It sounds totally reverbed out to me. The songs are good, they sound fine, but the production's not good.

"We did have Steve Jones of the Sex Pistols play on it," Mustaine continued, "so it had the makings of being a great song, and live it's still one of the staples of the Megadeth diet. The fans feel jilted if they don't hear it. But I look back and think of things I would have done differently – and one of them would have been to lock Jeff out of the studio. He was a great guy and a great guitarist, but I think I know what this band's supposed to sound like better than anybody else."

The breathtaking *Rust In Peace* featured songs such as 'Holy Wars... The Punishment Due' and 'Five Magics' and had a rounded, bass-heavy sound with riffs of extreme clarity. It is often voted the third best of all thrash metal albums, after Metallica's *Master Of Puppets* and Slayer's *Reign In Blood*, thanks to its near-perfect

1/100

combination of melodic elements and speedy, malevolent riffs. Mustaine and Friedman's leads are particularly outstanding.

On the subtle art of soloing, Mustaine explained: "If you understand that a solo should be used like spice, then you realise that there's not much space for it in the song. Marty's stuff with Cacophony was all solos. If you take away the solos and listen to the songs, the songs are mostly garbage. But for me, I write the song around the rhythm. And then I figure, OK, now the rhythm's here and there's a great lyric and a brilliant melody for the lyric, it's so complex to get the vocal and rhythm melodies to counterpoint. Then you've gotta figure out how to tuck a solo in there and where certain fills go. I think I'm blessed: I'm not an arranger, but a lot of times we try stuff and it just works."

As for riffs, he laughed, "I just make 'em. I just hold the guitar. It's weird, sometimes I'll do it on an acoustic, sometimes on an electric. I wrote most of *Peace Sells* on a bass. So much of Megadeth's music was written on different instruments. I'm no genius arranger or anything like that, but I am taking lessons from a classical guitar player. I know what I'm doing; I just don't know what it *is* that I'm doing. I'm self-taught. I don't know anything about the chords – I know some of their names, but I don't know the names of the scales or anything."

A combination of factors sent Megadeth into something of a decline from this point, including a series of bad decisions, an unwise shift in songwriting style, the turn of the wheel of fortune, Mustaine's personal problems, and his unfortunate propensity for alienating fellow musicians. Some high-profile tours should have sent Megadeth sky-high – the Clash Of The Titans in 1990 with Anthrax, Slayer, and Suicidal Tendencies, and a support slot with Judas Priest – but the band had only one critically-acclaimed record left in them: the *Countdown To Extinction* album of 1992. It was a Top Five hit in the USA and was followed by a successful tour with the then-new Pantera in support, but Mustaine's heroin addiction meant some cancelled dates in 1993. Meanwhile, the appearance of Megadeth songs in substandard action movies such as *Last Action Hero* dated them a little.

The new wave of darker heavy metal spearheaded by Korn and Tool made Megadeth's 1994 album *Youthanasia* seem laughably fake. It seemed as if written with an obvious desire for commercial acceptance. Mustaine blamed his band's shift toward radio-friendly blandness squarely on second guitarist Marty Friedman, but it was widely speculated that Metallica's successful leap into the MTV mainstream had been at least a partial inspiration.

A 1996 side project, MD.45, featuring Mustaine, Alice Cooper drummer Jimmy DeGrasso, and Fear singer Lee Ving, was briefly interesting as it revealed Mustaine's punk influences, but metal fans largely ignored it (as they had with similar punk covers by Metallica and Slayer) and it was of zero interest to devotees of Mustaine's guitar skills. As with the punk-themed recordings of other thrash metal bands, MD.45 didn't require much downstroke precision – leading to 'strummy' riffs rather than picked ones – or indeed much melodic soloing. This made it of interest to punk fans only.

A stint on the Ozzfest plus some high-profile TV and film soundtrack appearances helped keep Megadeth in the headlines. But Mustaine's music was decidedly mundane by this point. *Cryptic Writings* (1997) was reasonably well-received, but a slanging

> **I'm no genius arranger or anything like that, but I am taking lessons from a classical guitar player. I know what I'm doing; I just don't know what it is that I'm doing. I'm self-taught.**

1/100

1/100

match had developed between Mustaine and his former ally Kerry King, dating back to some prima donna behaviour by Mustaine on the 1991 Clash Of The Titans tour.

This is a book about guitarists, so you ought to go online if you want to read more details of Mustaine's feuds with other musicians such as Dimebag Darrell Abbott, Mike Muir of Suicidal Tendencies, and others. Let's just say here that over the years Mustaine has not made himself popular with many of his peers, although it should also be noted that he has apologised for many of his more incendiary statements.

In 1999 and 2001, Megadeth released two frankly awful metal-lite albums, *Risk* and *The World Needs A Hero*. Friedman bailed out between the two albums. Although his successor, ex-Savatage shredder Al Pitrelli, was a gifted player, it was clear that Megadeth had come to a turning-point. At the time, Mustaine was obviously convinced of the value of the new album. He said: "The music is probably a little bit more refined. It's still heavy, but it's much more melodic now. I think it takes a really developed songwriter to make heavy, melodic music. Anybody can write heavy music, and anybody can write melodic music, but to do the two is really hard. And it's even harder to write something that's your own. There's a lot of music around that's similar to the punk and new wave of 20 years ago."

Mustaine was forced to reconsider his career plans at this point. Fashions had changed, and he was under pressure to move his band in a different, more modern direction. Unfortunately, guitar solos and complex rhythm patterns weren't deemed cool at the turn of the millennium. The nu-metal wave was at its height and bands such as Limp Bizkit and Slipknot dominated the metal scene. Mustaine's key skills – fast, melodic solos made up of rapidly picked and swept licks, and complex rhythm parts – were almost redundant. What was he to do?

It was a bleak time for Megadeth after *Hero*. Ellefson, too, quit the band, and he sued Mustaine for unpaid revenue, although he lost the case. The final straw came in 2002, when Mustaine fell asleep in a rehab waiting-room with his arm over the back of a chair, compressing the radial nerve in his left arm and leaving it useless for several months. He had slipped back into heroin abuse after some years of sobriety, and during the resulting period of recovery and physiotherapy he split the band.

Mustaine later explained: "I'm pretty grateful that the healing took place in my arm. I didn't know if I'd play again. I fell asleep with my arm over a chair. The radial ulna nerve is right there, and it was right on the side of the chair. It cut the circulation off to the nerve, so the nerve stopped talking to the arm, and the muscle at the top of my elbow died. There was a little scoop out of it where the muscle had atrophied. It took four months to get the feeling back in my hand and another year of doing physiotherapy to make it work.

"But as you heard on *The System Has Failed* [2004], God saw fit to give me the ability to play again. It was humiliating. I heard people say that I slit my wrists. That's a fuckin' gutless way to go out. If I was gonna commit suicide I'd eat pussy to death or something. That's pretty rude, sorry about that. It was hard to tell people that I'd injured my arm by falling asleep on it. I wanted to say there was a fuckin' pram going down the road full of babies in front of a taxi, and I saved it and hit my arm – something like that. But the truth was, I fell asleep on it."

Looking back at that dark period, he told me: "I wasn't being a very good dad or

> **"** Let's just say here that over the years Mustaine has not made himself popular with many of his peers, although it should also be noted that he has apologised for many of his more incendiary statements. **"**

LEFT Dave gets his wings with his new Dean signature model.

1/100

a very good husband. I just wasn't showing up. I did hurt my arm in rehab, because I hated everybody in Megadeth at the time. And I started using again. When the lights would go off and the intro tape would go on, I would just be counting backwards from one to the last song, because it was all about money, to everybody but me. I would sit there for hours signing autographs, because these people who have supported me over the years, I owe them. When I became a public figure I made a transaction with them, to be available to them, although privacy is something that's been compromised too.

"The breakup ... I left before Marty did, really, because I didn't want to be in the band after *Risk* came out. The music scene at the time was all about alternative music, and instead of just sticking to our guns and being the mighty Megadeth, like AC/DC or Iron Maiden, everybody was pressuring me and the other three guys, and there's only so much I can take. [I was] getting it from two wonderful children that I'm not around, and a wife that I made a commitment to and I'm not showing up for, and then three other men and their families constantly wanting a piece of me. Then you got two other men who are managers and constantly wanting things from me.

"I just said, 'You know what? I give up.' I said to those guys, 'After *Risk* we're making another metal record.' Marty quit because he didn't want to make another metal record, and that's when I said, 'When *The World Needs A Hero* came out, if it doesn't outsell *Risk*, I'm done.' I was blinded at the time by all the madness."

When Mustaine returned to the scene two years later with a new line-up, new sobriety, a new album called *The System Has Failed*, and a much-ridiculed born-again Christian faith, he was playing faster and harder than he had for some years. 'Kick The Chair', for example, featured a fast, expertly-executed core riff that required every iota of Mustaine's picking skills, and 'Back In The Day' – a sarcastic nod to those critics who preferred Megadeth's earlier albums – contained a solo with as much venom as anything he had recorded in the 80s.

The album wasn't a match for vintage *Rust In Peace*-era Megadeth, but the pointless vapidity of the *Risk* era appeared to be gone forever, and the band regained a measure of respect from their fans. But, as always, things were not quite perfect. The recent Metallica movie *Some Kind Of Monster* had featured a scene in which a tearful Mustaine confronted Ulrich about his ejection from the band back in 1983. Mustaine hadn't wanted the scene to be used, but in the end it made the final cut, and he was furious.

As he told me: "They edited out a lot more stuff than was there, and they sent it to me for my approval. I said, 'I don't want you to use it.' It was two days after 9/11, on my 40th birthday. I was supposed to be at home getting a Mercedes CL55 AMG from my family as a present, and I'm here with one of the guys that I've hated the most in my entire life – my entire existence on the planet – making a videotape in San Francisco, because I can't fly to Phoenix to see my family.

"They sent me the tape, and I said: 'No, I don't want you to use it.' They went ahead and used it anyway. I'm like, 'Why send it to me for my approval if, when I say I don't like it, you go ahead and use it anyway?' They said that I'd signed the paper, so they figured, fuck him, he's signed the paper. You may remember September 13th: New York was still on fire, we'd been up non-stop watching CNN. Everywhere you went, people were freaking out over white powder, there were bomb threats

> **"**
> If I was gonna commit suicide I'd eat pussy to death or something. That's pretty rude, sorry about that. It was hard to tell people that I'd injured my arm by falling asleep on it.
> **"**

1/100

everywhere, you were having all kinds of fuckin' radical military manoeuvres and shit.

"I had aspirations at one point of becoming friends with James and Lars and doing something [with them] again some day in my career, but that door is shut now. That was the final betrayal. And if I ever see Lars again it'll be too soon. I don't care any more. He told me that this was supposed to be about healing. And it was more about furthering his career at my expense. I'm done with Lars Ulrich … I'm done with Metallica."

The feud appears to be back in place, unfortunately. Megadeth themselves were in the ascendant, however. *United Abominations* (2006) was another step up, with some world-class shredding from Mustaine, and there was a new commercial venture, an annual travelling festival, Gigantour, featuring Megadeth as headliners. Perhaps Mustaine was aware of the ticking of the clock – he is in his late 40s – but with this regular tour he has created a durable brand that may be a breadwinner for years to come.

Time may be flying, but Mustaine isn't quite done yet. "I don't look old," he said recently, "and I don't play like I'm old, and I'm in really good shape right now – but there are mornings when I wake up and it feels like someone's sucked the oil out of my hinges. I just creak back and forth until I get motion flowing inside me. But I think that's just an occupational hazard: this job is so strenuous on your skeletal system and your respiratory system that most people would be dead.

"I stay fit, though – I still work out, I go to the gym and do cardio stuff, and then of course there's the obligatory two hours of metal calisthenics every night. I'll know when it's time to stop – I thought it was time to stop before, when my arm got hurt. I honestly thought I'd lost the fire, but then I thought, well, I'll do this a little bit more, because there's something left unfulfilled inside me."

And so we come to the end of this book. You can safely assume that Dave Mustaine, a player of almost impossible skill, will keep guitar players and manufacturers guessing for years to come. After his years with Jackson, he moved to ESP in 2004 and, two years later, to Dean, leaving a flood of signature models on the market.

Of the various experiences he has had with gear manufacturers, Mustaine said: "Live, I still use Marshalls and Rocktrons, plus Hush silencers, Monster cables, Jim Dunlop Tortex picks, and JHS strings. My strings that I use are really heavy: I use 10-to-52s, and they'll eat your fingers up. If you bend a lot, you'll have a really hard time controlling the bends."

We like our guitar heroes to be a little unpredictable, as well as fast-fingered – and they don't come more mercurial than Big Dave. I asked him once if he thought he was a good guitar player. He said: "Yeah, I think I'm good. Even though there's hundreds and thousands of players who are better than I am, it's fun for me to push the limitations of my playing. I enjoy playing how I'm playing right now: I like setting the guitar down when I'm done playing the song and then looking at someone else, and going, 'Let's see you do that!'"

Dave Mustaine ticks all the boxes when it comes to the modern guitar hero. His playing skills are world-class; he has pioneered the art of riff delivery, without losing the tasteful bite of the songs; he's a charismatic character; and he has dabbled with the dark side more than you or I ever will. Without people like him, the guitar scene would lose its compelling edge. The world needs a hero? The guitar world already has one.

" Without people like him, the guitar scene would lose its compelling edge. "

1/100

APPENDIX 1 They also served — The next 50

Of course there are more than 100 great metal guitarists in the world. If we're honest, several hundred more players deserve to be in this book, but if I have to write about any more I'll pass out. Here's a select bunch of 50, just to reassure you that I know life doesn't stop with my little list.

101 ADAM 'NERGAL' DARSKI Behemoth	**114 HANK SHERMANN** Mercyful Fate	**126 MARTIN PERSSON** Dismember	**139 SHANNON HAMM** Death, Control Denied
102 DANIEL ANTONSSON Soilwork	**115 WILLIE ADLER** Lamb Of God	**127 BILL KELLIHER** Mastodon	**140 PHIL CAMPBELL** Motörhead
103 JESPER STROMBLAD In Flames	**116 PETER LYSE HANSEN** Hatesphere	**128 PETER TÄGTGREN** Hypocrisy, Pain	**141 DAVID BLOMQVIST** Dismember
104 ROB CAVESTANY Death Angel	**117 JOHN SODERBERG** Amon Amarth	**129 TREVOR PERES** Obituary	**142 CHRIS OLIVA** Savatage
105 PHIL FASCIANA Malevolent Creation	**118 ALEX HELLID** Entombed	**130 DANNY CORALLES** Autopsy, Abscess	**143 ERIC CUTLER** Autopsy
106 LUCA TURILLI Rhapsody Of Fire	**119 JON NÖDTVEIDT** Dissection	**131 JAKOB NYHOLM** Hatesphere	**144 CHARLES HEDGER** Cradle Of Filth
107 EMPPU VUORINEN Nightwish	**120 BRENT HINDS** Mastodon	**132 RICK ROZZ** Death	**145 JEAN-FRANÇOIS DAGENAIS** Kataklysm
108 DENIS 'PIGGY' D'AMOUR Voivod	**121 THOMAS 'QUORTHON' FORSBERG** Bathory	**133 SNORRE RUCH** Thorns	**146 BEN WEINMAN** Dillinger Escape Plan
109 LARRY LALONDE Possessed, Primus	**122 ROOPE LATVALA** Children Of Bodom	**134 RICHARD KRUSPE** Rammstein	**147 MARTIN HENRIKSSON** Dark Tranquillity
110 BILL STEER Carcass, Firebird	**123 THOMAS YOUNGBLOOD** Kamelot	**135 ADAM JONES** Tool	**148 OLA LINDGREN** Grave
111 MARK MORTON Lamb Of God	**124 TED 'NOCTURNO CULTO' SKJELLUM** Darkthrone	**136 PETER WICHERS** Soilwork	**149 JON OLIVA** Savatage
112 JIM MATHEOS Fates Warning	**125 OLA FRENNING** Soilwork)	**137 MICHAEL PAGET** Bullet For My Valentine	**150 GLEN DROVER** Megadeth
113 SVEN 'SILENOZ' KOPPERUD Dimmu Borgir		**138 OLAVI MIKKONEN** Amon Amarth	

APPENDIX 2 Shredders, not metallers

Just to expand a little on the point I made in my introduction at the front of the book that my Top 100 list is for heavy metal guitarists, not rock guitarists, I'm going to list here the phenomenal players whose work sometimes strays into the metal arena — but who are best known as fast and dexterous soloists rather than heavy metal songwriters. A few years ago they were often labelled as metal players, but today we know the truth. These are all amazing guitarists — but not known for playing in metal bands. Hence their absence from the Top 100. Your glasses, please, for:

1 EDDIE VAN HALEN Van Halen	**6 STEVE VAI** Solo, David Lee Roth, Whitesnake	**11 PAUL GILBERT** Racer X, Mr Big, solo	**16 JASON BECKER** Cacophony, David Lee Roth, solo
2 RANDY RHOADS Quiet Riot, Ozzy Osbourne	**7 NUNO BETTENCOURT** Extreme, solo	**12 VERNON REID** Living Colour	**17 CHRIS IMPELLITTERI** Impellitteri
3 YNGWIE MALMSTEEN Steeler, Rising Force, solo	**8 MICHAEL ANGELO BATIO** Nitro, solo	**13 JAKE E LEE** Ratt, Cutting Crew, Ozzy, Badlands, solo	**18 MARK TREMONTI** Alter Bridge
4 SAUL 'SLASH' HUDSON Guns N' Roses, Slash's Snakepit, Velvet Revolver	**9 GEORGE LYNCH** Dokken, Lynch Mob, solo	**14 GREG HOWE** Planet X, solo	**19 VINNIE MOORE** UFO
5 JOE SATRIANI Solo	**10 TONY MACALPINE** Solo, Mars, Planet X, Ring Of Fire	**15 BRIAN 'BUCKETHEAD' CARROLL** Guns N'Roses, solo	**20 ERIC JOHNSON** Solo

APPENDIX

APPENDIX 3 Lists of the list

The list by nationality:

USA	48	DENMARK	2
SWEDEN	14	FINLAND	2
UK	13	POLAND	2
GERMANY	7	AUSTRALIA	1
NORWAY	4	FRANCE	1
CANADA	3	SWITZERLAND	1
BRAZIL	2		

What does this ranking of countries mean? Simply that the USA is the current home of most of the world's best metal guitarists. The UK, where heavy metal was invented, has lagged sadly behind the States when it comes to producing new metal bands of high quality. The best British bands are probably Bullet For My Valentine (if you're under 20), Akercocke (if you're over 20), and Cradle Of Filth (if you're a goth). Sweden has a huge metal scene, of course, with fearsomely gifted guitarists thanks to the demands of the melodic death metal movement. I could have filled this book solely with Swedes, in fact. Meanwhile, Germany has always been the home of power metal (and some die-hard thrash acts), while Norway is a haven for black metal, which doesn't require its guitarists to shred too hard.

The list by genre:

DEATH METAL	31
HEAVY METAL	20
THRASH METAL	20
METALCORE, NWOAHM OR 'MODERN METAL'	12
POWER METAL	7
MULTIPLE GENRES	6
BLACK METAL	4

Over half of the list is made up of players from extreme metal bands (death, black, and thrash), because the music they make is usually faster and more technical than even the most abrasive traditional heavy metal. Fretting a riff, picking it cleanly enough for it to cut through the distortion, and palm-muting the unused strings – at, say, 250bpm – is obviously more tricky than doing it at slower speeds. Hence the profusion of extremists.

The list's age range

This book spans 36 years – two generations of metal guitar – as follows.

Oldest guitarist:
Glenn Tipton of Judas Priest, age 61 (born August 25 1947).

Youngest guitarist:
Corey Beaulieu of Trivium, age 25 (born November 22 1983).

Of the 100 guitarists, 96 were alive as this book went to press.

The list in alphabetical order:

'DIMEBAG' DARRELL ABBOTT, MIKAEL ÅKERFELDT, FREDRIK ÅKESSON, PAUL ALLENDER, CHRISTOPHER AMOTT, MICHAEL AMOTT, ALEX AUBURN, TREY AZAGTHOTH, MATT BACHAND, ROB BARRETT, COREY BEAULIEU, ANDERS BJÖRLER, RAND BURKEY MAX CAVALERA, DINO CAZARES, 'FAST' EDDIE CLARKE, CHRIS DEGARMO, PHIL DEMMEL, MICHAEL DENNER, KK DOWNING, JOE DUPLANTIER, STEFAN ELMGREN, EURONYMOUS, THOMAS FISCHER, ROBB, FLYNN, MARTY FRIEDMAN, GALDER, SYNYSTER GATES, BJÖRN GELOTTE, JANICK GERS, MÅRTEN HAGSTRÖM, KIRK HAMMETT, JEFF HANNEMAN, KAI HANSEN, MATT HEAFY, JAMES HETFIELD, GARY HOLT, SCOTT IAN, IHSAHN, TONY IOMMI , MATTHIAS JABS, RON JARZOMBEK , PATRIK JENSEN, WACŁAW KIEŁTYKA, KERRY KING, ANDREAS KISSER, ALEXI LAIHO, ANDY LA ROCQUE, MARTIN LARSSON, HERMAN LI, PETER LINDGREN, JEFF LOOMIS, MANTAS, JIM MARTIN, PAUL MASVIDAL, JASON MENDONÇA, TOM MORELLO, JAMES MURPHY, DAVE MURRAY, DAVE MUSTAINE, PAT O'BRIEN, ANDRE OLBRICH, JACK OWEN, ERIC PETERSON, MILLE PETROZZA, JOHN PETRUCCI, JESSE PINTADO, CHRIS POLAND, MARC RIZZO, MICHAEL ROMEO, JAMES ROOT, ERIK RUTAN, SAMOTH, KARL SANDERS, RALPH SANTOLLA, JON SCHAFFER, MICHAEL SCHENKER, RUDOLF SCHENKER, CHUCK SCHULDINER, ALEX SKOLNICK, ADRIAN SMITH, DAN SPITZ, NIKLAS SUNDIN, DAVE SUZUKI, DAN SWANÖ, MICK THOMSON, FREDRIK THORDENDAL, GLEN TIPTON, DALLAS TOLER-WADE, TIMO TOLKKI, SAM TOTMAN, DEVIN TOWNSEND, MATT TUCK, ZACKY VENGEANCE, JEFF WATERS, MICHAEL WEIKATH, MATT WILCOCK, KIRK WINDSTEIN, PIOTR WIWCZAREK, ZAKK WYLDE

INDEX

This index provides references to the guitarists and bands featured in this book. Page numbers for pictures are in **bold** type.

ACKNOWLEDGEMENTS

All interviews in this book were executed by the author between 1999 and 2008. The majority were conducted especially for this book, but a few excerpts have appeared in Total Guitar, Record Collector, and Metal Hammer magazines.

Fellow writers Neil Daniels, Bernard Doe, Malcolm Dome, John Doran, Ian Glasper, Hannah Hamilton, Bill Irwin, Maria Jefferis, Jake Kennedy, Christof Leim, Dave Ling, Joe Matera, Metalion, Greg Moffitt, Bob Nalbandian, Martin Popoff, Greg Prato, Jason Ritchie, Steven Rosen, Ian Shirley, Joe Shooman, Tommy Udo, Lois Wilson, Jonathan Wingate, Henry Yates.

Editorial staff Adrian Ashton (Bass Guitar), Bill Leigh, Brian Fox (Bass Player), Eugene Butcher (Big Cheese), Geoff Barton, Ian Fortnam, Sian Llewellyn, Scott Rowley (Classic Rock), Albert Mudrian (Decibel), Mike Carhart-Harris (DVD Review), Samantha Slater (Drummer), Michael Leonard (Guitarist), Neville Marten (Guitar Techniques), Jon Newey (Jazzwise), Terry Bezer, Alex Burrows, Caren Gibson, James Gill, Alex Milas, Jonathan Selzer, (Metal Hammer), Bill Miller (Modern Drummer), Mark Hoaksey (Powerplay), Jason Draper, Tim Jones, Alan Lewis, Ian Shirley (Record Collector), Phil Ascott, Chris Barnes (Rhythm), Robert Crampton, Dominic Wells (Times), Nick Cracknell, Claire Davies, Steve Lawson, Lucy Rice (Total Guitar).

Industry personnel Mike Exley (AFM), Darren Toms (Candlelight), Sarah Lees (Century Media), Joolz Bosson (Cooking Vinyl), Ron Veltkamp (Displeased), Talita Jenman, Dan Tobin (Earache), Sarah Vincent, Debra Geddes, William Luff, Tom Wegg-Prosser (EMI), Lars Chriss (Escapi), Andy Turner, Will Palmer, Andreas Reissnauer (Metal Blade), Zoe Miller (Mute), Jaap Wagemaker (Nuclear Blast), Matt Vickerstaff (Peaceville), Richard Dawes (Polydor), Michelle Kerr, Kirsten Lane (Roadrunner), Sabiene Goudriaan (Season Of Mist), Olly Hahn, Frank Uhle, Jay Lansford (SPV), Andy Lewis, Chas Chandler (Union Square), Daryl Easlea (Universal), Phoebe Sinclair, Ben Hopkins, Andy Prevezer (Warners), Laurence Baker, Sharon Chevin, Dave Clarke, Dan Deacon, Karl Demata, Ross Halfin, Cat Hollis, Mick Houghton, Dorothy Howe, Roland Hyams, Tina Korhonen, Gary Levermore, Kas Mercer, Nik Moore, Peter Noble, Marc Riley, Alan Robinson, James Sherry, Lisa Southern, Emma Van Duyts, Clint Weiler, Ian Whent.

Axe-wielders of the apocalypse Emma, Alice, Tom, Robin, Dad, John and Jen, Naomi, James, Tim and Moss Freed, the Corky Nips, Physt, Carlos Anaia, Jo Herbert, Jon Hoare, Tim Jolliffe, Jonathon Kardasz, Frank Livadaros, Billy Pilhatsch, Ian Salsbury, Louise Sugrue, David Thornell, Dora Wednesday, Elton Wheeler and the families Barnes, Bhardwaj, Bird, Cadette, Carr, Clark, Cooper, Edwards, Ellis, Eschapasse-Carr, Everitt-Bossmann, Foster, Gunn, Harrington, Hogben, Houston-Miller, Johnston, Knight, Lamond, Legerton, Leim, Maynard, Miles, Parr, Sendall, Sorger, Tominey, Tozer, and Woollard. Thanks to Glen Benton of Deicide for the foreword.

Picture credits (page number: source) 15: Andreas Hylthen; 37: Didier Messens/Redferns; 60: Andy Buchanan; 109: Rachel Rijsdijk; 129: Ebet Roberts/Redferns; 137: Angela Boatwright; 148: James Sharrock/www.burningeye.com.au; 155: Paul Bergen/Redferns; 169: Naki/Redferns; 176: Paul Bergen/Redferns; 179: Paul Bergen/Redferns; 187: Fin Costello/Redferns; 191: Mick Hutson/Redferns; 193: Robert Knight/Redferns; 199: Darren Edwards; 206: Peter Pakvis/Redferns; 209: Paul Bergen/Redferns; 211: Mick Hutson/Redferns; 216: Gary Wolstenholme/Redferns.

Updates, complaints, corrections? You can email the author at joel@joelmciver.co.uk or write to him at Metal 100, Jawbone Press, 2A Union Court, 20–22 Union Road, London SW4 6JP, England.

"Comparing guitar players is pointless. What is this, the Guitar Olympics?" Ian Gillan, 2005